"A delightful and lucid account of opening to the mystical in everyday life. Wise, yet down to earth, this book makes a very valuable contribution to the growing awareness that spirituality is not just for the religious."
—Peter Russell, author of *The Global Brain* and *From Science to God*

"A vitally important work that speaks eloquently to a yearning deep within the human heart. Rademacher's dual perspectives as trainer and minister make him uniquely qualified to write *A Spiritual Hitchhiker's Guide*—it is a deeply insightful examination of religion, spirituality, and consciousness. I hope it touches you as profoundly as it did me."
—Laurie Monroe, former president and chief executive officer of The Monroe Institute

"Giving this hitchhiker's book a ride made for a marvelous journey. Witty, eminently readable and absorbing, filled with lines urging to be underlined and quoted, this veritable parade of profound insights is surely a delight to read. As a long-time, antichurch Jesus freak, this treasure chest of observations and revelations concerning him was in itself richly rewarding, while even more spiritual insights unfolded, page after page. May the book flourish as profusely as its offerings, which surely deserve to be widely read."
—Joseph Chilton Pearce, author of *The Crack in the Cosmic Egg* and *Magical Child*

A Spiritual Hitchhiker's Guide to the Universe

TRAVEL TIPS FOR THE SPIRITUALLY PERPLEXED

PAUL RADEMACHER

HAMPTON ROADS
PUBLISHING COMPANY, INC.

Cover design by Steve Amarillo
Cover art © iStockphoto.com/Forest Woodward

Hampton Roads Publishing Company, Inc.
1125 Stoney Ridge Road
Charlottesville, VA 22902

434-296-2772
fax: 434-296-5096
e-mail: hrpc@hrpub.com
www.hrpub.com

If you are unable to order this book from your local
bookseller, you may order directly from the publisher.
Call 1-800-766-8009, toll-free.

Library of Congress Cataloging-in-Publication Data

Rademacher, Paul, 1952-
  A spiritual hitchhiker's guide to the universe : travel tips for the
spiritually perplexed / Paul Rademacher.
      p. cm.
  Includes bibliographical references.
  Summary: "A memoir and meditation book that explores the many paths of
enlightenment available to those looking beyond today's churches, temples,
and synagogues"--Provided by publisher.
  ISBN 978-1-57174-597-2 (tc : alk. paper)
  1. Jesus Christ--New Age movement interpretations. I. Title.
  BT304.93.R33 2009
  204.092--dc22
  [B]
                                                    2009001683

ISBN 978-1-57174-597-2
10 9 8 7 6 5 4 3 2 1

Printed on acid-free paper in the United States

To Jacquie, Sean, Jesse, and Stacy

CONTENTS

"I shall give you what no eye can see, what no ear has heard and no hand has touched, and what has not come into the human heart."[1]

—Jesus

ACKNOWLEDGMENTS

So many factors go into birthing a book that it's a puzzle to me who the real author is. Events and ideas seem to be orchestrated by forces great and mundane, visible and mysterious, sublime and ridiculous. There is the life-long, aching, interior compulsion which dogged me to say something of value. There are also the computer games Solitaire and Minesweeper which raised the crescendo of my self-loathing of procrastination to the point that I had no choice but to start typing.

But most of all there have been the precious people who have encouraged, inspired, and been exceptionally patient over all these years. My wife, Jacquie, has been the one true, steadfast, and guiding spirit. Without her constant gentle reassurance, her unflagging support as she read through countless drafts, and her belief in this project, it never would have come into being.

I also want to thank my children, Sean (Dirt 1), Jesse (Dirt 2), and Stacy (Dirtette 3), for the way they have embraced this strange journey of their father. You will never know how much it has meant that you cared so deeply about the tales of my curious adventures, took the time to read this book, and shared it so enthusiastically with your friends. No better PR could a father ever hope for.

I am extremely grateful to Janis Vallely, my agent, for taking a chance on this unknown author and to Nancy Hancock for recommending me to her. Bob

Friedman, my senior editor with Hampton Roads, has been an extraordinary guide who has shown an unusual grace and concern for me and this book.

My editors, Donna Beech (who labored tirelessly from Amsterdam and was an absolute wonder to work with in the early days) and Priscilla Stuckey (who took the wordiness of my manuscript and tightened it with remarkably little pain), were both gifts from the heavens.

To those who made special contributions when this was going to be a self-published book I can never begin to express my gratitude: Peggy and Ted Kemp for reading the manuscript, giving guidance about the publishing industry, and typesetting; my sons, Sean and Jesse, for their ideas and trial cover designs; Stacy and Jacquie for their feedback on titles and design.

There were many key people who read the manuscript, made suggestions, and gave me confidence: Frank DeMarco, John and Susan Rademacher, Mary and Sonny McDaniel, William "Twig" Branch, Lisa and Michael Tousignant, Laurie Monroe, Karen Malik, Fay and Skip Atwater, Ron Naylor, Barbara Bowen, Darlene Miller, Michael Sinkus, Carolyn and Curt Bartel, John McMichael, Kathy Bryars, Ken Smith, Sue Stickney, Kim Morris, Nancy and Lu Rudolph, Ann Walsh, Danielle Barcilon, and so many others. Please know that if I've forgotten your name, it is only because of the limitations of my memory and not for a lack of gratitude.

INTRODUCTION

A Tale of Two Psyches

For the sorcerers of don Juan's lineage, however, there is the cognition of modern man, and there is the cognition of the shamans of ancient Mexico. Don Juan considered these two to be entire worlds of everyday life which were intrinsically different from one another. . . . He explained . . . that it was energetically imperative for human beings to realize that the only thing that matters is their encounter with infinity.[2]

—Carlos Castaneda

A pastor is a poster child for all that is decent, true, trustworthy, and moral. After fifteen years in the ministry, I finally discovered that such sainthood leaves little room for joy. That's why I left preaching to become a building contractor and writer. Jesus probably hung out with sinners for the same reason: he liked to laugh.

But there was another reason for my walking away from the church. I found myself gripped by a fascination with things that are taboo for the clergy. Don Juan's *infinity* was one of those. Oddly enough, Jesus' kingdom of heaven was another. For me, they are one and the same.

Such things can't be said from the pulpit, not if you want to keep your job. Yet there comes a time in life when speaking the truth openly matters more than the security of a steady paycheck. So, for a number of years, I built during the day, wrote at night, and laughed whenever I got the chance.

ETERNITY AND INFINITY

But for most Christians, faith is no laughing matter. It's a deadly serious game, like the TV show *Survivor*. Heaven hangs in the balance, and the consequences of getting kicked off *that* island last forever, and then some.

So if you go to most contemporary churches, you'll find that they're concerned with *eternity*, rather than *infinity*. Countless Bible tracts left in public restrooms ask, "Where will you spend eternity?" Take your pick: heaven or hell. It's a proposition rooted in fear—fear of an Almighty who seems to be most interested in making people holy enough, so that God can stand to be around them. Our main task is to live good, wholesome, moral lives. We've heard it so often, it seems to be self-evident. And so the vast scope of human potential is concentrated on the narrow target of achieving time off for good behavior.

I'm convinced that we're meant for so much more. The "more" comes into play when we let go of our obsession with *eternity* and begin to entertain the possibility of *infinity*.

This infinity is not at all what you might think. Popular conceptions of the afterlife have colored our thinking so completely that we can scarcely look beyond threadbare visions of angels strumming harps, while perched on white billowing clouds. That stereotype is so sterile that it's little wonder we attempt to avoid death at every turn.

But infinity is infinitely more alive. It's teeming with activity, and, though we seldom realize it, it's interacting with this physical dimension constantly. When we become aware of that interaction, our self-understanding is radically transformed. The sacred nature of both the physical and metaphysical worlds becomes apparent. We begin to live in a truly multidimensional manner.

Jesus' name for this infinity was "the kingdom of heaven" or the "kingdom of God." Despite what many of us have been taught, that kingdom is not an after-death reality reserved for those who have been good. It is, instead, a state of consciousness, accessible to ordinary people in the present moment. Jesus knew that state intimately. We can too.

Once the kingdom of heaven is understood as a state of consciousness that can be experienced now, ordinary people like you and me can begin to do extraordinary things. It's then that Jesus' words begin to make sense: "The one who believes in me will also do the works that I do and, in fact, will do greater works than these."[3] And that, my friends, means much more than simply being good.

Suddenly, our motivation is no longer fear of eternal punishment, but the passionate exploration of hidden dimensions. We become driven by the euphoria of an intense curiosity. The heart is unleashed.

At the fringes of our awareness lies the encounter with infinity. In the twilight zone between sleep and wakefulness live vistas of breathtaking wonder. To brave that domain is to place our lives and this world in an utterly new context. It is to become alive, perhaps for the first time.

This book is the story of how I came to that understanding. It's a journey that has led through depression, anxiety, and doubt. Yet, that same journey has also allowed me glimpses of a splendor so exquisite that it propelled me on a passionate quest to recapture what I had discovered.

That quest has been anything but heroic. Despite my best efforts, I am still, and always have been, distressingly ordinary. My studies have been anything but orderly. Instead, the journey has been more like hitchhiking: sticking my thumb out and jumping into cars with strangers, having only the vaguest idea of a destination. And every now and again, I've opened the car door and been struck by enlightening. And that has made all the difference.

SUNDAY SCHOOL BADGES

My desire to become a pastor had its roots in a fondness for heavy metal as a kid. Not the rock music kind, but the heavy metal worn on the chest.

Those were the days when they would bribe us to go to Sunday school. Presbyterian lessons were basically about behaving decently, so God would like us. In case there was any question about who measured up, we were given medals to wear.

For near-perfect attendance in the first year, we would receive a red, white, and blue badge. After that, a new, color-coded bar would be hung from the badge for each succeeding year of faithfulness. With a full set, you were designated a world-class Sunday schooler. It was the Holy Grail.

Now, these weren't the kind of cheap plastic badges that you might get with a McDonald's Happy Meal. These were GEN-U-INE, 100 percent heavy metal—steel, to be exact. In our Sunday school pantheon, the real Champions of the Faith actually listed to one side from the weight of their hardware.

You could also tell the winners from the losers in the race for sanctity by noticing who was dressed appropriately to meet God. Some kids didn't even bother to wear much more than school clothes. Not me. It was a crisp, white shirt and clip-on tie or nothing. In my book, that was the kind of extra effort God deserved. And, besides, my chain of metals stood out best against a white background.

FLANNEL BOARD HEROES AND JOEY HEATHERTON

In Sunday school, we learned all about God and his favorite people. There were great stories about guys with interesting names like Jonahandthewhale, Noah Zark, and Jacob Sladder. The teacher put them up on the flannel board and acted out the stories right in front of us.

I knew my real calling was to be just like them, so that someday I could be up on the flannel board too, and God would be pleased. True, it would take some time. There was that whole Joey Heatherton thing to work out . . .

Joey Heatherton would come on the TV in cigar commercials, dressed oh-so-scantily, slithering around and singing in that sexy, throaty voice, "Hey, big spender! Spend a little dime on me."

Even though I was only ten years old, I was old enough to get an allowance, and I knew she was singing to me. When I saw her, my mouth would get dry and parts of me would start to swell up. But I pretended not to notice. As a world-class Sunday schooler, I had to be above such temptation.

Flannel board heroes know how to conquer sins of the flesh, no matter how silky smooth, supple, tender, and inviting that flesh might be.

According to my ten-year-old reasoning, God's cure for Joey Heatherton would probably kick in around my twelfth birthday. That was when I'd have my confirmation and first communion. I'd be so pure and sparkling on that day that God might even have to wear sunglasses. Besides, when you're twelve, you're practically grown up.

But my first communion came and went. To my surprise, Joey Heatherton still looked as good as ever, maybe even better. Well, maybe I would just grow out of it. There was no doubt that God wanted pure souls. The object was to be good and to do good.

But no matter how many medals I collected, the beast inside me never relented. My teenage years were a ceaseless parade of raging love affairs in my head. Women were an intoxicating brew of softness and heat. At night, I would toss and turn in the bed sheets fantasizing about being lost in their erotic embrace.

But, by day, I was too shy to do anything about it. Even as a teenager, my best friend and I would cruise through the streets of our hometown, hoping that beautiful women would simply leap into our twenty-year-old Rambler and snuggle under our outstretched arms. Many years would pass before I realized that an essential step for attracting members of the opposite sex is to actually talk to them.

The frustrations by day only served to stoke the fires of my fantasy life. It was a world unto itself that had nothing to do with God or being good.

But there was something more. Beneath my raging obsessions lurked a craving more dangerous than sex—it was a hunger for knowledge.

THIRD EYE BIND

That hunger began, oddly enough, with my father. He was an electrical engineer, a straight-and-narrow, by-the-book man who knew there was a right way and a wrong way to do everything. Life was like the transformers he designed. You either acted right or you got blown to smithereens. No warnings, no apologies, no explanations, no excuses.

I still carry images of sitting in the back seat of the car, with my brother and sister on either side, all of us dodging my father's flailing hand as he drove. We would bob and weave like prizefighters. That huge palm, swinging like an unattended fire hose, could level anything in its path.

We never talked much about God, my father and I. He was Catholic. My mom wasn't.

Mom wasn't Catholic because a nun came to our house shortly after my parents' wedding. The sister, dressed in her tidy black habit, informed Mom that her refusal to bring up her future children as Catholics was jeopardizing my father's salvation. My mother was so enraged by that visit that she vowed never to set foot in a Catholic church for the rest of her life. My mother and her children were Presbyterians.

Dad, on the other hand, continued to go to the Catholic church. He couldn't be a full-fledged Catholic, though. The little matter of fathering children who could not be claimed by the one true church had led to his excommunication. The joys of consuming the body and blood of Jesus were denied him. On Sunday mornings, Dad would drop us children off at the Presbyterian church with my mom, while he went to a Catholic mass that had cast him into outer darkness because of us.

Though the church he attended was shrouded in mystery for me, I still figured that his beliefs were pretty generic. You know—God, Jesus, Santa Claus, the Easter Bunny.

As I got into my later teenage years, we stopped going to church. But because we never talked about religion, I still suspected my dad's views were routinely conventional. So it was quite a shock when he suddenly handed me a book that introduced me to a completely new conception of God. It was T. Lobsang Rampa's *The Third Eye*.

"If this is true," he said, cryptically, "then this is really interesting."

It was the story of a man who entered a Tibetan Buddhist monastery at the age of four. Visions, astral travel, seeing auras, visiting other dimensions, communing with the dead, and more were all part of a day's work in his world. Rampa might as well have been describing the landscape of Jupiter. I was utterly captivated.

If this is true, I thought to myself, *it's much more than interesting!*

My father and I never spoke of the book again, but it tapped into a well-spring of curiosity and longing inside me. I just *had* to know about the won-drous worlds Rampa described.

Over the next few years, I read anything that promised to take me beyond the confines of my flannel-board religion. It was during that time that I came across Carlos Castaneda and his outlandish explorations under the tutelage of the Mexican shaman, don Juan.

His adventures were absolutely enthralling to me. But reading about them was ultimately unsatisfying. I wanted more. I wanted the experience for myself. Yet Mexico was a long way from the Pennsylvania steel town I grew up in. And even if I headed south of the border, it was unlikely I'd find shamans listed in the yellow pages.

And so I hungered for something I had no hope of ever finding. That longing never went away.

PART I

First Glimpses of the Kingdom

But whether small or great, and no matter what the stage or grade of life, the call rings up the curtain, always, on a mystery of transfiguration—a rite, or moment, of spiritual passage, which, when complete, amounts to a dying and a birth. The familiar life horizon has been outgrown; the old concepts, ideals, and emotional patterns no longer fit; the time for the passing of a threshold is at hand.[4]
—Joseph Campbell, *The Hero with a Thousand Faces*

CHAPTER ONE

A Crack of the Hip and Off to the Twilight Zone

When I was a building contractor the first time around, before I had any thought of becoming a pastor, I learned an important lesson: you have to be out of your mind to work with concrete. There are any number of ways to get concrete where you want it—all of them bad. You can shovel it, pour it, wheelbarrow it, dump it, pump it, use a conveyor, crane it, rake it, screed it, trowel it, push it, pull it, or even use a Georgia buggy. But no matter how you do it, the concrete will inevitably extract its pound of flesh, and then some.

It has its own timetable. Once the pour has begun, there's no stopping—no matter what—for load after load, truck after truck. Just when you think you can't stand anymore, a form breaks, a truck gets stuck, or a load spills. And when that happens, it's nothing but busted knuckles and rivers of sweat to set it right.

Bad days are the best you can hope for in concrete work.

Why would anyone want to make a living this way? If you'd asked my brother and me in 1979, we would've told you it was because we were smart. We were innovative and bold, with cutting-edge ideas.

We started marketing, doing trade shows, sending out flyers. We were on the radio. We were interviewed by the newspaper. We even spoke at the Kiwanis Club—slide show and all.

What we didn't know was that working with concrete is at the bottom of the food chain. So we learned the hard way that, in the concrete business, the best thing you can hope for is a bad day. My wife, Jacquie, had seen the strain on my face when I came home from work. She had witnessed, first-hand, the bruises, cuts, scrapes, and mangled flesh of the concrete business. She had become resigned to work clothes that could only be burned, because they were covered with form oil.

Knowing all this, why would she inexplicably begin praying one day that the concrete pour we had scheduled would go badly? Why would the love of my life, the mother of my children, my confidante, risk sending me, and our company, into the ravages of concrete hell?

She was looking for a sign.

In Search of a Sign

It had all started with the still, small voice.

While teaching Sunday school one day, these words popped into my head: "This is what I want you to do." The voice was clear and precise. I knew it was speaking of the ministry. It carried the kind of tone and purpose that made me sit bolt upright in my chair.

However, knowing the cost of such a move, I wasn't about to jump. We already had two children and lived in a community we loved. We were deeply involved in the life of our church. Our extended families were close by, and we wanted very much for our children to grow up around their grandparents. We had just begun building a new house. Going to seminary would have meant leaving all that behind.

After hearing that voice, Jacquie and I were invited to have dinner with our best friends, Steve and Kay. Steve was the associate pastor of our church. While driving to their home, I turned to Jacquie and asked, "What would you say if I were to go to seminary?" I knew there was no way she would ever agree to such a harebrained idea. After her veto, I could get on with my life and business.

No sooner were the words out of my mouth than, without batting an eye, she piped up, "Yes! Let's go!"

The quickness of her reply floored me. "But . . . but . . . what do you mean, 'Let's go'?"

"Well, I think you'd be really good at it!"

Before we had a chance to discuss it any further, we pulled into our friends' driveway. We shared a pleasant afternoon of raucous laughter, playing with the kids, and competing over video games. Then, after dinner, without warning, Jacquie looked at me and said, "Are you going to tell them?"

In that instant, Kay blurted out, "What? You're going to seminary?"

In the space of two hours, I'd received three separate, distinctive signs. Things were moving much too fast.

Years ago, there was a movie starring Steve Martin called *The Man with Two Brains*.[5] In it, he plays a famous brain surgeon who has lost his beloved wife.

His life is nothing but desolation until he becomes smitten with a woman who is the consummate gold digger. Martin is hopelessly infatuated and wants desperately to marry her. But, first, he must check for guidance from his deceased wife.

Hanging above the mantel is a portrait of his departed love. It's a shrine for him—the only place where he can find solace and comfort from his pain. In a touching scene, he poses the question of this new woman to his deceased wife.

"Becca, if there's anything wrong with my feelings for Dolores, just give me a sign," he pleads.

Suddenly, a great rush of wind comes out of the firebox, the sconces on either side explode, the wall cracks as the whole room quakes, the painting of his wife spins on the wall, and from within the painting comes a wailing voice that cries out, "NOOOO! NOOOOO! NOOOOOO!"

Then there's silence. Martin's hair is mangled from the wind. His neatly pressed suit is rumpled, and his necktie hangs over his left shoulder. Backing away slowly, he mutters, "Just a sign . . . any sign . . . I'll keep a lookout for it . . . In the meantime, I'll just put you in the closet."

When it comes to signs, we see and hear only what we want to. So Jacquie and I kept looking for more to convince us. There was just too much on the line.

One of the biggest hurdles was my brother, John. I knew that he couldn't handle the entire business by himself, not to mention the fact that he had little sympathy for my Christian faith. There was no way he would agree to my leaving.

I went to the senior pastor, looking for advice on the matter. He suggested that Jacquie and I schedule a dinner with John and his wife, then tell him about our struggle over going to seminary. "If he says something like 'I expected this,' then maybe you can take that as a sign from God."

Good advice, I thought, but I knew it would never happen. We scheduled the dinner anyway.

After eating, I broached the subject. John sat motionless as I laid out all that had been happening. When I finished, he leaned back in his chair, put his hands behind his head, and said calmly, "I expected this."

FALLING INTO THE KINGDOM

Still, Jacquie and I were unconvinced. We became desperate for signs.

One day, Jacquie decided to visit the construction site with our two boys, who were two and three years old at the time. (My boys liked to play in the soil so much that my friends began calling them Dirt One and Dirt Two.)

While driving to the site, Jacquie offered God a once-and-for-all, put-up-or-shut-up kind of bargain: "If Paul is supposed to go to seminary, then give us a sign that is unmistakable! Make the concrete pour go badly today!"

Then, realizing that the results of the concrete pour had a direct effect on our economic well-being, she quickly retracted, "No! No! Wait. Check that. Don't make the pour go badly, but please, please, give us a sign today that is unmistakable!"

Meanwhile, at the site, the pour was going suspiciously well. It was one of the best we'd ever had. A crane was doing most of the work, lifting the concrete in huge buckets to the roof.

Once all the concrete was in place, I looked over the forms and noticed a slight bow in one of the roof retaining walls. I pulled on one end of a brace to wedge the wall, and the 2 x 4 gave way. Suddenly, I found myself careening into space with no chance of saving myself.

As I fell, it was surrealistic to realize that *this body*—the one I came into this world with, the only one I have on loan, *this body* that had always been desperately allergic to pain, *this body* that is *me* in every shallow sense of the word—was about to be crumpled, broken, or maimed.

It was odd, because *this mind* that is attached to *this body* didn't have enough time to make a physical adjustment to cushion my impact, but it did have enough time to lay out vivid scenarios of my years ahead spent in wheelchairs and iron lungs, tethered forever to some machine that spells out yes-and-no answers to questions when I blink my eyes, because they're the only muscles still functioning.

This mind also had ample time to wonder at the absurdity of God's non-intervention, because how in the world could God allow this to happen to *me*? After all, what good is it if God isn't available for simple lifeguard duty? All I needed was for God to look down from that heavenly perch and cast even the smallest sideways glance, to make the wind shift (just slightly) so that, instead of hitting the rocks below, I might end up on a—

Pow!

My body slammed into the ground. My head missed the base of the crane by some six inches. I rolled over, then couldn't move my leg. Pain washed over me like a tidal wave.

The other workers called an ambulance. I was rushed to the hospital. Every time the ambulance moved, I nearly blacked out from the agony.

In the meantime, Jacquie had arrived at the construction site. Her brother, who was working with us, rushed to her car. "Paul's all right. Don't worry; they've taken him to the hospital. He fell off the roof."

Jacquie immediately turned the car around and headed to town in search of me. As she drove, she knew that this was the unmistakable sign for her. In my fall, God had spoken.

When she finally found me, they were about to move me from the emergency room bed to a wheelchair. X-rays had shown that there was no fracture in my hip; I could be moved by ambulance to a hospital nearer to my home.

The orderlies closed in to lift me up. With the movement, a wave of nausea swept through my body, as I slammed into a wall of pain. Everything turned black.

To my surprise, the blackness brought a blissful state that was free of pain. There was total stillness and, for the first time, relaxation. It was such a joy to be released from the pounding agony of my hip.

But Jacquie is a nurse. Cool, calm, she saw me slumping in the chair and did what all nurses are trained to do: she put her cupped hand over my mouth and nose so that my lungs would take in more carbon dioxide. This stopped my hyperventilating and brought me back to full awareness of the crushing pain. I was furious at her.

DOORWAY TO ANOTHER DIMENSION

That night, I was placed on a gurney in the corridor of a hospital because of a nurses' strike. I would call for help, or a glass of water, or a trip to the bathroom, only to be neglected because I wasn't "a real patient" until I got into a room with a number. The incessant throbbing of my hip faded in and out with my consciousness.

The next day, when I nearly passed out again, more specific X-rays were ordered. Sure enough, there was, after all, a fracture.

Questions followed. The figure coated in white with stethoscope stood at the foot of my bed and fielded them. How long will I be in traction? "One week." How long off work? "Six weeks." Will I fully recover? "Sometimes yes, sometimes no. You might be OK for a while, then fifteen years down the road need a hip replacement. We never know."

I thought to myself that it would be great if I could build houses under those terms.

Customer: "Will this house stand up after you leave?"

Me: "Sometimes yes, sometimes no. You might be OK for a while, and then a beam could crash in on your head and kill you. We never know."

When the doctor left, all I could think of was the prison term of one week immobilized on my back with a weight attached to my leg. Six weeks off work? There was no way. This was the busiest time of the year. My brother couldn't possibly handle all the jobs we had lined up. This couldn't possibly be happening.

I entered into a cycle of pain and anxiety that led me deeper and deeper into a downward spiral. It was the loneliest of feelings to watch helplessly as everything unraveled. During that time, my fear took on a life of its own.

Then, in the briefest of moments, I broke through. Exactly what I broke through, I can't even say to this day. It was as if the downward spiral had a bottom, and the bottom itself wasn't an impenetrable barrier. Instead, it was, once pierced through, a doorway. Suddenly I found myself in another dimension.

All my life, I had been convinced that pain led to no place other than more pain. The only thing to do, when confronted with it, was to endure. I knew this from childhood visits to a dentist who didn't believe in novocain. The most horrifying words I ever heard were, "Oh, that's just a small cavity. We won't need to use anything for the pain. This'll just take a minute."

That minute was a journey into the depths of hell. For me, pain had never led to other dimensions. It was a black, bottomless void. But now, for the first time, there was a door in the wall of pain.

The momentum of my agony and anxiety blew me into an utterly new realm. To my amazement, the pain vanished, and I was surrounded by complete peace. And even more surprising, I was fully alert and conscious.

THE PEACE BEYOND ALL UNDERSTANDING

To put words to that dimension would never do it justice. There was a stillness that was charged with potential. Questions were irrelevant, for everything was self-evident. The air seemed to vibrate with life and consciousness.

Never had I experienced anything remotely like it. This life that I had called my own was clearly linked to all of existence. Barriers disintegrated, as the web of creation became intertwined with my body.

A being of light stood in front of me, radiating streaks of white and gold in all directions. I couldn't make out the face, because it was similar to viewing a faint silhouette made by light shining from behind.

This person was strangely familiar to me. At the time, I equated him with Jesus, but, in retrospect, I'm not so sure. I don't recall him ever using that name; it was simply my own association.

There was no sense of time. Gone was the unyielding regularity of seconds and minutes. In some ways, it felt as if we had been standing in front of one another for all eternity. We communicated efficiently, yet without words.

To stand in that presence was to be fully known and completely loved. It became abundantly clear that this accident of falling off the roof was no accident at all. In fact, there were no such things as accidents. Every moment, every experience, was filled with purpose and intention. In that state, I knew that I knew that I knew.

The apostle Paul had a similarly transcendental encounter on the road to Damascus, when he was blinded by a great light and confronted by a dead man—Jesus of Nazareth. Later on, he would label that experience "the peace that passes all understanding."[6] In that encounter, Paul saw the direction of his life change toward a whole new purpose.

For me, the shift was indeed beyond all understanding. It was not a function of rational thinking that moved in linear progression. It was, instead, something that transcended thought altogether.

Standing in that light, I knew I was to go to seminary. It was the unmistakable sign.

In that moment, it seemed that the sole purpose for my mystical journey was to answer our question about seminary.

Over time, it was to become much more. An intense desire began to take root in me. It was the desire to touch that realm again, to understand it, to work with it, to travel between dimensions.

Naively, I thought that studying to become a pastor would lead me in that direction. After all, what is the religious life if it's not uniquely intertwined with the divine pursuit? What better way to discover the nuances of this other dimension than through the ministry?

The issue had finally been settled. I left with my family to enter Princeton Theological Seminary.

THE PEARL OF GREAT PRICE

Jesus once told a parable about a person who found a great treasure hidden in a field owned by someone else. Excited beyond belief, because he knew that the treasure was priceless, he then did something that must have seemed positively bizarre: he sold everything he had.

Imagine the gossip:

"He's crazy! What will become of his retirement plan?"

"Oh, he's always been a dreamer."

"What a disgrace! Selling the family heirlooms. Look at him; they mean nothing to him!"

Yet, within his own level of experience, the man's actions made perfect sense, for what he intended to do was to buy the field in which the treasure had been hidden. What he had found was so valuable that he was willing to trade everything for that prize.

Jesus began this parable with the words, "The kingdom of heaven is like a treasure hidden in a field."[7] To reinforce his point, Jesus then told a second parable, very similar to the first.

This time he started by saying, "The kingdom of heaven is like a merchant in search of fine pearls."[8] Coming across a pearl of extraordinary value, this merchant too sold all that he had in order to buy it.

In both cases, the kingdom of heaven is compared to something of ultimate worth. It is so priceless that all one's worldly goods would gladly, even gleefully, be sold in order to buy it. What could possibly be of such infinite value?

It wasn't until I fell into the mystical realm that I finally understood what Jesus was talking about. What would you pay for ultimate peace? While engaged in the pursuit of happiness, what would you give to stop chasing after joy and suddenly attain it?

For the first time, the kingdom of heaven became a living, present reality. For me, it was a reality open not just to a select few, but to everyone.

UNCOMMON SENSE

The problem is that, even though it might be open to everyone, most of us simply don't have the eyes to see it or the ears to hear it. Though the kingdom of heaven is all around us, we're preoccupied with a thousand other things, locked in a consciousness that denies anything out of the ordinary.

When I was younger, at times, I would slip into another realm unexpectedly. Without warning, my attention would drift into sublime reveries, and my awareness of this world would fade.

But these states, I learned, got in the way of focused attention. That was bad news.

If I got into trouble as a kid, my dad would usually demand, "What were you thinking?" And before I had a chance to answer, he would offer the withering accusation, "Well, ya *weren't* thinking, were ya?"

So the message was hammered home. I should always be thinking. But it wasn't just any type of thinking that was needed. Thinking had to be rooted in common sense. So, gradually, I learned to discount my own experience and to forget that mystery and wonder ever took a detour into my neighborhood. The world was what everyone else said it was. No more, no less.

But when I fell off the roof, I couldn't forget anymore. Spiritual amnesia was obviously nonsense. In that moment, I discovered that there is a world beyond description, flourishing at the edge of consciousness.

Falling off the roof allowed me to peer into a realm of uncommon sense. That wasn't my first encounter with mystery. It was just one that I couldn't ignore.

CHAPTER TWO

Hitching a Ride to the Kingdom

One of those previous encounters happened to me in 1974, at the age of twenty-two. In those days, my motto was, "If it scares you, do it." One of the things that scared me most back then was hitchhiking. For some reason, the very thought of being on the open road, completely at the mercy of passing motorists, sent shivers up my spine. So, of course, I had to do it.

An opportunity came when my sister moved to Arizona and needed help with her furniture. We packed up an orange-and-white U-Haul, put the hideaway bed in the back so we could take naps on the road, and headed west. My plan was to hitchhike home to Pennsylvania via California.

After unpacking her stuff in Tucson, I hit the road with nothing but my thumb and my backpack.

When you're hitchhiking, everyone who stops to pick you up knows they'll never see you again. It's amazing how quickly people open up in those circumstances. You can get the fluff out of the way in the first twenty minutes: jobs, in-laws, kids, that sort of thing. In forty-five minutes, they're talking to you about their sex lives. Inside of two hours, they're telling you about their last bank robbery and where they hid the money.

My first ride was with a psychologist who liked me so much that he put me up for the night at his home, gave me dinner, and then breakfast the next morning.

My second ride was with a band of hippies, driving a broken-down Ford Fairlane with no air-conditioning. Four of us were crammed into the back seat, with all of our belongings. With the windows open all the way in the desert heat, there was a sea of whipping hair—mostly from armpits.

As it turned out, they'd picked me up to see if I had any money for gas or food. In my naiveté, I was expecting a dawning of Aquarius reception from them. Maybe they would offer a garland of flowers as a token of their love for me and the universe.

But soon it became clear that they were expecting me to bankroll the whole excursion. To make matters worse, it wasn't at all clear that they had any interest in sharing my money with me. But before we could finish the one-sided negotiations, the universe intervened and killed their car. It sputtered to a stop on the roadside, and I got away as quickly as possible. The nerve! Wanting a hitchhiker to pay for something!

It was the middle of the desert. My head felt like it would explode from the pressure of the sun's heat. Still, it was far preferable to the company of my last ride.

Standing alongside the baked asphalt, a dusty semi pulled over. The driver was three hundred pounds of redneck stuffed into a sweat-soaked "wife beater" undershirt. Tobacco juice trickled down a greasy, gnarled beard. His belly oozed over his huge metal belt buckle, as he leaned on top of a horizontal steering wheel.

I knew from *The Hitchhiker's Handbook* that it was illegal for truckers to stop for hitchhikers. So with a manufactured cheerfulness, my first words, as I climbed into the cab, were, "Gee, I didn't know you guys were allowed to pick up riders . . ."

He looked over at me with steely eyes and a toothless grin. "Don't worry," he growled. "If we get stopped, I'll just bury you."

A chill shuddered down my spine. But before I could open the door to get out, he'd ground the transmission into first gear. As the cab lurched forward, the diesel roared. The seat back slapped me so hard, it practically knocked me into the windshield.

In the first twenty minutes, the driver told me about his career as one of the original Hell's Angels. There were stories of Harley choppers, wild women, bar fights, drugs, parties, the riot at the Altamont rock concert. It was all black leather, silver chains, and the wind in your face.

And, eventually, he told me where they hid the money.

As the white lines flashed by, his tales took on the staccato rhythm of the cab seats pounding us hard in the kidneys. When we stopped at a truck stop, he bought me lunch. We laughed, hung out together for a couple of hours, then climbed back into the cab and let it beat on us some more.

By the time he dropped me off at Big Sur, in California, it hurt to say good-bye. The good part about hitchhiking—and the bad—is that you're never going to see these people again. But we were heading in different directions. I was going straight. He wasn't.

As the last echoes of the diesel died away, the quiet rattled around inside me. The only sound was the hiss of tires from an occasional passing automobile. Loneliness settled over me like a fog.

Hours drifted by with no one stopping. It was nearly sundown, and the temperature was falling fast. There was no shelter in sight. The scene was short on romance and long on bad options.

It looked like I'd finally gotten what I had come for: I was scared.

Then the strangest thing happened. It took me by surprise. At a time when everything was fraught with uncertainty, when I was completely at the mercy of forces beyond all my control, when I had no friends or family to come to my aid, when I had no visible means of support—just then, I was surrounded by the deepest sense of security I had ever felt.

It began with the music of wind sifting through redwoods. Light filtered through the green canopy in diagonal shafts of dancing brilliance. The forest took on a sheen of soft radiance, as if I'd stumbled into Eden.

But it was more than what I saw. Something was changing in my body. It was a feeling—like warmth, but much more.

I hesitate to call it a presence, because there was no apparent being. It was larger and more encompassing than that. All at once, the barriers that had always separated me from the world evaporated in a dancing swirl of light and color. Yet, it was subtle—the kind of thing you could walk right past without noticing if your mind was in a muddle.

But, even more, there was a knowing. In the most uncertain of circumstances, I knew beyond a shadow of a doubt that I was cared for, deeply and profoundly. I was safe and secure in this most vulnerable of situations.

For just a moment, the world turned out to greet me—to remind me I was anything but alone.

Standing among the redwoods of Big Sur, I heard the voice of creation calling to me, not in words, but in spirit.

What had happened? Why had the world waited for that moment to radiate its glory? Was it necessary to be stripped of all my security before I could be bounced on the breast of Mother Earth? Had all the air-conditioning, vinyl, and elevator music so separated me from her nurturing embrace that I had become dead to her song? Regardless of the reason, I knew that she was alive and that her caring was complete.

A Bush Burning in the Wilderness

Joseph Campbell pointed out that the act of moving away from one's family and heritage is essential to the hero's journey.[9] Culture is a tool that educates us into a particular way of seeing. We learn to split creation's unity into a thousand distinctions, simply because our parents told us so. Our vision becomes clouded.

In fact, it is not *our vision* at all, but the vision of countless generations before us. To see on our own, we must move away from all that we once assumed to be true. Only when we are alone in the wilderness can silence speak.

To move into the wilderness is to risk direct contact with the earth. When we're alone with the land, there is no culture to split our vision. Absent are the human voices that tell us who we are. Gone are the obligations that muster us into the line of duty. There is only the naked call of being. When we've been stripped of all, the song of creation springs forth. Only then do we have ears to hear and eyes to see.

This theme of moving away from our familiar surroundings is played out over and over again in the Bible. Abraham was called to leave his own country and family and go to a land that would be shown to him. Joseph was taken by slavery into Egypt. Elijah climbed to the top of the mountain to catch a glimpse of God passing by. Jesus spent forty days in the wilderness as a prelude to his ministry.

When Moses stumbled upon a bush that was burning in the wilderness, he heard the voice that would change him and his people. You have to wonder how many times he had taken his little flock of sheep past this very spot without noticing that bush.

But, this time, he saw. This time, he heard. This time, Moses knew he was on holy ground, as the sacred burst into his life. In that red-hot minute, all that he thought he was, all that he was told about the world, all that he knew about the gods vanished in a blaze. His vision penetrated the external to gaze upon the dancing light of essence.

Suddenly Moses was privy to God's view of the world. Where the Hebrews knew only slavery, God saw freedom. In a situation where Pharaoh held all the cards, the Creator offered a different kind of power. While Moses's people were languishing in despair, divine insight saw profound hope.

It seems that a fundamental aspect of the kingdom of heaven is the capacity to fashion unimagined possibilities out of what, at first glance, is apparently worthless. Divine insight is able to perceive an infinite abundance, even in the most desperate of circumstances. Human insight, on the other hand, is hemmed in by assumptions of inadequate resources. Words to the wise ring in our ears:

"There's no such thing as a free lunch."

"If it sounds too good to be true, it probably is."

"The early bird catches the worm."

"One good turn . . . gets most of the blanket."

Because things are scarce, we all want to get our share of the blanket, and then some. We hoard and save for a rainy day. Our hoarding actually produces the very scarcity we fear.

But hitchhiking into the wilderness puts us on a collision course with scarcity. And, in the wilderness, there are no spectators.

Personal Experience versus Hearsay

Years ago, a circus performer named Blondine decided that the ultimate feat was to walk a tightrope across Niagara Falls. Crowds came from all around to watch him traverse the thin line in the swirling mist and wind.

As part of his act, he pushed a wheelbarrow out over the chasm. Inching his way along the narrow strand, he tipped and teetered on the brink of disaster, as the crowd held its breath. When he returned safely at last, the tension gave way to thunderous applause.

Once the cheers died down, Blondine asked the crowd if they thought he could place the weight of a man in the wheelbarrow and safely complete the journey. The crowd egged him on. Placing two eighty-pound bags of grain in the wheelbarrow, he made the dangerous trek high above the thundering waters.

Upon returning safely to the crowd, Blondine asked how many thought he could take a real person over and back. As before, the throng cheered with delight at the prospect.

Then he asked for volunteers. The only one ever to accept the offer was Blondine's manager. No matter how much the crowd respected Blondine's skill, they didn't trust him with their lives.

In the wilderness, we have no choice. When surrounded by nothing but deprivation, like it or not, we've already hitched a ride in a very precarious wheelbarrow.

Ironically, it is that very deprivation that sets the stage for the sacred to break into the world. And with it can come a completely unexpected form of nurture.

But it's not the kind of thing you can understand from the sidelines. That's why not only Moses, but all those who followed him, needed to wander in the wilderness for forty years.

Only then would they cease to be bystanders hawking their "eyewitness" version for the news cameras. It became their story when it was *their* throats that were parched with thirst. When *their* stomachs were wracked with starvation, it was no longer a fairy tale. When they realized that *these bodies—*

the only ones they had come into the world with—were about to be wasted, suddenly their attention was riveted.

So when Moses rapped on the rock with his staff, and a stream came gushing forth in the midst of the desert, the mad dash to water's edge became the stuff of legend. And when, on the verge of their starvation, manna came raining down from the heavens, suddenly they knew it in their bones that there was more to this world than meets the eye.

ABUNDANCE

This history formed the backdrop of Jesus' understanding of the kingdom of heaven. When he proclaimed, "I came that they may have life, and have it abundantly,"[10] he was evoking the heritage of his own people in their wilderness sojourn. But what gave his words such compelling authority was that he had had his own confrontation with scarcity and lived to tell the story. He had seen an inexplicable provision during his own trek into the desert.

So when Jesus said, "Seek first the kingdom of heaven," it wasn't abstract theory. For him, the spiritual world was primary, and it contained a hidden abundance that could be relied upon in all circumstances. It wasn't merely a nice, earth-friendly philosophy he was espousing. His words were an exposition of the way the universe was structured. In fact, creation itself was always reflecting this plenty:

> Therefore I tell you, do not worry about your life, what you will eat or what you will drink, or about your body, what you will wear. Is not life more than food, and the body more than clothing? Look at the birds of the air; they neither sow nor reap nor gather into barns, yet your heavenly Father feeds them. Are you not of more value than they? And can any of you by worrying add a single hour to your span of your life? And why do you worry about clothing? Consider the lilies of the field, how they grow; they neither toil nor spin, yet I tell

you, even Solomon in all his glory was not clothed like one of these. But if God so clothes the grass of the field, which is alive today and tomorrow is thrown into the oven, will he not much more clothe you—you of little faith! Therefore do not worry, saying "What shall we eat?" or "What shall we wear?" For it is the Gentiles who strive after all these things, and indeed your heavenly Father knows that you need all these things. But strive first for the kingdom of God and his righteousness, and all these things will be yours as well.[11]

While he spoke, Jesus drew attention to birds circling aloft, or he plucked a lily from the ground and turned it in his hand, as if the whole world were at his disposal for teaching.

Indeed, it was. He had so trained his attention that he could see beyond duality and gaze upon the spiritual dimension permeating this material reality. It was apparent to him, even on this side of death, and had appeared in the midst of extreme vulnerability.

It was this same reality that opened up to me while standing, backpack in hand, beside the pavement of California's State Highway 1. For the first time in my young life, there was nothing to protect me from the outrageous nurture of creation. A deep joy swelled up from within me and spilled out among the redwoods. In return, the harmony of creation's inner song played over me.

CHAPTER THREE

The Genius of Our Multiple Personalities

Highway 1 emerges from Big Sur's forest and snakes along the razor's edge of California's coastline. It's a two-lane ribbon, pinned precariously against the vertical rock walls. To one side, the mountains shoot skyward. To the other, a stark void plunges into the Pacific.

Shortly after my moment of communing with creation, a young woman drove by, eyeing me suspiciously. She pulled off at a diner, just a few yards up the road.

While she was eating, I walked on past, still hoping for one last ride. After half an hour, she got back into her car and pulled quickly out of the parking lot, as if to drive by.

In a gesture of mock distress, I placed my palms together, pleading for her to stop. To my surprise, she did.

THE OLD MAN AND THE SEA

I threw my backpack into the rear seat of her late model Tercel, and we headed north on Highway 1. The serpentine route took us to breathtaking vistas high above the crashing surf. The sun was just beginning to set, the clouds slowly turning first golden, then pink, and then magenta, as the last rays bounced off them.

At one point, we were driving in the shadow of the mountain when we rounded a hairpin turn in the slender road. The sun suddenly burst toward us in a blinding flash. At that very spot, in the center of our lane, was a huge boulder.

There was no chance. We didn't even have time to swerve. We smashed into the boulder and went airborne. I wasn't wearing a seat belt, so I jammed my hands to the roof, wedging myself in place.

The car started to flip in space. We turned over once, twice, and then a third time, all in slow motion. It gave me plenty of time to think.

I knew that the ocean was on the other side of the road, hundreds of feet below. The road was too narrow. We had no chance of avoiding going over the edge. Clearly, this was the end of my life.

Like many people in a near-death situation, I felt oddly serene. There was no panic, no surprise, only calm. *So this is what it's like to die in a car falling off a cliff,* I thought. *Interesting . . .*

Suddenly, I was no longer a twenty-two-year-old hitchhiker from Western Pennsylvania. I was an observer—old, wise, captivated by this moment of possible destruction, and totally unafraid.

I had never met this person inside me before. He had absolutely no use for worry. For him, all of life, including death, was fascinating. As the world spun around the axis of that car, that old man was able to hold a center that was unmovable. There was no need for concern of any kind. This was just another sampling of the vast cornucopia of life.

I had the impression that this old man was well acquainted with life and death. He had seen many lives. For him, it was simply the appointed route for returning to something beyond. It would be quick and painless; the blink of an eye, and everything would change. There was no doubt about it. He knew about the other world. It was his home. And so he gazed upon the impending tragedy not with horror, but with unbridled fascination.

Strangely, the car didn't go over the edge, but flipped straight down the narrow road as if guided by an unseen hand. The driver was held in by her seat belt. I continued to wedge myself in place by pushing hard against the car top as the Tercel rolled over and over.

The car came to rest on its roof, and both of us found ourselves looking at the world upside down. The engine was still sputtering. Plumes of smoke belched from the tailpipe.

"You OK?" I asked her.

She nodded, numbly.

"We'd better get out of here." I had seen too many movie cars blow up in moments like this to want to stick around. We struggled through the side windows and hurried away as quickly as possible.

A few yards ahead, an RV was parked at a scenic overlook. The owner took us in and cleaned us up. We had a few minor cuts and bruises, but no significant injuries.

The car, despite the fact that it didn't explode, was totaled. I felt sorry for my driver. She had borrowed the Tercel from her brother. Now she'd have to break the news to him that his shiny new ride was scrap metal.

But, through it all, the old man inside of me was perfectly calm, perfectly accepting. He was somewhat puzzled as to why death hadn't won out, and found himself chuckling over the improbability of our narrow escape.

"Such a strange world," he muttered to himself.

Strange indeed. The young woman and I parted ways, never again to make contact. It seems so odd, given the intimacy of our brush with death.

The wise old man, on the other hand, continued to live in me. His visits were infrequent, to be sure, but his presence was always unmistakable.

THE INNER PANTHEON

As I get older, I'm often awed by how many distinct personalities seem to emerge in the strangest of circumstances. Sometimes I wonder how many different people actually reside within my psyche.

In my early years as pastor, I never had much time to reflect on this idea. It never even occurred to me that we could be anything more than just one distinct human being.

All that changed one day when a young woman came into my office for counseling. She began to explain that she suffered from multiple personality disorder. Day after day, she contended with a variety of people vying for control of her body. They would emerge without warning and seemed to be completely independent from one another.

I could hardly believe what she was telling me. It seemed absurd. Apart from the scars on her arms, she seemed perfectly normal.

She came back several more times, and I was naive enough to think that I was helping her. Pastors rescued people, right? (What better way for the eight-year-old boy in me to earn medals?) About the fourth time she came to my office, though, I noticed a definite change. Her pupils were like pin pricks. She spoke as if from a great distance away. Her movements were awkward and halting.

I called her by her name, but she corrected me, saying she was "Sarah." Slowly, I began to realize that I was talking, not to the woman I had come to know, but to a completely different personality. As we spoke, her eyes grew increasingly clouded and distant. I felt like I was losing all touch with her.

We weren't trained for these kinds of things in seminary. Still, rather than calling for help from the senior pastor, I decided to stick it out.

She gradually regressed in age, until finally melting down into a fetal position. For hours, she lay on my couch, motionless. I didn't have a clue as to whether she was dead or alive, except for the occasional breath. Clearly, I was in over my head. The only thing that kept me in the room was my utter fascination and foolishness.

Eventually, I was able to get in touch with her psychiatrist, who answered my panicked questions, but did little to bring her back to the realm of the living.

As the hours passed, she gradually returned. But she was like a shell, hollow and exhausted from the ordeal. I helped her get home.

Later I came to understand that the scars on her arms were from the war that raged in her psyche as one personality and then another wrestled for control. Some were so possessive that they would even seek to kill the body that carried them all, taking knife in hand to slash her wrists, rather than relinquish command to the others.

It wouldn't be the last time I would see her multiple sides. One time, she called me long distance and asked me to talk her through the process of dying, after she had intentionally taken an overdose of sleeping pills. She wanted nothing more than a friendly voice to accompany her transition into the next world.

Fortunately, I was able to put her on hold and contact paramedics near her home. While I waited for their arrival, I clicked back over to her, only to hear her voice becoming more and more faint and disoriented. While we were still on the phone, the rescuers arrived and I could hear them, rushing in to pump her stomach and bring her back to life.

I was badly shaken. I wondered if I had done the right thing. Had my intervention only served to prolong her suffering?

But somehow, through it all, she managed to stay alive and even to become self-supporting. She was and is one of the most courageous people I have ever met. She began to open my eyes to the fact that there is much more to each of us than what we allow the world to see.

LEGION

When I was a child in Sunday school, my teacher once recounted Jesus' encounter with just such a person.

It happened right after Jesus had calmed the storm, and he and his disciples were reaching the far side of the Sea of Galilee. No sooner did their feet touch the sandy beach than a "demoniac" came charging toward them.

Now, people didn't have demons when I was growing up. They had a screw loose. They needed to see a shrink. They had a social disease. They had an inferiority complex. But no one had a demon in them.

People must've been ignorant and superstitious in Jesus' day. But we were different. Even as children, we understood ourselves to be enlightened, because we were scientific. Our world could be explained.

Still, it made a good story. And if Jesus could calm the storm, he could probably beat up on this demon guy too.

The demoniac madman lived in the graveyard. The locals, who were terrified of him, tried, in vain, to shackle him. Time and again, he snapped his chains. Finally, the townspeople gave up, and the madman roamed free, howling among the tombstones.

When Jesus asked his name, the words flew out of him, like something from *The Exorcist.* "My name is Legion, for we are many."

With these words, the teacher raised his voice to make it sound scary, but I wasn't impressed. Wandering around in graveyards, rattling chains? That's just a Hollywood movie scene—the part where they tell you to put on your 3-D glasses.

It would take many years for me to lose my sophistication. After I had seen one personality after another take up residence in my friend's body, the figure of Legion suddenly came to life. Then I knew, personally, why that madman had inspired such fear in those who met him.

The Legion in Each of Us

One of the insights of depth psychology is that we are indeed many personalities. As we encounter impossible circumstances, the psyche becomes overwhelmed. We come to grips with this by assigning subpersonalities the task of holding the traumatic experience.

We then split these personalities off into the unconscious, so that we can continue to function day to day. Not only do these forgotten others carry our trauma, but they also can be repositories for grief, shame, rage, or any other emotion that we think is unacceptable.

As a child, I had an imaginary friend who was small enough to slip into my shirt pocket. He was supposed to love me at all costs, but I made it very difficult for him to do so.

At night, I would force him to hang from the rail of my top bunk, torturing him with the agony of cramping arms growing weak with fatigue. If he made it through the night without letting go, I would love him in return. But if he fell into my cupped hand while I slept, I would feel him hit my palm and punish him severely for letting go.

I never actually decided what the punishment would be—it was the situation that fascinated me and held my attention. I knew he was imaginary, so I never really took it seriously. Still, I savored the godlike euphoria that comes with absolute control over another person.

On one level, it's uncomfortable for me to write about this now. On another level, I recognize that it was a brilliant way of dealing with an impossible situation. In real life, I was the pocket-sized imaginary friend.

Though it wasn't evident to me then, it was a perfect depiction of my relationship with my own father and his unpredictable rage. I was supposed to love him no matter what. But his love was tied to my performance. Could I hang on to the railing all night without falling? His anger hung over me like a cloud. This imaginary exercise was one way I could retain some sense of power in the face of my own helplessness.

I'm still amazed that a child could think of such a creative solution. My imaginary friend eventually disappeared into the murky waters of my unconscious. But I suspect that he still lives on in some hidden fashion, carrying the weight and fear of a lonely child.

As effective as this maneuver is, the splitting comes at a great cost. Though hidden, these subpersonalities continue to demand energy for their maintenance.

NUMBING OUT

But there is an even more basic cost: the world outside of us loses its glory. Why? Because the energy devoted to our unconscious personalities is designed to keep them hidden. We want to numb out to them, because the story they have to tell is far too painful. In a sense, they become dead to us.

But this numbing carries over into our relationship with the world. Because we live with the constant fear of stumbling across an unwanted inner memory, we live in a persistent anxiety that the external environment also holds the capacity to do us harm. Numbing out to our inner landscape desensitizes us to the external environment as well.

As I discovered in the redwoods of Big Sur, the world does have the capacity for speaking to us. Though we may hold some romantic notions about the nature of this communication, we're terrified of what we might discover. We've been taught that it's best not to know. And so the spirit within creation recedes from our awareness, and we end up howling in a graveyard of our own making.

PROJECTION

These subpersonalities don't always disappear into the unconscious. Quite often, we appoint other people to play their parts for us.

One of the telltale signs of this maneuver is rage. When others inspire an irrational and uncontrollable anger within us, it's a clear indication that such a person is carrying our dark side. It's the psyche's way of shoring up the boundary. We become consumed by the need to persecute or destroy the offender.

Not only does this happen at the personal level, but, in an even more devastating manner, it surfaces on a national level as well. We can see it in the persecution of the Jews, the enslavement of blacks, the violence of homophobia, the injustice of sexism, the slaughter of Native Americans, and so many other forms of bigotry and rage. Each is a product of our inability to deal with our own cultural darkness.

This is the real reason why Jesus said, "Love your enemies and pray for those who persecute you."[12] He wasn't laying out an impossible challenge, nor was he advising us to become sugarcoated do-gooders. He wasn't even suggesting that we should bury our anger and pretend that all is well.

What he meant was that every person around us, especially our enemy, is a mirror for who we are. When we fully understand this, every person becomes our teacher. They show us, in three-dimensional Technicolor, what resides unconsciously within us. We truly are not aware of these other personalities when we swear up and down that they have no part in us. Yet, denial doesn't make them go away.

A prime example, of course, is the almost universal vow never to be like our parents. Even if a father or mother has died years before, it can be one of the most startling things to suddenly hear yourself speaking with the same words, voice inflection, and posture of the very parent who was never to be imitated. Why does this happen? It's because that person still lives within us.

When we're aware of this dynamic, then the world becomes a place of unparalleled teaching. Those who enrage us most have the potential to become our greatest allies. They're the ones who can break through our game of hide-and-seek and show us who we really are, and so move us along the journey toward awareness.

THE SHADOW AND POPULAR RELIGION

That this world can be redemptive and that our enemies might actually play an indispensable role in our growth are ideas that are usually overlooked by popular Christianity. Because of the preoccupation with eternity, salvation and the kingdom of heaven are pictured only in terms of the afterlife. Either you're going to Heaven or you're going to Hell.

Any genuine healing in the present seems trivial by comparison. Your eternal fate hangs on good behavior, or acceptance of Jesus Christ as Lord and Savior, or choosing the right denomination. Those who choose rightly go to Heaven, and those who don't go to eternal punishment.

But when you think about it, isn't this a rather odd view of God? Rather than exhibiting the beautiful Old Testament quality of *hesed,* most often translated as "steadfast love," the God of this theology seems to be highly conditional. It's an either/or proposition, backed up by threats. We all hang from the bed rail in an impossible double bind.

What kind of God says, "Love me or I'll kill you. No, wait . . . I won't kill you, I'll torture you for longer than you can possibly imagine"? How is it possible to truly love someone who extracts affection by intimidation? Yet this is precisely what this theology asks us to believe.

The unfortunate part is that it avoids the real problem, which is that it doesn't lead us to genuine wholeness. Because, for many of us, the only means of dealing with enemies is to seek their destruction; it never occurs to us that such adversaries are actually mirroring our own rejected parts. These dark aspects stay hidden and unacknowledged, split off into the unconscious. Rather than seeking wholeness, which would require the recovery and integration of these lost parts, we're convinced that "evil" lives on the outside and must be eliminated in the name of purity and holiness. This results in lives that are tragically fractured. We become so focused externally that we live in blissful ignorance of our own inner demons.

The paradox is that the preoccupation with rooting out evil in the external world requires that the list of enemies be inexhaustible. If the final victory were won, if the last adversary were defeated, there would be no one left to live out our unacknowledged inner darkness. Unable to embrace a genuine wholeness that would reclaim our inner demons, we manufacture a synthetic wholeness, instead, by forcing others to live out our rejected lives. We persecute them, but we also need them, for they allow us the luxury of avoiding the inner journey.

In condemning others to eternal punishment—not even offering them the grace of some sort of conclusive death—there is the assurance that there will always be someone to carry our rejected darkness. Since that's the underlying motive, it's easy to see that the punishment of an actual once-and-for-all death would defeat the purpose.

In his famous book, *The Gulag Archipelago,* Aleksandr Solzhenitsyn put it well when he wrote:

> If only it were so simple! If only there were evil people somewhere, insidiously committing evil deeds, and it were necessary only to separate them from the rest of us and destroy them. But the line dividing good and evil cuts through the heart of every human being. And who is willing to destroy a piece of his own heart?[13]

Only hard-won wisdom has the capacity to see that "the line dividing good and evil cuts through the heart of every human being." The basis for peace can only be understood when each of us confronts the question, "And who is willing to destroy a piece of his own heart?"

But if salvation is understood as recovering a lost wholeness, then everything shifts. The task then becomes not the achievement of an otherworldly ticket to a plush Radisson, complete with cloud-filled pillows, en suite Jacuzzis, and winged room service. Instead, our essential mission becomes the recovery of those lost and hidden parts. The by-product of this journey is that the shining vibrancy of the present world begins to open to us.

This journey implies becoming ever more aware of those dimensions of ourselves that we have consigned to unconsciousness or have asked others to carry for us. Even more, it asks us to entertain the mystery of who we truly are.

MISSING PARTS

Judging by his remarks in Matthew, Jesus seems to have been aware of this.

> Those who are well have no need for a physician, but those who are sick. Go and learn what this means, "I desire mercy and not sacrifice." For I have come to call not the righteous, but sinners.[14]

To make that statement, Jesus had to be aware that everyone around him was a part of himself. In calling sinners, he was intentionally moving toward wholeness, gathering up all the parts of himself that might otherwise disappear into the unconscious.

In the parable of the sheep and the goats, he drives home this same point when he says, "Just as you did it to the least of these who are members of my family, you did it to me."[15]

The catch is that we have to first be aware that something is missing, to know that we each possess unhealed—even elusive—parts within.

When Jesus cast out Legion's tormenting hoard, they entered into a herd of swine, which then rushed into the sea to their deaths. Since pigs were unclean animals to the Jews, they are a metaphor for our own unwanted memories. We believe them to be unclean and unacceptable. The only solution is to destroy them—let them plunge into the sea to their deaths.

THE SIN EATER

Many have looked at this story with dismay over the injustice of Jesus killing off a herd of innocent animals to save the sanity of one person. It's difficult to reconcile, until we realize that Legion was the appointed "sin eater" for his village.

I first came across this term in a short story by Christianna Brand titled "The Sins of the Fathers." Through the end of the seventeenth century, and possibly longer, sin eaters were common in Welsh culture.

It was the sin eater's vocation to ingest the guilt of the recently dead by eating food that was placed on the corpse. It was a banquet with only one guest. The worse the sinner, the better the food. The witnesses in the room would know that the sin had passed from the dead person when the sin eater gave out a blood-curdling scream. Only then was the transaction completed.

The sin eater, then, was trading his salvation for a meal and a few coins. His future was hopeless.

In the story by Christianna Brand, sickness had gripped the land and the sin eaters were kept exceptionally busy. It became increasingly difficult to find someone who could take on the iniquities of the dead before burial.

On one dark and damp evening, there was a knock on the door of a sin eater's home. The house was in ruins, with cracked mortar and shingles falling in. Only those requiring the morbid services rendered inside dared to approach.

The sin eater's wife answered the door, only to find yet another anxious relative seeking release for his departed kin. But, this time, the sin eater was sick. At first, the wife said he couldn't come.

But the visitor was persistent; there simply was no one else available. Finally, they struck a deal. As long as the sin eater could ride on the visitor's horse both to and from the funeral, then she would allow her husband to make the trip.

Knowing that her husband could never survive the journey, the woman suggested to her son that he go in his father's place. The boy was horrified. "Me? Eat the sins of a dead man?" His protests erupted into tears.

But his mother assured him that the sins would pass to him only if he ate the food from the body. She urged him to go and tell everyone they had to leave the room because he only worked alone. All he had to do was to shove the food into his pockets, wait a while, and then scream. Then he could bring the food home and safely eat it there.

The family was starving. And when she explained that they would also pay him, he decided, after much coaxing, to do his mother's bidding.

When the boy arrived at the funeral riding on the horse, he had a shawl covering his head to hide his youth. Some of the onlookers were suspicious, especially when he spoke in such a high voice. But there simply was no other sin eater available. This one would just have to do. Reluctantly, they agreed to his unusual demand that he be alone with the corpse.

Once everyone left the room he began shoving fruit, vegetables, and hunks of greasy meat into his pockets as fast as he could. His heart raced with terror, as he recoiled from the possibility of touching the body. Suddenly, he tipped over a tray and began hysterically screaming as he went lurching out of the house, not even pausing to pick up the coins that had been thrown into the mud as his payment.

He scurried back to his own home, staggering through streams and thick woods, his clothes sagging from the weight of the stolen food. Finally, he arrived. He had made it without tasting even one scrap.

After delivering the bounty to his frantic mother, she turned toward the back room with the food in her arms. The son protested that she had promised that he could eat what he brought back. She reassured him that he would have all of it for himself. The son stood stammering in protest, unable to make sense of the delay.

Finally, his mother reappeared and took him by the hand to the room where his father had been lying ill.

As he came through the door, the room seemed to spin around as he struggled to make sense of the bizarre scene. There was the feast collected by his own hand: piled upon his dead father's naked torso. The village had a new sin eater.[16]

THE BLACK SHEEP AND THE SCAPEGOAT

The concept of the sin eater is not as crazy as it sounds. It has its roots in the Old Testament, in the tradition of the scapegoat.

To deal with their collective sin, the high priest would choose two identical goats—one to be sacrificed and the other to carry away the communal guilt, as the scapegoat. A red cord was tied around its neck to symbolize the sins it carried on behalf of the people. It was then driven from the camp to its death. If the sacrifice was accepted by God, the red cord found the next day in the wilderness would have turned white—proof that their sins had disappeared along with the goat.

When a person has been designated to be a scapegoat, he or she must bear the guilt of the larger community or family. The real tragedy is that, by confining this unfortunate to such a limited range of character traits, each family member must assume an equally constricted, artificial role in the drama.

As a result, none of them are able to make any conscious choices about their behavior. The role they're acting dictates everything. It's as if they were all sleepwalking.

Because the villagers living near Legion were unaware of their rejected aspects, they had no way of seeing how much of themselves they had forced him to carry. For Legion to truly become whole, each person who feared and shunned him needed to reclaim his or her projections.

Because they were unable to take that step, the "demons" exorcized from Legion couldn't return to their place of origin. Instead, they were consigned to the collective unconscious, symbolized by the unclean swine.

From this perspective, it wasn't Jesus who caused the destruction of the herd. Rather, it was the residents of that area. Because they couldn't receive back their own unclean spirits, the swine became a convenient repository for all they had rejected in themselves.

But the enactment of this drama brought the villagers too close to their own darkness. Their reaction to Jesus' miracle was fear. They immediately asked him to leave.

Reclaiming our own demons, both individually and collectively, is one component of the journey toward the kingdom of heaven. The inability to do so always results in some form of destruction: either our own or someone else's.

FRATERNIZING WITH THE ENEMY

Curiously enough, the encounter with Legion didn't seem to unsettle Jesus. How he was able to rid the man carrying the unclean spirits of his burden is something that I don't understand. How he achieved such power is a mystery. But that he understood the human psyche is clear.

In the political climate of his day, the dividing line between good and evil was extreme. Legion lived in non-Jewish territory. In daring even to set foot in that forbidden land, Jesus, as a teacher of Judaism, was seriously compromising the purity demanded by the Pharisees.

In healing a Gentile, he was also taking what was assumed to be rightfully reserved for the Jewish people and giving it to those considered to be unworthy. For Jesus, this was a persistent tactic. He was continually coloring outside the lines of his own tradition by fraternizing with foreigners and outcasts. To the political leaders of his day, it was nothing less than an act of treason.

Those wishing to wage war have always outlawed fraternization with the enemy. War itself depends upon demonizing the unseen foe. If the populace can be convinced that the citizens of a foreign nation are all murderers, rapists, bloodthirsty terrorists, and part of an evil axis, then military action can be not only justified—it can be virtually assured.

The one thing that can dispel the image is face-to-face encounters. It's far more difficult to kill those we're looking at, because we can't help but notice how much they're like us.

Jesus understood that the kingdom of heaven can be found in the most unlikely of places—even in the embrace of our worst enemy. It's the enemy who tells the true story of what we've rejected. And so the enemy holds the key for our wholeness.

KNOW THYSELF

For centuries, the admonition to "know thyself" has been a hallmark of wisdom. This counsel is also a road map to the kingdom of heaven. It means coming to grips with the Legion living within each of us.

The old man who suddenly appeared in me as our car flipped over and over in Big Sur was part of my own inner Legion. I was quite surprised to meet him. It was even more surprising to find out that, for him, living and dying were all one piece.

In the end, his calm acceptance of all that happened was well founded. The owner of the RV parked at the scenic overlook not only took us in, but he also drove us to a place where my friend could get help and make contact with her brother. Once assured that she was well and in good hands, we dropped her off.

My new friend then invited me to come along with him on his journey to San Francisco. Upon arrival there, he took me on a tour of the city and introduced me to his friends. They gave me a place to stay and even treated me to a meal.

After staying for a few days, the driver of the RV and I headed back out onto the road. He was a gourmet chef, and, every once in a while, he asked me to take the wheel while he cooked up something special in the back.

"Here, try this," he would say after a while, his hand reaching around from behind the driver's seat to pop a new delicacy into my mouth. "How do you like it?" I would nod my enthusiastic approval, wanting to know if there was more, all the while keeping my eyes dutifully on the road.

We drove to Yellowstone National Park and camped there for a few days. Then we drove all the way to Illinois. I trusted him and his hospitality completely. He was one of the kindest, most generous people I have ever met. It was, as we say in the hitchhiking business, "one hell of a ride."

CHAPTER FOUR

Jonah and the Unified Vision

"Do you believe that Jonah survived three days in the belly of a whale?"

The search committee had drawn their chairs into a tight circle. They were firing questions at me to determine whether or not I was "their boy." The gloves were off.

I had already passed the first-impression test. They had thoroughly examined my resume and checked my references. Jacquie and I had been treated to a tour of downtown Minneapolis and had assured them we were hardy enough to survive the biting winters. So far, I was a suitable candidate to be their pastor/poster child. But the real examination was just beginning.

Ironically, I wasn't even sure I wanted this job. But it was a good-faith gesture to Jacquie, who couldn't see bringing up our children in the Texas panhandle, at a church I'd accidentally fallen in love with.

I was a senior in seminary at the time. Along with all the other graduating seminarians, I was deeply into the process of interviewing for a church position. Competition was keen, as committees came from all over the country to Princeton to sift through resumes and make initial contacts with promising candidates.

We had been advised to practice interviewing with many different search committees, whether we were interested in a particular church or not. Repeating the process helped to build confidence. That way, when we came across a congregation that seemed like a good match, we could shine.

Banking on that advice, I had signed up to meet with a church group from Hereford, Texas. Now, nobody wanted to end up in Hereford, Texas— not me, not my friends, and certainly not Jacquie.

As I went out the door for that meeting, she reminded me, "Now, remember, this is only a *practice* interview!"

"No problem," I vowed. "I have no intention of taking a church in the middle of nowhere."

But once I began speaking with the committee, I became thoroughly enchanted. These were the nicest, most genuine, most loving people I had ever met in my life!

"Jacquie!" I shouted, bursting through the door after the interview. "They want to take me to breakfast in the morning! And they want you to come too!"

Jacquie groaned. "Paul, I told you not to get involved. You promised this was only for practice!"

"I know. I know. But just come and meet these people."

Before we knew it, we were on a plane to Hereford, Texas. Once again, they were wonderful people. Slowly, I began to muse over the idea of becoming their pastor. While we were there, they offered me the job. I said we'd need to pray about it.

On the plane home, Jacquie had looked at me and said, "What do you think?"

"Well, I never thought I'd say this, but I'm actually considering it."

"And who would be your wife?" she'd asked.

A LITMUS TEST

So here I was, being grilled by another church in Minnesota—because it was about as far away from Texas as we could get.

When they asked me about Jonah, I knew it was a litmus test. If I answered that I believed a man could live for three days in the belly of a whale, then, in their eyes, I could be trusted to be a true, Bible-believing,

God-fearing, fire-and-brimstone, tough-on-sin, Praise-God, Haaaaaleluia, Thankya JEESUUUS literalist.

If I didn't, they'd put me down as one of those no-good, mealy-mouthed liberals, who didn't believe in the Bible—or God for that matter—just another communist in disguise, the product of a socialist, atheistic, heathen church. Why, I might even be willing to marry gays!

It was a tense moment. Though I wasn't sure this church was a good match for me, it seemed prudent to keep my options open. Any hedging about my answer would disqualify me.

To this day, I don't know where the words came from, but suddenly a deep calm came over me. It was like the wise old man came to visit out of nowhere.

"To tell you the truth, I'm not nearly so interested in arguing about the Bible as I am in reading it. That's where I would start. Let's see what's really there first, because most people have no idea what the whole story of Jonah is about in the first place. Mostly, they only know about the whale, and the whale is just a very small part."

In the next few minutes, I went on to tell the story of the radical nature of Jonah's odyssey. I was shocked to notice something I'd never seen before. The whole committee was listening intently. Even the man who had been the most suspicious of my theology was leaning inward, so as not to miss a word.

It was my first encounter with the disarming power of storytelling. There was a softening on each face, even an occasional silly grin. Their testing, confrontational demeanor had given way to the thrill of a mutually shared journey. Apparently, it was the first time any of them had actually heard the saga in its entirety. Their predetermined positions melted into the childlike curiosity to hear how it ends.

But another, even more surprising, thing began to happen—I actually started to listen to the Jonah tale with new understanding myself. Though I couldn't realize the full impact at the time, his story would become one of the most profound, unsettling, and vital passages I would ever read.

JESUS AND THE SIGN OF JONAH

Apparently, Jesus felt that way about the story too. When he had a search committee approach him one day, looking for a sign, his only reply was, "No sign shall be given to this generation except the sign of Jonah."[17]

It was an odd response. Surely, a man who could heal intractable diseases, feed thousands with a few scraps of food, and even breathe life back into cadavers could stoop to a minor display of power to entertain his new audience. It was a simple, straightforward request. Why complicate things with a mysterious reference to an obscure prophet?

But Jesus was after something bigger than putting on a magic show. He wanted to shift their way of looking at the world. The story of Jonah asked them to do just that.

Who was this Jonah character? And how could he, in the space of four Old Testament pages, become so central to Jesus' mission and self-understanding?

By our standards, Jonah was crazy. If we had lived in his day, none of us would have taken him seriously. Yet, when the cute little story of Jonahandthewhale is told to countless toddlers every Sunday, Jonah is held up as a paragon of obedience and virtue.

The tale is told by teachers who, themselves, have no understanding of the radical implications of his journey. Yet, if fully grasped, the story of Jonah challenges our understanding of God, reality, and human consciousness.

Make no mistake though—Jonah was insane, and dangerously so. That's why Jesus' response to the Pharisees was such a thunderclap.

In Luke, his reference to Jonah is embedded in a series of condemnations against the scribes and Pharisees. As the story goes, "When he went outside, the scribes and Pharisees began to be very hostile toward him and to cross-examine him about many things, lying in wait for him, to catch him in something he might say."[18] Why the hostility? What could possibly be so offensive about the innocent story of a little man caught in the belly of a big fish? And why did Jesus mention Jonah when they asked for a sign?

Matthew provides an easy answer by linking Jonah to Jesus' death: "For just as Jonah was three days in the belly of the sea monster, so the Son of Man will be three days in the heart of the earth."[19]

But that was not what the scribes and Pharisees were reacting to. Jesus had not yet died, so any connection to his resurrection would have been meaningless to them. It certainly would not have inspired them to such open hostility.

Jesus' audience was much more biblically sophisticated than we are. They had the whole Old Testament committed to memory. The mere mention of a name or a phrase would evoke for them the entire history and context of the passage in question.

To understand what Jesus was getting at, we need to be just as familiar with the story as they were. Only then can we see why it sparked such unbridled fury.

THE PERFECT ENEMY

Jonah was a good Jew. From the time he was a child, he was taught one thing: the Jewish people are the chosen ones of God.

They didn't need Sunday school attendance medals to get on God's A-list. That favored position was their birthright. Because of their special place in God's eyes, anyone who was their enemy was also the enemy of God. God played favorites, and the Jewish people were on the winning side of that favoritism.

That's why it was such a crazy thing when Jonah started hearing voices telling him, "Go at once to Nineveh, that great city, and cry out against it."[20] And that's also why Jonah ran as far as he could in the opposite direction from Nineveh when he heard them. The people of Nineveh were the enemy.

Nineveh was the capital of Assyria. In 721 BC, the Assyrians had attacked and defeated the northern half of Israel and slaughtered thousands. Those whom they didn't kill were taken into captivity. For Jonah and his fellow Jews, the only good Ninevite was a dead one.

The idea of preaching to these heathens was not what disturbed Jonah. It was the possibility that the preaching might work.

Jonah knew that the character of God was based in forgiveness. If the Ninevites accepted Jonah's warnings, they might repent, and then God might forget about punishing them. It was a possibility that was totally unacceptable.

To understand the depth of Jonah's rage, consider the feelings of Americans after the World Trade Center was destroyed. As far as many were concerned, death would have been too kind a punishment for the perpetrators. Had God commissioned someone to preach to Osama Bin Laden's network so they might be forgiven, that person would have been publicly condemned, beaten, or even killed.

The outrage over Assyria's domination was even more passionate during Jonah's time. Jonah and his fellow Jews wanted nothing less than annihilation of the Ninevites and their nation.

So Jonah ran away, booking passage on a ship bound for Tarshish. He couldn't possibly trust the unpredictable nature of God's forgiveness.

While they were sailing, the wind started to howl through the rigging. Whitecaps broke over the bow.

The small boat was beginning to sink. It was clear to everyone that somebody on board was responsible for this calamity. They cast lots to see who it was.

Sure enough, the lot fell on Jonah. They tossed him overboard, and the raging torrent fell silent. That's how Jonah ended up in the belly of a great fish.

When the monster of the deep vomited him up on dry land after three days, that's where the story usually ends. It's a nice, neat lesson in always following God's will. That's the part we all know.

MORE TO THE STORY

But if that were the end, we'd miss the point altogether, as most people do. You see, what Jonah discovered on the rest of his journey disturbed him immensely. It shattered all of his comfortable notions about God's intentions for the world.

God called him, once again, to preach to the people of Nineveh. Not wanting to spend another three days in the belly of who-knows-what, this time Jonah obeyed.

Through the streets of Nineveh he wandered, screaming out at the top of his lungs, "Forty days more and Nineveh shall be overthrown!"

He looked like a wild man. No one could communicate with him. His words seemed to erupt from a cauldron of pain and anger. His eyes darted around in paranoia. His clothes hung from his body in tatters. He spoke constantly to an invisible partner.

In many ways, he looked and acted much like a contemporary street person. In almost every city, there's a hidden population of homeless people ghosting about. They push shopping carts containing all their worldly goods. They rant and rave while staggering along the sidewalk. They huddle in cardboard boxes and under bridges at night, finding sustenance in fast-food Dumpsters.

We accept them, ignore them, and then move on with our lives. We take comfort in knowing that we won't intersect with them in any meaningful way. We feel secure in being insulated from their world.

There are times, however, when we can be drawn into their drama, even against our will.

THE MAN WITH DISAPPEARING LEGS

Dusk was settling over the city. The last red-and-gold streaks from the sunset were reflecting in my rearview mirror. Sitting at a red light in my Ford F-150, minding my own business, I was lost in thought. I barely noticed the rumpled figure moving toward the curb at the intersection.

Then something gripped my attention. He was arguing with an invisible partner.

His words were audible, even strident, as if he were doing battle with unseen forces. His hair was matted, and his greasy clothes hung loose and tattered.

Suddenly, his head disappeared below the fender of my truck. Though I couldn't see it, I knew instinctively that he was lying down with his legs stretched out in front of my tires. If I started forward, his legs would be crushed under the weight of my truck.

The light turned green. The cars behind me began tapping their horns. I didn't move.

Another light change. Still there was no sign of the man who had hunkered down beneath my front bumper. Drivers started laying on their horns in anger and frustration.

The light changed back to red, then green again. I threw the transmission into park, opened the door, and waved the snarling drivers behind me to go around. When I made my way to the hood of my truck, my suspicions were confirmed. Here was a man I had never met, stretched out, sitting on the curb with his legs directly in front of my Goodyear Wrangler radials.

I tried to communicate with him, but he kept up a monologue about his missing shoes. He didn't even acknowledge my presence. The voices in his head were much more real to him.

Finally, a shopkeeper came out and began shouting, "Johnny! What the hell ya doing? You can't just sit in the middle of the road! Get up!"

Johnny acted as if his legs were useless. So the shopkeeper and I gathered up his limp form and carried him through the intersection, depositing him on the opposite curb in a heap. Johnny then proceeded to scoot along the sidewalk on his behind, toward a destination known only to him.

As I made my way back to my pickup, the bizarre nature of our encounter washed over me. Johnny lived in a world that was totally separate from mine. Though our physical forms had touched, the encounter had never registered for him, even though our meeting could have maimed him for life.

By all traditional assessments, Johnny was crazy. His "illness" would be diagnosed as a form of schizophrenia. He talked to people, or entities, that obviously were not there, and his actions were guided by invisible information.

In every city, there are people like Johnny claiming that they speak to God. They perform actions of the most preposterous nature. And we, in turn, call them crazy and pay them little attention.

Yet, oddly, when biblical characters demonstrate these same behaviors, we applaud them as heroes. Being in the Bible somehow changes everything. They're in there to teach us how to be good, aren't they?

The truth is, if they were living today, we would see them ranting and raving on street corners and sleeping on park benches. We would know they were crazy, no matter how insistently they claimed to be speaking to God. We would walk away, glad to avoid any contact with their madness.

A MADMAN AND A KING

But Jonah's culture was quite different from ours. It wasn't assumed, in those days, that such people were mad. Those who displayed unsettling behaviors were often considered to be the mouthpiece of a god. And so, when the king of Nineveh heard Jonah's preaching, the words had greater impact than they might have had if uttered by a homeless person hunkered beneath a car fender today. Because Jonah was taken seriously, a great fast was proclaimed, and, at the king's insistence, the whole city began its rites of repentance.

God was so moved by this collective act of contrition that the creator of the universe repented from his intention to destroy them: "When God saw what they did . . . God changed his mind about the calamity . . . and he did not do it."[21] What happened next is terribly clever. When he saw that the enemies of the Jews were spared, Jonah flew into a rage and began railing against the divine nature. It was the consummate "I told you so!"

> Is not this what I said while I was still in my own country? That is why I fled to Tarshish in the beginning; for I knew that you are a gracious God and merciful, slow to anger and

abounding in steadfast love, and ready to relent from punishing. And now, O Lord, please take my life from me, for it is better for me to die than to live.[22]

In this passage, Jonah is quoting words that were sacred to the Jewish people. These were the very words revealed to Moses on the mountaintop, when he came within a hair's breadth of seeing the Lord: "The Lord, the Lord, a God slow to anger and abounding in steadfast love and faithfulness."[23]

This is so clever, because the author is using this sacred description of God to show the absurdity of the Jewish notion that God cared only for them. It was a subversive way to force them to confront a steadfast love that was much bigger and more inclusive than they had previously acknowledged.

Jewish history was replete with instances of God demonstrating mercy in dealing with the Jewish people. As long as mercy and steadfast love were displayed to those who were the favorites, the world made sense and God seemed rational.

But the thought that this same God could love those who were clearly the enemies of God's people was bizarre, to say the least. It was so unsettling that Jonah would rather die than consider the possibility.

Jonah's world and theology were shipwrecked on the rocks of an insane God. Unable to die, Jonah did the next best thing. He went outside the city, sat on a hilltop, and set up camp, hoping God would repent of his repenting. Maybe there was still a way for Ninevite blood to be spilled. Jonah wanted a good vantage point to view the carnage.

As luck would have it, it was a very hot day, and the sun beat down hard. Yet, God's mercy came in the form of a great plant, which grew rapidly above Jonah to give him shade.

Jonah was pleased about the plant. It seemed appropriate that he, a good Jew seeking the destruction of God's enemies, should be rewarded. The world was beginning to make sense. Maybe Nineveh would be destroyed after all.

But, in the blink of an eye, everything turned upside down again. A worm killed the bush that was giving Jonah shade. What's more, a withering east wind blew up, and the brutal sun beat down all the more intensely. For Jonah, it truly was better to die than to face such a crazy world.

> Then God said, "You are concerned about the bush, for which you did not labor and which you did not grow; it came into being in a night and perished in a night. And should I not be concerned about Nineveh, that great city, in which there are more than a hundred and twenty thousand persons, who do not know their right hand from their left, and also many animals?"[24]

The story ends with this question. It ends this way precisely because we too are meant to consider its implications, for God's question put to Jonah is ours as well.

In a beautifully crafted little tale, we are invited, almost without our knowing it, to ponder the very nature of the creator. And, when we do, we're confronted with something that is both profound and disconcerting. For at the very heart of this tale, we are shown *a God who chooses and yet has no favorites, a God concerned for the whole world.*

This, then, was the sign of Jonah that Jesus offered to his listeners.

THE RAGE OF THE PHARISEES

The Pharisees knew exactly what Jesus was driving at. In those days, Israel was under Roman domination, and the occupiers were hated with white-hot fervor. Roman boots were treading on holy ground. Clearly, these intruders were God's enemies. By calling the story of Jonah a sign, Jesus was asking the Jews to consider the possibility that God cared about the welfare of these Romans just as much as the Israelites.

It was tough to swallow then. It's just as tough today. Take away our enemies, and what is there to live for?

Worse still, what is there to die for? When the implications of this simple quality of God are realized, the entire nature of life is altered.

Yet, for many, enemies are so obvious, so dangerous, that to propose that God is *not* constantly calling us into a holy war against them seems patently absurd. It's not just the Jews who can be convinced that God is on their side. Virtually every country that goes to war does so with the belief that it is acting on God's behalf. Quick to point out the inhumanity and evil of the enemy, the combatants rarely recognize their own nation's capacity for corruption and malevolence.

Americans, for instance, are aghast at the idea of jihad, or a holy war, as it is conceived in some Islamic cultures. To us, it seems like a despicable marriage of faith and militancy that degrades the sacred nature of religion.

Yet, when we choose to go to war, there is no hesitation to call upon God to bless our soldiers and our country. Our own marriage between war and religion is just as pervasive in many ways. This sentiment is captured in bumper stickers like these:

"It is up to God to forgive Osama Bin Laden. . . . It is up to us to arrange the meeting."

"Praise God. Pass the ammunition."

The ubiquitous American flag paired with the words "God bless America" has become so prevalent that, in the minds of most people, God is exclusively concerned with the welfare of citizens of the United States. It is a rare person who would dare to ask if we might not have fewer conflicts if we began asking God to bless *all* nations instead.

Politicians have long recognized that the easiest way to solidify support is to propose armed conflict with a foreign nation.

George W. Bush didn't have to work very hard to sell Americans on the idea of wars in Afghanistan and Iraq. Despite the fact that weapons of mass destruction were never found in Iraq, the mere assertion that Iraq was a threat to us unleashed a torrent of patriotism and outcry in favor of mobilizing our military. Bush's popularity skyrocketed.

But enemies come in a variety of forms. It's not just conflict with foreign nations that underscores the hunger we seem to have for naming an adversary.

In his book *Blinded by the Right,* David Brock reflects on the unexpected consequences that victory over communism had on the Republican Party:

> When the Berlin Wall fell, ushering in an era of post–Cold War politics, the reliable Republican issue of anti-Communism . . . was also lost. Everywhere Communism was collapsing . . . . Anti-Communism, as the conservatives conceived it, was never supposed to be a winning crusade. Now, the passion behind our politics was gone. The loss of anti-Communism as a rallying point "left [conservatives] in a sinking boat without a motor," said Thomas Fleming, editor of the conservative magazine *Chronicles.*[25]

It was Rush Limbaugh and Newt Gingrich who recognized the danger to their party inherent in the loss of an enemy. Their genius was to supply a new one and to sell it to the American public: liberalism. *Liberal* became synonymous with *satanic* in the minds of many. Yet, if liberals should one day cease to be a threat, like communism, another enemy would be required to take their place. The same could be true of the demise of conservatives—both factions are needed. Without the term *liberal, conservative* has no meaning.

Therein lies the value of an enemy. Our enemies define us. They give us a reason to live, if only to fight against the evil we project onto them. If the enemy goes away, we are faced with the task of defining ourselves in a vacuum.

The need for an enemy is certainly not limited to foreign relations. It is just as prevalent in the church.

In the Presbyterian tradition, groups of churches come together to form Presbyteries. It's astonishing to find out how much of these meetings is spent in fighting. If it weren't for the prayers and preaching, there would be little difference between a Presbytery gathering and a congressional filibuster.

There are the same old feuds, the same behind-the-scenes maneuvering in smoke-free rooms. Sides are drawn up even before debate begins. There is exasperation with the opposition at its inability to see the obvious. Votes are taken, issues are decided by narrow counts, only to have the losers vow to fight on, with the victors incensed that their win isn't recognized as God's final decree. For a church that was founded on the idea of love, there is an amazing amount of animosity and even outrage.

One issue that refuses to go away is sexuality. Like a worn-out family joke, it keeps coming up—long after it has ceased to be funny. Whether it's ordination of homosexuals, sexual expectations for pastors, definitions of morality, or family values, the arguments are so well rehearsed that they don't even need to be voiced. The combatants are intense crusaders fighting for the purity of the church, utterly convinced that God is on their side.

Few seem to notice that, for all their hairsplitting and posturing, for all the hours and days spent in preparation and debate, the pronouncements made are irrelevant. Despite their best efforts, sex is here to stay in all of its kinky, extravagant, and taboo variations.

Seldom, if ever, does anyone check on the latest General Assembly guidelines before embarking on a forbidden sexual exploit. Still, the fights rage on, coming back year after year, as surely as the change of seasons. The fight *has* to go on. Without an enemy, the combatants are unable to define themselves in any meaningful way. Ironically, the very thing that is hated is essential for giving order to the lives of most people.

Is it possible to live without enemies? Can we see our lives as having positive value in and of themselves, without the need of an enemy to define us?

Jonah's story asks us to consider just that. It's not an easy proposition, however, especially for those who have based their lives on the conviction that they are doing God's work.

GOD THE ENEMY

Telling the Jonah story to that Minnesota search committee had turned the tide. Though I hadn't elaborated on the implications of the Jonah story, the very fact that I knew the story from memory seemed to impress them. I could almost see them saying in their minds, "Well, at least he knows the Bible. He can't be *too* far off base."

Afterward, the questioning turned from theology to pastoral care. The guy with the perpetual sour look took the lead.

"Are you a good listener?" he mumbled.

"I'm sorry. What did you say?" I replied, tongue-in-cheek. Nobody laughed. In fact, I was quite sure that nobody even got it. He repeated the question.

"Are you a good listener?" the prune face mumbled, louder this time, for my benefit.

I decided to play it straight. "Oh, yes! Listening happens to be one of the things I do best!" Everyone breathed a sigh of relief, assured that I was a capable listener, as long as they remembered to speak loud enough.

It began to dawn on me that I would be explaining myself a lot to this group. By the end of our time together, it was clear to me that we weren't a good fit. I gracefully bowed out of any further discussions and focused my job search on other churches.

One by one, though, my leads ran out. Suddenly, I was faced with the prospect of graduation with no job.

The thought was paralyzing. Jacquie, pregnant with our third child, was becoming more rotund by the day. Dirt One and Dirt Two were growing like crazy and needed to be fed constantly.

How would I support my family? Where would we go? What would I do with my life? The anxiety swirled around me like a tornado, and, with it, an intense anger began to build.

One night, unable to sit still in the face of mounting pressure, I went for a walk alone to vent my rage. With each step I screamed at God—mostly in my mind, but sometimes even out loud.

"How *could* you? How *dare* you? I leave everything I have, I come to this place to follow a calling that *you* chose me for, and now you abandon me? Is this some kind of joke? Do my prayers mean nothing to you? Is this the reward I get? Nothing? Don't you care anything about my family? Answer me! You have no right to do this!"

And so the raging went. I must have looked like a wild man, pacing furiously, eyes darting everywhere. Engaged in battle with someone who was obviously not there, I became oblivious to my surroundings.

The irony was lost on me. I had turned into Jonah, railing against God because my position as a chosen one couldn't be cashed in for special privileges. Deep down, I had expected that my journey through seminary would make me a favorite son. Surely, God would see to it that a spiritual person's earthly needs would be satisfied. It was shocking to find out otherwise.

In that moment, God became the enemy. In a way, it felt good. I needed someone to blame. By making God the bad guy, I helped to define myself: I was the one being wronged, the hero standing up to the ultimate adversary.

And how much more dramatic it was that my enemy wasn't a mere mortal, or even a nation, but the very creator of the universe! My rage was of biblical proportions! I might not have had a job, but at least I was special enough to do battle with the Almighty.

By the time I arrived home, I was exhausted from the fight. I walked through the door utterly spent, but somehow cleansed.

As soon as I got back, Jacquie announced that a pastor from Muncie, Indiana, had called wanting to interview me. We had never even heard of the pastor, the church, or the city.

I picked up the phone and dialed, little suspecting that Muncie would be the place we'd spend the next seven years of our lives.

Limited-Sight Distance Ahead

Part of the problem with selecting an enemy is that we do so on the basis of flimsy data. We think we know what's best for us, only to discover that our assumptions are misguided. Circumstances change, and we suddenly realize that the very person we hated has become our greatest teacher. We nurse our pet peeves, as if they were ordained from on high, only to find out that we've been blind to grace.

Such is the dilemma of the dualistic mind. With holy fervor, it splits the world into a thousand distinctions. Then, in the aftermath, it either grieves its choices, when they're shown to be inadequate, or it goes to war to defend them, so as not to have to face contrary evidence.

That's why it's not easy to live with a God who is equally concerned about the welfare of our enemies. It undermines our worldview.

The way we understand our lives is the product of countless choices, most of them made unconsciously. Because we assume God sanctions our judgments, it gives us a sense of security, even power. It gives order to our lives. Conversely, if our worldview becomes unraveled, we're lost in a raging sea of uncertainty.

Is it possible to live without enemies? Is there a way to look upon the world with eyes that can see value in everything, even in that which we would seek to destroy?

In truth, that is a very difficult proposition for normal Western consciousness. We've been taught from the earliest age to discriminate between good and bad, right and wrong, truth and falsehood. The filter of judgment we place on the material world largely determines even the nature of our perceptions.

But there is a way around this limitation. It requires that we shift out of the mind of duality and to embrace, however fleetingly, an entirely different state of awareness. In this other way of perceiving, the world is no longer a series of isolated things and events. Instead, it's a web of interconnections that is ultimately one.

From this perspective, the idea of an enemy is laughable. The old saying, "We have met the enemy and they are us" becomes exceedingly apparent.

When Jesus pointed to the sign of Jonah, he was calling for a dramatic shift in awareness. That shift forms the basis for the kingdom of heaven.

But before we can grapple with such a change in consciousness, we must more fully understand the nature of our own perception. For that story, we must begin at the beginning.

CHAPTER FIVE

How We Split the World

When my boys were teenagers, they had a saying that drove me nuts. Whenever I would try to correct some of their more irritating tendencies, they would respond flippantly, saying, "It's all good, Dad."

"Is your homework done?"

"Don't worry. It's all good."

"You're going to be late if you don't hurry!"

"It's all good, Dad."

"Your underwear is showing, and I can see your butt crack."

"It's all good, Dad."

But for parents, it is *not* all good. Parenting is the dirty, thankless job of relentless nagging until our children outgrow their foolishness. For us, the world is divided between the good and the bad. The only thing that keeps our children from certain calamity is our frantic splitting of reality into ever finer distinctions. But such is not the way of God. If there is one aspect of the creation story in Genesis that stands out, it's the refrain: "And God saw that it was good." After each day's hard work of creating, the text says, "And God looked upon everything that he had made, and indeed it was very good."[26]

Could God be like a misguided teenager responding to our incessant worries and concerns by insisting it's all good?

Deadly Earnest

Sadly, the creation story itself has become a sort of litmus test. If a speaker takes a literal interpretation of creation, some people will rest assured that he or she can be trusted to speak the truth about the rest of the Bible.

Other people, who are unable to dismiss years of scientific research supporting evolutionary theory, may consider the same speaker ignorant.

Yet, neither side is willing to challenge its fundamental reading of the text. For both sides, the story is no longer alive. The Bible has become a club used to bludgeon one's enemies. All joy and laughter are lost in the hand-to-hand combat of biblical interpretation.

Something Out of Nothing

If the issue of literal truth can be put aside for just a moment, we just might hear something entirely new. If we can examine the creation story with these more gentle eyes, then perhaps we can stumble upon profound wisdom.

"In the beginning God . . ."

Who can even imagine what things must have been like before the first act of creation. A world in which there was nothing. *Nothing.* No thing. Nada. Zilch.

It's odd, because we really want a God who thinks as we do, who understands our special point of view and validates it fully, unquestioningly. We want, in other words, a God who is just as we are.

If, indeed, the divine being were like us, then the creator must have spent many a sleepless night worrying about inspiration. "Where can I get the ideas for making a new world? What if it's no good? What if I look like a fool?" His or her self-esteem would have been hooked to the outcome of this project in a big way. Literally, the whole world would have been waiting to pass judgment on the resulting handiwork. Talk about writer's block, the artist's terror of the blank canvas, or the fear of public speaking!

CREATIVE PLAY

Yet, because God is different in nature from us, the act of creation was not fraught with fear. Instead, it carried the joyful enthusiasm of a child picking up a crayon for the first time. That childlike enthusiasm is the essential energy of creativity. It's an energy that is built into each of us. Studies have shown that a rush of endorphins, producing a state of temporary euphoria, often accompanies the process of creating. Could it have been anything less when the universe came into being?

Almost as if God were scribbling around, just to see what would happen, creation was started; then there was a separation.

It must be understood that the biblical stories were first used for instruction. This teaching began with small children, and because this was before the advent of printing, stories were communicated by word of mouth.

Unlike our modern English, which is highly visual, the books of the Bible were intended to be a language of the ear. This oral culture certainly was predominant in Jesus' day. That's why he would often say, "Those who have ears to hear, let them listen." Hearing, not seeing, was at the center of communication.

IN THE BEGINNING WAS THE WORD

It comes as no surprise, then, that the word was the vehicle for bringing the world into being. "And God said, 'Let there be light'; and there was light."[27]

It was the word, too, that was the vehicle for passing along knowledge—often through stories.

To make an oral story work, you had to memorize it accurately. This was crucial, if it was going to be handed down to succeeding generations intact.

One aid to memorization was (and still is) repetition. The passage was rehearsed over and over. That was why the scribes and Pharisees of Jesus' day knew the Old Testament by heart.

The passage itself was fashioned to aid memorization. Repetitive elements were used as hooks for the mind.

The creation story bears this repetitive imprint. A rough pattern was established in the first act of creation:

Command: God said, "Let there be light."

Result: And there was light.

Assessment: God saw that the light was good.

Separation: God separated the light from the darkness.

Naming: God called the light Day, and the darkness he called Night.

This pattern was mirrored in the following days of creation. The author used repetition to draw the hearer's ear to the most significant elements of the message.

HAIRSPLITTING

The most noticeable repetition is the phrase, "And God saw that it was good."

This phrase is crucial to the message, because what is introduced is a God who chooses, even separates, yet has no favorites. The separation of darkness and light is followed by the separation of the waters. This was, in turn, followed by a series of separations to complete creation. The final separation was between male and female.

At the end of each series of separations and/or creations, there was the voice of God assessing it all with approval. "And God saw that it was good." But when God had viewed the whole thing as a totality, suddenly, it was no longer just "good," but "very good." All those distinctions. All those separations. All those dualities. All those potential antagonisms. All those opportunities for us versus them, you against me.

Not once in the whole story does anyone say, "This town ain't big enough for the both of us."

"It's my way or the highway."

"You're not from around here, are ya, mister?"

It would have been so tempting to declare one side of the separation as good and its opposite as bad, but it never happened. When the stunning variety and diversity of the earth was surveyed, it was all, every bit of it, "very good."

God's ways truly are not our ways. In his book, *The Power of Now,* Eckhart Tolle makes this same point:

> Do you truly know what is positive and what is negative? Do you have the total picture? There have been many people for whom limitation, failure, loss, illness, or pain in whatever form turned out to be their greatest teacher. It taught them to let go of false self-images and superficial ego-dictated goals and desires. It gave them depth, humility, and compassion. . . .
>
> Seen from a higher perspective, conditions are always positive. To be more precise: they are neither positive nor negative. They are as they are. And when you live in complete acceptance of what is . . . there is no "good" or "bad" in your life anymore. There is only the higher good.[28]

It's from this higher perspective that God viewed creation. When the outrageous variety of creation was assessed, there was nothing but divine approval. The essential message of the creation story, then, is designed not to communicate *how* the world came about, but rather its *quality.*

Reading it as a blueprint for the cosmos misses the point entirely. If this were understood, the whole debate between creationism and evolution could have been avoided.

EDEN AS A STATE OF CONSCIOUSNESS

Apparently, there was a time when human beings could see clearly the wonder and beauty in all of creation. It was precisely this awareness that constituted the Eden experience.

As such, Eden was not located at a particular place or time. It was, rather, a state of human consciousness that was open to the spirit within creation.

It was this awareness that dawned on me in the redwoods of Big Sur in the midst of profound insecurity. It was the consciousness that overtook me, even as death hovered over that car, lunging toward the abyss of the Pacific Ocean. It was this dimension that broke in, as I was swept into that vortex of pain and anxiety in the hospital after falling off the roof.

Each of these moments was a shift into the kingdom of heaven. Each was a new awareness found in present time. I didn't need to die to experience it.

From this perspective, the entire world is alive with consciousness. Every moment is pregnant with possibility and learning. Creation is speaking to us all the time. The voice of God is everywhere.

THE GREAT SPIRIT

Indeed, there are still cultures that hold this perception. Years ago, I went to a conference held by the Presbyterian Church. One workshop dealt with the issues of ecology and environmentalism. In the discussion that followed, we traded ideas about how we could better care for the world in which we lived.

Sitting in the audience was an older Native American man who wore his hair in braids, dangling over each shoulder. His face was tanned and leathery, his eyes piercing, yet serene. He remained quiet through the discussion. Finally, the leader called on him, wanting to know what he thought of the issue.

The man chuckled a little and then said, "You have to understand that we approach this from an entirely different perspective. You see, for me, the whole world is sacred. When I look at that mountain over there, it's something that is alive to me. The Great Spirit lives in the trees, the animals, and the very air we breathe. For us, it's all one."

This is a point of view that is quite foreign to the Western industrial mind. Our education is biased toward reducing things to their smallest units, then isolating them into discrete categories. The oneness of the world is not at all apparent to us, as it is to the Native American tradition.

To make matters worse, we feel compelled to grow up fast. Our self-worth is tied to how much responsibility we can shoulder; we lose perspective with noses that are pressed so close to the grindstone.

Thoreau's description of his fellow citizens who inherit farms, only to find themselves pushing their barns before them with each step, is just as apt today as back then. As he so famously observed: "The mass of men lead lives of quiet desperation. . . . A stereotyped but unconscious despair is concealed even under what are called the games and amusements of mankind. There is no play in them, for this comes after work."[29]

And so it was one day, when I found myself pushing my own barn before me as I was walking on the beach. My spirits should have been high, because the ocean is a place I find tremendously invigorating. But on this day, my mind was heavy with a thousand weighty concerns.

To add to my misery, the beach was littered with dead jellyfish, millions of them. For days I had been waiting for the tides to reclaim them, but the blobs of translucent gel seemed to be anchored into the sand. Seagulls would occasionally peck at them. But even they soon gave up. Every step I took had to be chosen with care.

Suddenly, I looked up to see a girl who appeared to be about four years old. Her golden frizzy hair was swirling around her face as her beach dress billowed and twirled around her body. She had chosen one jellyfish and was dancing circles around it, arms flapping gaily in the breeze.

As I drew closer, I could make out her high-pitched voice singing into the wind, but her words were swallowed by the crashing surf. As I came within several yards of her, she suddenly stopped dancing for a moment and eyed me.

Then she burst into song, all at once, and shouted, "Jellyfish for sale!"

I had to laugh. It was so ludicrous. I contemplated how I might explain to her the laws of supply and demand, so as to educate her in the ways of commerce. You can't sell something nobody wants—especially when there are millions of them for free, especially when they're nothing but disgusting, icky, jellyf . . . Then it hit me. In that most precious of moments, I found myself gazing on the infinite possibility of a child's mind. It is a mind where there are no barriers, no barns to push, no tomorrow to care about. It is a world where even jellyfish can be sold to total strangers. And it was all good.

Had I had my wallet with me, I would have gladly given her twenty dollars for her dead jellyfish. I suspect she could have sold one to every straggler who happened along the beach that day. Her joy was that compelling, her delight that irrepressible.

As Jesus said, "Suffer the little children to come unto me, for such is the kingdom of heaven."[30] They can see that which we, as adults, have lost.

We may catch glimpses of such wonder on occasion, but it is difficult for us to sustain it on a daily basis. It can be frustratingly elusive.

But there is another trap. Obsessed as we can be with control, after catching a glimpse of this ethereal spirit, we can find ourselves assuming it will always be at our beck and call.

But the kingdom of heaven is beyond our ability to master it, often eluding our most desperate grasping.

Although in some cultures there is a great emphasis on teaching and sustaining an awareness of sacred unity, it's a rare thing in Western education. We're faced with a constant parade of distractions that continually pull us back into a mind-set that splits the world. Even if we feel ourselves called individually to the path of a new awareness, we must usually do it with little external support. Our dawning consciousness then fades away all too quickly.

On occasion, we can reconnect with these sublime states, in spite of our cultural distractions. Such fresh contact can sustain us in the spiritual quest.

There are, however, periods that can last for years, even decades, during which all contact with the world beyond seems utterly futile. Though heartrending to endure, it is a necessary phase to go through, if we are to give up our desire for control over that which is, by nature, limitless.

When all seems to be lost, that's the beginning of the dark night of the soul. It's a state well documented in mystical literature. Though it seems to be a crucial rite of passage, no one chooses it voluntarily.

It may feel like a meaningless void, hemmed in by walls of despair. Yet, even in this, the learning continues.

PART II

Stumbling into the Dark Night

The most highly developed branches of the human family have in common one peculiar characteristic. They tend to produce . . . often in the teeth of adverse external circumstances—a curious and definite type of personality; a type which refuses to be satisfied with that which other men call experience, and is inclined, in the words of its enemies, to "deny the world in order that it may find reality." We meet these persons in the east and the west; in ancient, mediaeval, and modern worlds. Their one passion appears to be . . . the finding of a "way out" or a "way back" to some desirable state in which alone they can satisfy their craving for absolute truth. This quest, for them, has constituted the whole meaning of life.[31]
—Evelyn Underhill

CHAPTER SIX

Unlearning the Habit of Doctrine

In so many ways, it was ironic that I should have been starting a career as a pastor. If I had been paying attention in seminary, it might have become clear that the ministry really wasn't going to fit me very well.

As incoming freshmen, we were required to begin working in a local church as student assistants. It was a way for us to get adjusted to the role and rhythms of clergy life. For a modest stipend, we did the things the regular pastors didn't want to do, and, in return, they provided us with informal mentoring.

My first Sunday as a student assistant was a shock. It was in an old church in Maplewood, New Jersey, with gothic stone architecture and leaded stained-glass windows. When the sanctuary was empty, the click of your heels would echo with each step, as if the walls were talking, telling the stories about all the stern faces that had lined the pews through the generations.

Since it was my first Sunday, and since I didn't know anything at that time, I figured I'd just be introduced to the congregation and then sit back down in the pew. But the senior pastor had other plans. Just before we went into the worship service, he threw a black robe in my direction and said, "Here. Put this on."

There was no time to protest. The organ was already launching into the prelude. The stern faces were seated and waiting.

It was an identity crisis of the first order, with no time to process. One minute, I'm a contractor with calloused hands and dried-out fingernails, reeking of form oil. Then, in the blink of an eye, I'm a *holy man!*

I'd assumed it would take me three years of seminary and a master's degree to get scrubbed up enough for a clerical robe. But it had only been three weeks since I'd started school and, already, I was in a black robe, headed for the podium.

Nothing could have prepared me for this. I felt like a fraud, but I had no time to explain to the congregation that this was a serious mistake.

As I walked down the aisle for the processional, Jacquie glanced in my direction. Her jaw dropped. If there hadn't been people on either side, she might have fallen out of the pew. That robe had implications for her too. It meant that she had suddenly slipped into the restrictive role of the minister's wife. Neither one of us was ready.

Originally, the black robe was adopted during the Protestant Reformation. It had been a deliberate reaction against the ostentatious clerical garb of the Roman Catholic priesthood. In the eyes of the reformers, Catholic clergy had been corrupted by the enormous wealth that poured into the church coffers, often via highly questionable fund-raising tactics.

The black robe became a symbol that distinguished the wearer from such extortion in the name of God. But it also did something that was subtly corrosive. In an era when priests carried enormous influence and were the celebrities of their day, pastors of the Reformed Tradition donned the black robe as a way of hiding the person. In the act of preaching, the human element was meant to disappear, so that the voice of God could become the sole focus. Though the intent was admirable, it was one small step toward a message that became progressively disembodied.

Pastors became talking heads, separated from anything below the neck. The dividing line was punctuated by the clerical collar. It was a black band that choked out any life, save for the little white square over the throat, the voice of God shining in the darkness. The robe and the collar emphasized that the church was no place for passions of the flesh. It was not the heart that mattered, but the brain.

As the voice of God, the pastor was only partly human. The head and the hands were the only parts visible.

The divine message could not be entrusted to a mere mortal. Mortals have feet of clay, knees that tremble, spleens that need to be vented, spines that are weak. But, most of all, they have—God help us—genitalia.

Not so for pastors.

When I donned that robe for the first time, the weight of those expectations bore down on me. The split between who I knew myself to be and the role I was to play was enormous. If I had been paying attention, it might have been clear that something was terribly wrong.

SKIPPING CHAPEL

The robe was only one challenge. Preaching was another one. When my fall off the roof convinced me to go to seminary, it never occurred to me that I might actually have to speak in public.

I was the kid who always sat in the back of the room. When I did verbalize, it was smothered in self-consciousness. I never asked any questions in class and mostly mumbled when spoken to.

Now, to my utter dismay, I was being asked to come out of my protective shell and verbalize in public . . . out loud . . . so that others could hear . . . so that strangers could critique me!

The first time I preached from the pulpit, it was an exercise in sheer terror. I didn't sleep a wink the night before, spending the whole time in the bathroom vomiting and with diarrhea. I literally prayed to die.

Jerry Seinfeld once remarked, "According to most studies, people's number one fear is public speaking. Number two is death. Does that sound right? This means to the average person, if you go to a funeral, you're better off in the casket than doing the eulogy."[32] To me, it was no joke.

Though I made it through that first sermon, preaching would continue to be exhausting and traumatic for years to come. I hated it, especially when God saw fit to send this talking head into the pulpit Sunday after Sunday with nothing to say. *Nothing!* Nada! Zilch!

It didn't help when people told me I was a wonderful preacher. I never could see myself in that role. A storyteller? Maybe. But not a preacher. Despite my best efforts, the heart's passion kept peeking out from under the robe. I should have known it would never work.

Then there was the issue of chapel. Every day I would watch as my classmates trudged dutifully into the sanctuary to hear another sermon and sing a few hymns. I went the first few times, but soon I discovered that the chapel service was a profoundly empty time for me. The preaching was eloquent but devoid of meaning for me. The singing was beautiful but failed to touch my soul. I began to wonder what was wrong with me.

Each day, watching that parade into Miller Chapel, I would vow, "Tomorrow I'll go." Tomorrow would come and the guilt would rush over me. After all, good pastors go to church. But I couldn't do it. Something was missing. Terribly so.

A New Reformation?

Occasionally, I would talk with some of my closest friends about the need for a new reformation. When I read the Bible, there was, at its very core, the transcendent experience.

From Abraham to Moses, from Elijah and Elisha to Jesus, from the Apostles to Paul—every one of them found the beginning of their relationship with God in the unexplainable event. It was the shattering encounter with the divine that had not only shaped who they were and what their mission was, but had also radically altered the community in which they lived.

Yet, the generations that followed had become progressively more removed from the firsthand encounter with God. Lacking the experience of the personal vision, those who followed sought to capture its power and essence in ritual, law, custom, and language.

These elements eventually displaced the divine encounter as the hallmarks of the faith. What ensued became a matter of faith, to be taught and enforced.

Gradually, persistently, that mystical dimension was obliterated from common thinking. Because it was feared and misunderstood, it became an object of ridicule. All that remained were its echoes. Gone were the power and majesty of the first encounter.

For me, it was this personal encounter that held the key for everything. Yet, when I would speak of a new reformation that could emphasize the mystical journey, even my friends would look at me blankly.

Perhaps they hadn't had an encounter that could open such sweeping vistas. Or, perhaps, their encounter had been crushed by our society and had withered in the face of unceasing skepticism.

They couldn't make the connection that, to me, was so obvious: if it weren't for the mystical encounter, we would have no tradition to study at all! There would be no pastors, no churches, no governance, no Bible.

That mystical encounter was the very thing that had sent me to seminary. It began to seem like a cruel joke that seminary was the last place I could find it.

For the most part, I had understood my encounter with the mystical world as little more than a sign, an answer to my question, "Should I or should I not become a pastor?"

But the experience of falling into that other dimension had left a legacy that stayed with me long after my question had been answered. Even though I adjusted to wearing the robe, and even to preaching, I never adjusted to the loss of the kingdom of heaven.

SEEING IS BELIEVING

In the Gospel according to John, the disciples, too, were forced to deal with the loss of the kingdom of heaven when Jesus died. For them, it was Jesus who carried all the hopes and dreams for a new world. When his lifeless body was laid in the tomb, everything came crashing down.

But then, miraculously, some of the disciples began reporting that they had seen Jesus alive, even after his crucifixion.

For Thomas, this was shattering news. He hadn't been present during the first reappearances of Jesus. Locked in the ravages of grief, he had gone off on his own to deal with it the best way he knew.

It wasn't comforting when tales of Jesus' survival of death came to him on the excited lips of his fellow disciples. He wasn't about to be swept up in misguided exuberance again, only to be crushed by disillusionment. "Fool me once, shame on you; fool me twice, shame on me," as the old saying goes.

There is seldom any way to describe the devastation that comes with the loss of a loved one. The stages can be described academically, but such words have no power to capture the rage and anguish that can come over us.

The most honest portrayal of grief I have seen came from the hand of C. S. Lewis, while he attempted to deal with the loss of his beloved wife, Joy:

> Meanwhile, where is God? This is one of the most disquieting symptoms. When you are happy, so happy that you have no sense of needing Him, so happy that you are tempted to feel His claims upon you as an interruption, if you remember yourself and turn to Him with gratitude and praise, you will be—or so it feels—welcomed with open arms. But go to Him when your need is desperate, when all other help is vain, and what do you find? A door slammed in your face, and a sound of bolting and double bolting on the inside. After that, silence. You may as well turn away. The longer you wait, the more emphatic the silence will become.[33]

Thomas knew the bitter sound of that silence. He had believed too much in something that turned out to be a mirage. His was not only the grief of losing a loved one; it was the unbearable rupture of hope for the future. Swearing that he would never allow himself to be crushed that way again, he retreated into an efficient pragmatism. It was the only solace he could find.

From then on, Thomas would trust only the evidence of his five senses. "Unless I see the mark of the nails in his hands, and put my finger in the mark of the nails, and my hand in his side, I will not believe."[34] Who can blame him? To come close to the kingdom, and then to lose it, is to mistrust all that has gone before. "Perhaps it wasn't so after all. Maybe it was just my imagination," we tell ourselves. We make vows to protect ourselves in the aftermath of disappointment:

"I'll never let my heart be broken like that again!"

"It'll be a cold day in hell before I do business with them!"

"I'll never be poor again!"

In the same way, Thomas swore that he would never again be swept up in the hysteria of others. But when Jesus appeared to him, all of his vows were undone. Despite Jesus' invitation to touch the hands and to explore the wound in his side, Thomas refused. There was no need.

Jesus replied with words that have become famous, yet tragically misunderstood: "Have you believed because you have seen me? Blessed are those who have not seen and yet believe."[35]

THE BEGINNING OF DOCTRINE

After the first generation of followers died away, the power of primary experience became muted. Lacking the impact of direct encounter, these later adherents were faced with carrying on a tradition through the memorized stories of their predecessors.

Eventually, these oral tales were elevated to the role of holy scripture. Once cast in the stone of sacred writing, a gulf was placed between the recorded experiences of those first disciples and the possibilities for ordinary people.

Gradually, the church looked to the scriptures as the vehicle by which God spoke. The hope that one could personally touch transcendent realms faded. Because the kingdom of heaven no longer was possible in the present, it became an afterlife reward for good behavior.

In the silence of that loss, the church seized on Jesus' reply to Thomas to explain that, even though we can't see the kingdom, we can still find blessing in our belief. Eventually *belief* came to mean *beliefs*, a set of doctrines and creeds that helped to distinguish the true church from imposters.

There was right belief and wrong belief. Priestly authorities made that determination. They did all the thinking. They paved the way. They alone maintained the elusive connection to the voice of God. The laity only needed to obey.

After a while, no one even wondered if seeing beyond the ordinary world was possible. The five senses would suffice. Seeing was disconnected from believing.

It was dogma that prevented error. If questions arose, it was the priest who held all the answers. But, it was best not to question in the first place. After all, "Blessed are those who do not see, and yet believe."

A PORTABLE PRESENCE

But it was not belief in doctrine that Jesus was speaking of. There was no Christian dogma in his day. There was only Jesus pointing to—and embodying—the kingdom of heaven.

That was the challenge. If Jesus were to embody the kingdom in the present, could it be seen apart from him? Once he was dead and gone, could there be any divine connection still available to workaday, bill-paying, car-pooling, muddling-through-life slackers like you and me? Jesus' words to Thomas were aimed at precisely that issue: "Blessed are those who do not see, and yet believe."

Not seeing seems to be shared by the vast majority of people. The evidence of our senses testifies constantly to the absence of anything beyond physical reality. Even if we do catch a glimpse of the kingdom, it most often remains maddeningly elusive thereafter.

Eventually, it fades from sight, leaving us with a deadening silence. That silence can last for years, even decades.

In the meantime, we're left on our own to search desperately for it. In retrospect, we sometimes can see the blessing of the search. But while we're in the midst of the silence, we know only the bitterness and grief of an inconsolable loss.

This is as it must be. If the vision didn't fade, we would be tempted to identify the kingdom with the package in which it came.

Moses, for instance, could have mistaken the burning bush itself for the divine presence. Rather than returning to Egypt to free his people, he could have built a shrine around the bush and charged an entry fee for others to come and see. Or, he might have uprooted it, put it in a glass case, and taken it on tour.

The kingdom would then become a commodity, rather than a way of life. Moses's vision would have depended on the bush. If the bush had died, the vision would have disappeared with it.

THE CLOUD OF UNSEEING

To make room for the unpredictable nature of the mystical realm, we must inevitably move through a period of losing contact with the world that lies beyond the five senses. It is a time of unseeing, when the interaction we once took for granted fades from our perception. This loss eventually breaks the encrusted mold of our expectations. It disrupts our naming, our use of nouns, and the judgments that inevitably accompany them.

Historically, this experience of losing touch with the life-giving mystical realm has been known as the dark night of the soul. It seems to be a rite of passage.

Knowing this doesn't make it any easier. To behold the priceless pearl, and then become blind to it, creates such desperation that one is tempted to give up the search entirely. Getting lost in the cares of mundane life can become all the more attractive to us. At least, then, we can be distracted from the pain of a lost glory.

In mentioning those who believe without seeing, Jesus was not lobbying for allegiance to future church doctrine. His words were meant to inspire faith in the kingdom of heaven itself, even in those inevitable times when it was invisible. "Just because you can't see it, doesn't mean it's not there," he seemed to be implying.

There is blessing, even in the search, no matter how hopeless and desperate that search may seem to be, no matter how it can be smothered under clerical garb. The pearl can still be found in the most unlikely places.

But, in order to find it again, we must first understand how it was lost. For that, we might return once again to the biblical narrative and look at it with fresh eyes.

CHAPTER SEVEN

The Fruit of Duality

In the Eden story, what went wrong is disarmingly simple. A young couple ate something from a tree that they were expressly forbidden to even touch, and they got into a whole bunch of trouble. So the lesson today, kids, is, "Always do as you are told."

I just love the Bible, don't you? It's all so clear, so straightforward. You got questions? God's got answers. All you have to do is trust and obey.

But aren't you just a wee bit curious about the fruit they ate? Oh, I know we aren't even supposed to touch the thing, but what harm can there be in just poking it with a stick a little. Look at it . . . it's just lying on the ground there, turning brown at the edges. Adam and Eve are standing naked outside the garden, and God's over there yelling at them. Who's gonna notice if we just kinda flip it over. I mean, it's not made of kryptonite or anything.

Well, would ya lookit that! I always thought it was supposed to be an apple. But it doesn't look like that at all. I wonder what it is.

Wait a minute. There's a sign under the tree. It says, "This is the Tree of the Knowledge of Good and Evil. If you eat of it, you will die. So keep your hands off. No trespassing. This means YOU!"

Hmmm . . . Maybe we'd better quit poking at it. Quick! I think the Big Kahuna's coming back! Drop the stick!

Whew! That was close. Did ya get a look at it? Surprised me too. Where did all that talk about the apple come from? That was no apple, was it?

And what about sex? I thought it was the fruit that made Adam all horny and everything, and that's why we call it original sin. Sin is mostly about sex, isn't it?

But look at Adam and Eve standing outside the garden. They look pretty torn up. Why are they crying? I wonder where they'll spend the night. The sun's setting, and it's getting cold. They're both shivering.

Is this what happens just from disobeying? It seems so harsh, especially when you look into the future and see that all of their children for all of the generations will be punished for that one indiscretion. It doesn't make sense. Besides, I thought God was supposed to forgive.

KNOWING GOOD AND EVIL

Oh, look! Here's the instruction manual that came with the tree. It states very plainly that the forbidden delight Adam and Eve ate was "the fruit of the Tree of the Knowledge of Good and Evil." There's no mention of an apple. Nothing at all about sex. Not a word about original sin.

So what exactly *was* that fruit?

Maybe the fruit was exactly what it says it was—"the Knowledge of Good and Evil." Those words can't be an accident. Yet, we treat them as if they were. We fill in every alternative we can think of while dismissing the one that's the most obvious: the fruit is the result of our judging of the world, dividing it up into good and evil.

If that's the case, then eating the fruit wasn't a matter of disobedience, but a matter of perception. It represents our internal compulsion for dividing everything into two categories: one that we accept and one that we reject. (This, despite the fact that the Eden story follows on the heels of creation, during which God judges everything individually as good and everything together as very good.)

We can't see from this larger perspective, as God can. Still, that doesn't dampen our enthusiasm for straining all of creation through the filter of our value system. Even though our standards for judging good and evil may be highly arbitrary, we insist that they're mandated by God and seek to impose them on all others.

But such knowledge has no place in a world that's only good. The fruit of the tree in the midst of the garden produces an awareness that is utterly foreign.

To judge things critically in a world that is only "very good" is to find flaws where none exist. It's one thing to notice the polarities that comprise the variety of this world: light/dark, hot/cold, earth/sky, male/female, you/me.

It's quite another to insist that half of any given pair is good, but the other is evil. Such capricious judging leads to a faulty perception of reality and contributes to an unconscious paranoia. The world is no longer sacred, but must be resisted, because at least half of what we see is seeking to do us harm.

FOR THE BEST

There's a traditional Eastern story that illustrates the futility of such pre-judging. Hans Wilhelm adapts this tale in his children's book *All for the Best*.[36]

It's the story of a carpet weaver who lives in a small village. One dark night, a thief steals one of the weaver's sheep. His neighbors are incensed and come to console him in his loss. The weaver's only reply is, "It will be for the best."

Soon the thief is caught and is required to bring back not only the stolen sheep, but also must give a horse as restitution to the weaver. Once again his neighbors come to express their joy in his good fortune.

"It will be for the best" is the only response they receive.

One day, the horse breaks from its stall and runs away. The neighbors parade over to the weaver's shop, expressing their deep sorrow over his misfortune.

"It will be for the best," he replies yet again.

Soon the horse returns, with two wild horses behind him. The villagers are stunned by this turn of events and can't resist expressing their joy for the weaver's good fortune.

To their puzzlement, the weaver keeps quietly working on his carpet and gives the same assessment as before.

A few days later, the weaver's grandson is training one of the wild horses and falls off, breaking his leg. The neighbors are shocked at the weaver's insensitivity when he assesses the situation with the same, uncaring summation, "It will be for the best."

One day there is weeping and wailing in the village from all the mothers. The king is coming through and forcing all the young men into his army. The weaver's grandson is not taken because of his broken leg.

Curious to understand his grandfather's wisdom, the grandson asks the weaver about his saying. The weaver replies that life is like his carpets. When viewed from the back, they seem to be a senseless hodgepodge of random threads. But when viewed from the front, they form a beautiful pattern. It's just a matter of seeing from the right perspective. Seen from the front, all is indeed for the best.

ONE

To judge good and evil is to split a world that is one into two parts: the good guys and the bad guys, the truth and the lie, the sacred and the profane, the divine and the human, the spiritual and the mundane. Each of these pairs forms a whole. However, in rejecting one side of the polarity, we partake of duality, and we must then suffer the consequences of the imbalance we've created.

It's interesting that the most famous set of laws, the Ten Commandments, begins with the assertion, "Hear, O Israel, the Lord our God, the Lord is one."[37] Most often, these words are taken as an assertion of monotheism— the idea that there is only one God, as distinct from many gods. Monotheism has been the touchstone of Judaism for generations.

Yet, there is another, more vital, interpretation possible. These words are a fundamental assertion concerning God's unity: *one, not two.*

It's true that one translation reads, "The Lord is our God, the Lord alone." This is not an assertion of monotheism, but a declaration of *which* God Israel will follow exclusively.

The other translations seem to be emphasizing something altogether different. The second part of these translations generally reads, "our God is one Lord" or "the Lord is one." The emphasis is on the number one as a description of God. Rather than an attack on polytheism, this is an assertion about the undivided nature of the Godhead.

This God makes choices, and even distinctions, and so brings variety into this world, but inexplicably has no favorites. Why? It's because all variety is based in the oneness of God.

It's tragic that this is the same God who is invoked against our enemies. Therein lies the cost of misunderstanding the Eden story.

In seminary, we took a class that dealt with what was called the problem of evil. The course revolved around a central question: How could a good God, who is all-powerful, allow evil to exist in the world? Since evil seems to be a fact of life, all the arguments boiled down to one of two propositions: either God is not all-good or God is not all-powerful.

If God has unlimited power, why hasn't evil been defeated? If God is only good, how did evil get started in the first place?

During that class, we read a variety of books on the subject. The authors would tip the balance one way or the other. In the end, none of them were satisfactory, because all of their arguments were merely intellectual.

Intellectual arguments can never explain suffering. Suffering is born of experience. Intellect is born of abstraction, disconnected from the reality of pain. None of them could explain it, because none of them spoke a language that touched the real problem.

TWO

The real problem in the Garden was something that changed us from within. When humans took upon themselves the right to judge good and evil, they traded the unity of divine perception for duality.

This division of the world into right and wrong blinded us to the world as it is. This skewed way of perceiving has become like the very air we breathe. It's so much a part of us that we can no longer notice it. For us, judging between good and evil is what it means to be human.

So, when we come to the story of Adam and Eve, we fail completely to see any significance in the name of the tree in the garden. "The fruit of the Tree of the Knowledge of Good and Evil" is something we skip over with no awareness whatsoever, because our judgments are so ingrained. We can't conceive of any other way of dealing with the world.

Dividing creation into categories of good and evil is only one mode of perception. There are others. When we fail to grasp this, we also fail to understand that the issue is essentially an internal one. It's a legacy of the mind that insists on filtering all experience through the sieve of past judgments. As a result, we no longer perceive the world around us at all.

NOSES AND BUMPERS: THE ARTISTIC EYE

When my children were younger, Jacquie and I encouraged their artistic efforts. Often, they would try to get me to draw for them. "Dad, I don't know how to draw a nose. Would you do it for me?"

Believing that it was important for them to experience art for themselves, most often I refused. But I also encouraged them to move beyond the preconceptions in their minds about noses. There is no such thing as a universal nose. There are only individual noses, each one utterly unique. Some are long, some are pug, and some are bulbous and veined. For this reason, I would usually encourage them to first have a look at the particular nose they were trying to depict. Drawing begins with seeing.

But seeing is not at all easy. To really see, it was first necessary for them to unlearn everything they already knew about noses, about faces, even about their own ability to draw. Without this unlearning, they would always be pulled away from the nose in front of them to some symbol they carried in the back of their heads. Such symbols are actually preconceptions that would keep them from seeing.

Gradually, with practice, they began to draw, not some symbol, but the uniqueness of the feature they were studying. Every nose has a story to tell, a history that is unlike any other.

One day, my son, Sean, was getting frustrated trying to draw a chrome bumper so that it actually looked like a shining, chrome bumper. After trying several times without much success, he came to me, saying, "Dad, how do you draw a bumper?"

"Well, first of all, you have to forget that it's a bumper and draw what you see," I suggested. We started to look together. It then became apparent that what our minds call a chrome bumper is, in fact, a series of different-colored, curving shapes produced by the reflected light.

When he drew those curving shapes and shaded them, forgetting it was a bumper, then the surface took on the elusive, reflective qualities of shiny metal. It was like magic. The glistening piece of steel sprang to life on the drawing paper.

In order to draw, we must first see beyond our mind's labels. The noun the mind uses to name an object must be disregarded, because this labeling brings a static quality to the perception. What is perceived, then, is not the thing itself, but a composite of all the noses or chrome bumpers we have ever encountered.

If you think about it, even a chrome bumper never looks the same way twice. It depends on the angle of the light striking it. The time of day has an impact. So does the environment in which we see it. Move the car to a new location, and the bumper will reflect an entirely different landscape. Labeling the object misses all of these dynamic changes.

This, then, is the problem of the Garden of Eden. When we jump to rash judgments, we no longer can perceive the world around us. What we experience is not the uniqueness of each thing or event, but the symbol we carry in our heads. We're blind to creation and, so, live in a state of numbness.

THE MIND IS A TERRIBLE THING TO USE

In college, a professor of mine often reminded us that experiments have shown that we perceive, on average, only 4 percent of our environment. "It makes you kind of wonder what the other 96 percent looks like," he would say, wistfully.

The reason we can't see is because our naming has become tainted with judgment. Not the judgment of God, but the world-splitting bias of the human mind.

We're still living in the Garden of Eden; we just can't see it. Our minds are preoccupied with forcing every aspect of creation into predetermined categories, dividing experience into ever finer distinctions. We have neither the time, nor the interest, to see the unity that binds all things into one.

This is where Jesus' words to Thomas are crucial. "Blessed are those who do not see, and yet believe." Change your point of view, shift your awareness, and the very thing you're missing snaps into view. It was there all along.

But it can't be perceived by a mind locked in duality. Rather than seeing as if for the first time (what Zen Buddhism calls the *beginner's mind*), we bring shopworn expectations. The richness and variety of the universe become muted to a dull gray, because we never are able to engage anything beyond our assumptions.

This is one reason why the name of God is never spoken in Judaism. The sacred letters for the name YHWH—often pronounced "Yahweh" in the Christian tradition—are replaced instead by a pronunciation altogether different in the Hebrew tradition.

When coming upon the holy name, a Jewish reader will intone "Adonai" instead, to preserve the uniqueness of the Godhead. The blinding capacity of language is well understood. It's better to leave the name unspoken, in order to preserve the mystery.

Indeed, in ancient times, there was great hesitancy to offer one's name, for to possess someone's name was to gain a sort of power over them. If this were true of humans, it was also true of divinities.

Naming, when it's connected with the human habit of judging, is no longer a creative act, but one that mitigates the inherent quality of wonder. The shining glory of the world recedes into a hollow, aching depression. The internal posture of judging the world robs it of its wondrous, even outrageous, variety.

In his autobiography, *Balancing Heaven and Earth,* Robert Johnson relates how he stumbled across what he calls "the Golden World," after a horrific night of labor inside the bowels of a tin-roofed cannery. It was five years after he had lost his leg in an automobile accident. He had been assigned a grueling task that tested his frail sixteen-year-old frame to the limit. He was told to push a four-hundred-pound cart, stacked high with cans, and he had to do it while being chewed out unmercifully by the foreman.

Through the night he labored, until the stump of his amputated leg was bleeding so profusely above the artificial limb that his sock was wringing wet. In exhaustion and despair, he clocked out at 4:30 a.m. and drove off into the darkness.

> I parked the car and hobbled onto a promontory just in time for the sunrise. The sun began to inch its way over the horizon, and—unbelievably—the Golden World shone forth with all its glory. . . . I can't really say whether I heard, saw, smelled, tasted, or touched that sunrise. No matter. It was an antechamber of heaven, and it was my native land. It lasted for about thirty minutes of clock time, but was an eternity in that heavenly realm.[38]

Notice that Johnson uses the word *heaven* to describe his experience. It's an experience that comes on the heels of the hellhole of that cannery. But even more importantly, he ties the perception of that heaven to his state of consciousness.

Whether we perceive it or not, the Golden World is always around us, waiting to be discovered. The human condition is such that we're simply blind to it. We're locked into the static qualities of our labels.

Labels allow us to conveniently categorize the world around us. We take comfort in the fact that a nose is a nose is a nose. There is a sense of safety in familiarity.

For most of us, the world seems much less threatening when it can be tamed by our judgments. Labels allow us to put the world into a headlock and then pin it under the weight of a category that is the same today and for all time.

Judge Not

It's ironic that Jesus, who supposedly pronounces final judgment upon us when we die, makes this declaration: "Even if I testify on my behalf, my testimony is valid because I know where I have come from and where I am going, but you do not know where I come from or where I am going. You judge by human standards; I judge no one."[39]

Because Jesus was able to view things in their wholeness, he could transcend the limited human perspective that splits the world. Thus, he not only knew the beginning and end of his journey, but he also was able to see the futility of judging.

This is why he could see the kingdom of heaven when it was so elusive to his contemporaries. The kingdom of heaven is grounded in the oneness of creation.

From this perspective, Jesus' admonition in Matthew takes on a whole new meaning: "Do not judge, so that you may not be judged. For with the judgment you make you will be judged, and the measure you give will be the measure you get back."[40]

He wasn't speaking of an afterlife reward and punishment here. He was simply stating the nature of reality. Split creation with your judgments, and you'll live in a world forever fragmented.

Is it possible for us to see beyond the veil of our own prejudices? Can we view firsthand the divine spark playing peekaboo? Can we catch a glimpse of the spirit radiating from within?

Countless mystics have insisted that we can. Jesus called such perception the kingdom of heaven or the kingdom of God. For him, it was a reality springing to life in the here and now.

But, in order to see, we must first become blind to all that we know.

CHAPTER EIGHT

A Mystic in Middletown

I was sleeping soundly in my bed when I was suddenly awakened by a clear and deliberate voice. There was no chitchat leading up to it, no social introductions. There were only the words from someone I could neither see nor feel—spoken once and with unmistakable purpose: "You must read Steiner."

I sat bolt upright. No one was in the room. I'm sure that, had Jacquie been awake, she would have heard nothing. But I know, without a doubt, that the command was not my imagination.

I also knew immediately that the voice was referring to Rudolf Steiner, an early twentieth-century Christian mystic I'd been introduced to six years earlier as an undergraduate at Goddard College. But I was hardly about to run out and purchase his books. After all, I was four years into ministry in Muncie, Indiana, with a loving family, and life should have been at its fullest.

Yet, I was sick with despair and couldn't talk about it with anyone. The ministry had, by this time, lost its shining promise. Buried under endless committee meetings, hospital visits, sermons, and Sunday school lessons, my time seemed to be owned by everyone else.

Occasionally, the world would crack open in a flourish of light—especially when I was away from my work.

There was the time I came to pick up Sean at school. He was in the second grade then, and he came running across the schoolyard, dressed in blue, his backpack bobbing up and down, as it hung from his shoulders. It was a bright day, and the sunlight glistened atop his shock of brilliant, blond hair. He was lit up like an angel.

It was his smile that caught me. When Sean smiled, it was like bringing a spotlight into the room; everything would start to glow. It was the smile of childhood innocence, the sheer delight of discovery. To see that took my breath away. I was awestruck at the depth of love I felt for him.

I wanted so much to catch that instant of wonder, to bask in the delight of that unbridled joy. Instead, I found myself groping blindly in the dark. Frequently, I would get up in the middle of the night, unable to sleep, haunted by something I couldn't name. While Jacquie slept, I would silently dress and walk the streets of our neighborhood, asking myself over and over, "What am I doing? Why is my life such a waste?" The walking would bring no answers. Finally, exhausted, I would make my way home and slump back into bed.

The silent ache was made all the more impossible for having touched the brightness of that other world. I knew it was there. I had seen it and touched its glory. For a brief moment, I had been to the mountaintop and been wrapped in the stunning elegance and beauty of something beyond description. Where was that world now?

In shock, I wandered aimlessly, hungry for nourishment of the soul. There was no name for the void I felt. *I can't go on like this,* I thought to myself.

THE MASK OF COMPETENCE

I'm often asked why the spiritual journey is so difficult. If we're called to mingle with the life springing from other dimensions, why are those dimensions not more accessible? Are depression and despair prerequisites for sacred insight?

One of the reasons for the difficulty is that truth has a nasty habit of getting in the way. By this, I don't mean the truth of the Bible, or the truth of religion, or absolute truth, or even the truth of God. Rather, it's the truth about who we are that is the most unsettling.

That's because it challenges our carefully cultivated mask of competence.

By most accounts, I was a great success in the pastorate. It was fairly easy to manipulate the applause meter in my favor. The rewards included personal praise, financial compensation, increased responsibility, and a nice big office, to name a few.

When the rewards for performance increased sufficiently, it became all too easy to back away from whatever was risky or innovative and to fall back instead on sure-success formulas. Every word, every gesture, every step was measured by its potential for approval. Gradually, I no longer approached the world with openness and spontaneity, but from the programmed image of the "competent pastor." This image was a caricature. At times, I felt as if my face would crack in two from wearing a perpetual smile.

Having reveled in the presence of a being whose light penetrated to my soul, having lived and felt the "no accident" nature of existence and, hence, the perfection of this world, I was lost when that experience faded.

I couldn't know it then, but that very hunger would begin, gradually, to overtake my old fake-it-till-you-make-it strategies. It wasn't a conscious decision on my part. There was no heroism involved. There was just no choice. The loss and desperation were simply too great to ignore.

THE INTERNAL MELODRAMA

I'm not alone in carefully crafting a presentable persona. The business of being human is steeped in the art of deception. Breath mints, Wonderbras, flashy resumes, hair coloring, makeovers, tailored suits, Rolex watches, little red sports cars, bathrooms with bidets are all designed to hide the truth about us. And those are just the surface qualities.

There are deeper issues. They are little lies we tell ourselves about how generous we are, how good-natured, how loving, how loyal, trustworthy, and true. Each of us carries around an adoring internal audience that cheers and coos when we score points that, if others could only see, would surely make them insanely jealous of us. Those are the bright lies.

Then there are the dark ones. These are the ones that are the hardest to break through. These are the lies that come from our chorus of internal detractors.

"You'll never be good enough."

"Who do you think you are, anyway?"

"You really screwed that up!"

"How could you be so stupid?"

The dark critics are so hard to silence, because we secretly treasure them. Despite our protests, they provide us an indispensable service. They shield us from having to confront our unique destiny.

Though we scarcely realize it, we're far more terrified of our genius than we are of our darkness. To embrace fully our deepest calling requires sacrifices and courage that few of us can muster. So the dark voices inside keep us from having to try. That's why we love them.

But the dark voices don't own the truth. Neither does the internal audience of praise. Each of these is but one more piece in the mosaic of the false image we show to the world.

To speak in our own true voice is our deepest calling. Because it requires the shattering of all that we have crafted so diligently and yet so falsely, we turn away from it at every opportunity. To live honestly costs so much, because it means turning a deaf ear to the voices that would call us to more socially acceptable and profitable pursuits.

That's one reason why the spiritual journey is so difficult. As one's true calling wrestles with the false image, the disorientation of the dark night sets in.

It would take years to shatter my pastoral persona. In the end, it turned out to be the healthiest thing that could happen to me.

FALSE IDOLS

False images are as old as the Bible. Ask any number of people in the West what standard they live by, and a majority will swear by the Ten Commandments. Ask those same people to name those commandments, and you'll be greeted with embarrassed confusion.

Though few could recite it, one commandment that is relevant to our discussion is, "You shall not make for yourself an idol, whether in the form of anything that is in heaven above, or that is on the earth beneath, or that is in the water under the earth. You shall not bow down to them or worship them."[41] Now, we all know that this is the one that's easy to keep. Gone are the days when idols of wood or stone had any hold on our imaginations. To give special power to a lifeless, miniature statue would be ridiculous. We've come a long way from ancient superstitions, and this prohibition against idol worship clearly doesn't apply to our modern sensibilities.

But what if the idol cited here is equated with the false mask we show the world? Could we then say so glibly that we don't worship false idols? What if the deepest reading of this law isn't so concerned with offending God, but instead with offending our truest self, which is the highest gift from the creator?

If this is a possible interpretation, then making contact with the sacred must, at some point, mean the shattering of the false image. The journey toward wholeness means that there is "nothing that is covered up that will not be uncovered, and nothing secret that will not become known."[42] That's why Jesus said: "You are the light of the world. A city built on a hill cannot be hid. No one after lighting a lamp puts it under the bushel basket, but on the lamp stand, and it gives light to the whole house. In the same way let your light shine before others."[43]

When we hear children singing, "This little light of mine, I'm gonna let it shine," we smile, because it's so darned cute. But if we understood the profound implications of these words, it would make us shudder. Us, revealed? Finding ourselves naked before the world is our ultimate nightmare.

Yet, to be true to our core essence, to live in the utterly unique manner for which we were created, means that we must inevitably disappoint the expectations that others have for our lives. It means that all the lies we've strung together to craft our false image to gain acceptance, approval, and love must be unraveled.

A Simple Kindness

The year was 1975. I was a new student at Goddard College. Goddard was an exotic place in those days, a haven for hippies, subterranean politics, and experimental lifestyles. The sexual revolution was in full bloom, and so were feminism, environmentalism, the drug culture, vegetarianism, radical politics, and more. The wild freedom was reflected in a campus landscape dotted with naked bodies working in the organic fields or lounging nonchalantly by the dormitory doors. Whimsical architecture could be seen everywhere in buildings often designed by the students. The buildings delighted the eye but were often less than successful at keeping out rain.

Shortly before matriculating at Goddard, I had gone through a Christian conversion experience. With my fresh new faith, I was excited to know that I was, once and for all, "right with God." My cheeks freshly scrubbed with holiness, I looked to the future with the greatest of confidence, knowing, without a doubt, that I was clearly on the winning team.

A more ridiculous clash of lifestyles could not be imagined. When I set foot on the Goddard campus, I was no longer surrounded by people who told me what to think or how to act like a good Christian. The sights and sounds of this strange new school set off an inner cacophony.

One day, while walking along one of Goddard's tree-lined paths, I found myself plodding along behind Jim Nolfi. Jim looked like a mountain man, with thick bushy hair, a beard that birds could nest in, and the OshKosh overalls that, most of the time, he wore without a shirt—or, as far as anyone could tell, underwear.

But, he was my professor, so I held him in great esteem. In many ways, he was brilliant. To my surprise, he invited me to walk with him.

There are times in life when the simplest act can communicate the most precious kindness. Jim's invitation probably meant very little to him, but to me it was like a hand reaching down to a man sinking beneath the waves. At that time, I was very shy. When I was speaking with strangers, words were difficult to come by. But Jim had a disarming way about him, probably because he really cared about his students.

To Jim, I confided that I had been having a struggle bringing my theology together with the campus life all around me.

Jim listened with keen attention. He then began to tell me about his wife, Ann, who had been on a spiritual journey of her own.

It had begun with a serious illness that had put her in a coma for weeks. Around her hospital bed, blinking machines measured everything that modern science could monitor. There was talk among the physicians that she might not make it.

In the early morning, the night shift was gathered at the nurses' station. Their muffled chatter was all that broke the silence.

Suddenly, Ann saw a great light enter her room. As it drew near to the foot of her bed, she woke up, as if for the first time. No words were exchanged, as the brightness enveloped her body. She could feel a vibrant new energy coursing through every cell, as rapid healing processes were unleashed.

No sooner had the light finished its work than Ann rose from her bed and quietly disconnected the wires tethering her to the myriad machines. Strangely, this act didn't trigger any alarms.

Slipping into her robe hanging in the closet, Ann began strolling through the halls. Through one door she noticed another woman who was also comatose. Mucus was draining from her nose; her skin was pale and gray. There seemed to be little life force still in her.

As Ann slinked into the room, she felt like she was floating. Drawing close to the woman, she leaned over the steel bed rail and whispered in the woman's ear, "I've got some extra energy. You want some?"

Ann then touched the patient's hand. The woman's eyes fluttered open. There was a smile.

The next thing they knew, these two patients began strolling through the hallway, arm in arm, giggling and laughing out loud. When they came to the nurses' station, pandemonium broke out. Not one, but two hopeless cases had virtually risen from the dead!

Jim explained that this experience had put his wife on a journey to understand what had happened. She too had come from a Christian faith, but had had trouble finding a home church where she could talk about her experience openly. In a tradition that had retreated into the intellect, there was little room left for the miraculous.

He explained to me that the best explanations she found were the writings of a twentieth-century mystic named Rudolf Steiner. Also a deeply committed Christian, it was Steiner who began to explain the mystical side of Jesus' work.

When Jim invited me to dinner with his wife, I was captivated by what she said. Still, I wasn't quite ready to integrate the radical ideas of Rudolf Steiner into my own shaky theology.

Only years later, when I heard that voice speaking in the middle of the night, could I begin to take in the wonder of the mystical tradition. When I heard that voice, I recognized that it was time to embark on a new leg of my journey. But, at the same time, I was skeptical enough to laugh.

After all, we were living in Muncie, Indiana. The town had been the focus of several famous sociological efforts called the Middletown Studies. Muncie was chosen for this research, because the authors felt it represented the very middle of American life—not just geographically, but morally, economically, spiritually, and socially. The thinking, apparently, was that if they could characterize the nature of existence in Muncie, then they could extend their graphs equally in opposite directions and capture all of American life. Being in the exact middle, Muncie residents began to think of themselves as representative of the American way. If you wanted to tap the essence of Americana, then, like a pilgrimage to Mecca, a trek to Muncie, Indiana, would be in order.

Muncieites not only reveled in this vaunted status of being in the middle, but it became their duty to preserve this cultural icon of mediocrity. It's still one of the few places in the continental United States that has chosen not to go on daylight savings time. As more than one person has remarked, "They're so conservative in Muncie, they won't even change the time!"

So when a voice came to me in the middle of the night, telling me to read Steiner, in ordinary, mediocre, middle-of-the-road *Muncie, Indiana,* I had to laugh.

I knew full well from my conversations with Jim and Ann Nolfi that reading Steiner would take me into the far reaches of theological inquiry and well beyond the fully extended graphs of the Middletown Studies.

I thought to myself, *Yeah, right. Where am I ever going to find a copy of Steiner?*

PORNO IN THE SEMINARY BOOKSTORE

Several weeks later, I went back to my alma mater, Princeton Theological Seminary, for some continuing education. I attended several lectures and heard a few renowned preachers trumpeting from the pulpit, who then gave workshops on how we could sound just like them. None of it touched me.

Restless and fidgety, I decided to take a tour of the seminary bookstore. I was walking past one of the shelves, when a book practically reached out and grabbed me. Only the binding was visible, but, even so, it stopped me dead in my tracks. The title was *A Steiner Primer*.

It was like discovering *Playboy* in a church parlor. Pulling it off the shelf, I could feel it burning in my hands. My only thought was how I could buy this thing without anyone seeing me. Some part of me expected this contraband to draw a crowd. I rehearsed lies about how I was doing research and that I didn't really believe any of these things.

To my surprise, not so much as an eyebrow was raised. I carried it back to my dorm room in a brown paper bag, hoping I wouldn't run into any of my clergy friends.

I stopped going to classes or lectures. The rest of my time there, I spent reading.

Reading Steiner was a relief. Finally, here was somebody coming from a Christian perspective who not only took the mystical tradition seriously, but also tried to interpret it for the modern world. It was like finding pure gold.

Steiner insisted that nothing he said was to be taken on faith. There was no doctrine to believe in, no endless monologues on morality. Everything he wrote about came as a result of his own experiences. Instead of accepting the fact that we're incapable of peering into spiritual realms, Steiner urged his students to go see for themselves; then he even told them how.

He constructed maps of hidden dimensions and delineated the invisible energy fields of the body. For Steiner, soul and spirit were as real as the physical body and just as crucial to understand. He laid out stages of human evolution that reached back into prehistory and claimed that he received his information from a great spiritual library that he called the Akashic Records.

At the center of that evolution was the person of Jesus, who brought about a monumental transformation of human consciousness.

Needless to say, this was all new to me. Though I had no way of verifying what he said, I was captivated by the possibilities. I wanted more than anything to catch a glimpse of the vista that was an integral part of his daily life.

The problem was that I still lived in Muncie, and I was still a Presbyterian pastor. Reading Steiner aggravated the split all the more. I had to keep up appearances, if for no other reason than to support my family. It was like living in a straitjacket.

And so I continued to shuffle through the streets of my neighborhood in the wee hours of the morning, wondering what I was doing with my life. The pull between my inner and outer worlds was becoming excruciating.

Over time, I read—or attempted to read—ten or twelve of Steiner's books, hoping that they would lead me to what I was seeking. But his style was so confusing, and his ideas so out of my reach, that I finally gave up. I wanted to see for myself. To my disappointment, reading Steiner—as exciting and invigorating as it was—didn't get me any closer to the kingdom of heaven.

So the tension was ratcheted up even more. How does anyone continue to function, when the very essence of what they hold dear must be denied? Perhaps someone with more courage would have simply walked away and started a new, more authentic life. But I couldn't.

My search would last many years. At every step of the way, I had the feeling that my mystical experiences were the essence of what Jesus had spoken of as the kingdom of heaven. Yet, it was difficult for me to make the connections.

As a result, I found myself looking for answers far outside the Christian tradition. It was heartbreaking to suspect that the very theology that was my heritage and birthright seemed to be so lacking in insight regarding the words of its own founder.

CHAPTER NINE

Death and the Glass-Bottomed Boat

Freddie was twelve years old the first time I met him, but his body looked like he was six. His baldness revealed a thick purple scar running down the back of his head and neck. His arms and legs were spindly and looked far too frail to support any weight. Translucent skin was stretched tight and thin over a delicate skeleton. Except for his distended belly, skin and bones was about all there was to him.

His mother first came to my office telling me that she was running away from her husband. In a drunken rage, he had tied up their younger son in a chair and had threatened to kill him with a kitchen knife.

Alice had intervened, only to be brutally beaten. Mother and children had all survived, but, after the incident, she'd gathered up her kids and, with only a few belongings, left town in their beat-up Chevy. She'd come to the church asking for help.

She explained that, at about the age of six, Freddie had started having intense headaches. A series of tests revealed a brain tumor. Doctors performed surgery, then radiation, followed by more surgeries, and eventually chemotherapy. Still, the cancerous tumor grew.

When I visited them in their small, rusting mobile home, Freddie was sitting at the table. By this time, it was very difficult for him to walk, so he had to be helped over to the stained sofa. The floor was littered with papers, scraps of food, and children's toys. The wind whistled through gaps in the jalousie windows.

Looking at him was surreal. Nothing seemed to fit. His head was far too big for his body. Propped in the corner of the couch as he was, he could barely sit upright. He had the look of an infant. Not sure of what to do, I hesitated. It was Freddie who spoke first.

"How're ya doin'? I'm Freddie."

He stuck out his hand to shake mine. His skin was startlingly soft, his grip light. But there was a disarmingly robust character about him. Even in his suffering, there was an unmistakable spark of life.

As we sat and talked, it seemed as if I were conversing with someone my own age. Freddie had no hesitation in answering my pointed questions about his illness. Even after all that he'd been through, he spoke with wit and humor.

That cheerfulness would be sorely tested over the next few years. As Freddie's suffering escalated, I would try to help as best I could, but my efforts always seemed inadequate. Nothing I, or anyone else, did could diminish the sense of death's inevitability stalking ever closer.

It wasn't just the cancer we feared. There was always the possibility that Alice's husband might find them. There was no way of knowing whether he was lurking in the shadows, waiting for an opportunity to pounce. Day after day, they lived with the dread, terrified that he would find their trail if they stayed in one place too long. But because Freddie's care demanded continuity, moving was out of the question.

At that point in my career, I could see nothing positive about Freddie's suffering. Even when we would receive a tidbit of good news, it was followed all too quickly by the return of the tumor. Even temporary hope turned into a cruel joke. To think that his trauma was part of God's all-good world was out of the question for me.

I couldn't help wondering if Freddie's tumor wasn't the result of growing up under the extreme stress of his father's murder threats. If so, then maybe cancer was actually a sane way of exiting an impossible situation. Still, the injustice of such suffering made no sense to me.

And then, there was the paradox. Even as ill as he was, there remained something radiant about him—an underlying calmness, a quirky wisdom that allowed him to be amused by circumstances that would have broken a man three times his age. It wasn't there all the time, but often enough that it caught my attention.

It was then that I began to think that there is more to death and suffering than meets the eye. Questions arose that I had never considered before: What is it about the nearness of death that sparks so much life? Do those facing an abbreviated life compensate by packing more into the time they have? Is there a strength that comes through when the body is failing? Are we, in fact, more nearly alive when closest to dying?

DEATH DEFYING

For many of us, the first glimpse of death catches us by surprise—in an unexpected accident, a rare disease, or the light fading from the once vibrant eyes of the generation ahead of us. But, until then, we all tell ourselves that these things happen to others, not us.

As a pastor, I often noticed that impending death brought out a refreshing frankness, at least for the person who was dying. The family, on the other hand, usually continued trying to push the thought of death from their minds until the last possible moment, to keep their spirits high.

"You'll be up and about in no time!"

"Oh, don't talk like that! You'll be fine!"

"Don't you give up on me now!"

Because of this, whenever I was confronted with a patient who was dying, I usually couldn't wait for the family to leave so I could be alone with the person. Then we both could breathe a sigh of relief. It can be immensely frustrating for someone embarking on the mysterious journey of dying to have no one who will even acknowledge it, much less speak of it.

Yet when the family can acknowledge the obvious, a new depth of relationship can emerge. People can drop their old games and begin to speak from their hearts. As old scores are settled and forgotten, people can relate to one another, essence to essence. Priorities can snap into focus. Memories can be sifted and savored, as if they were panning for pure gold. Laughter and tears can flow unceasingly. When it's approached with this degree of honesty, impending death has the capacity to illuminate life.

THE GLASS-BOTTOMED BOAT

Several years ago, one of my close friends, Porter, was undergoing heart surgery. The news from the doctor was anything but encouraging. If everything went very well, we were told, he could expect two more years of life at the most.

But things did not go well at all. During his recovery, an unexpected infection started. At first, they tried to drain his chest cavity, hoping to eliminate the bacteria. But his heart was struggling to pump.

At last, it was decided that the only hope was to open his chest up again and keep it open until everything had had a chance to heal internally.

Porter was wheeled back into surgery and sliced through the sternum once again. In the intensive care unit, he was kept under constant sedation, his rib cage propped open with jacks. The yawning cavity was covered over with clear plastic to maintain his chest pressure and to keep infection at bay. He stayed that way for two very long days.

There is something unsettling about peering into an open chest and seeing a beating heart, especially when that heart belongs to a close friend. Yet, there it was, Porter's heart, open for view—his innards made suddenly public.

It was as if he were one of those glass-bottomed boats that allow you to watch barracuda and coral formations up close and personal.

It might have been a chance to witness the hidden wonders of nature, a spectacle of teeming life. But it wasn't the wonder of nature that caught my attention. Nor was it the technology that pushed the breath in and out of his lungs. What was shocking was that I couldn't find Porter, the person, anywhere. I could see his body all right, but clearly some crucial ingredient of the recipe that was Porter, as I knew him, was missing.

We're accustomed to thinking of people living inside their bodies, as if their true essence were something encased within their flesh. We speak of intimacy as the ability to get inside someone's skin, or to get into their head, or to touch their heart.

But here I was, literally peering into the interior of my friend, and I couldn't get over the fact that he was nowhere to be found. As I stood over this lifeless body, the heart fluttering openly, there was no point of communion. It was like dialing the phone, only to hear ringing, ringing, ringing . . . with no one to pick up on the other end.

What did I expect to see? I don't really know, but I didn't expect to be confronted by this absence. My reaction was visceral, beyond rationality.

But if Porter wasn't there, where was he? I probed intellectually. I thought in terms of the spiritual. But at each point, the window in the glass-bottomed vessel failed to show me anything.

It was a moment of great learning. We often speak glibly of leaving the body after we die, but these are mere words. To stand by the vacated form, to feel the absence of spirit, to sense how trivial the physical is without the soul enlivening it, is to know that we don't live in our bodies. Our bodies live in us.

Where Do We Go?

Porter eventually came back to life and was still functioning some six years after that ordeal. By that time, he had already tripled the meager time he had been allotted.

But for two whole days, while his heart lay beating open to the world, Porter went somewhere else. I wanted to find out where. Our relationship was such that I could ask him about these things. But, to our mutual disappointment, he could remember nothing of what had happened.

And so the questions chased after me. Where does a person go when under sedation? What happens when we become comatose? From what unseen regions of silence and confusion does the Alzheimer's patient emerge intermittently to unexpected flashes of clarity? Are we able to drift back and forth between realms? If we could stay conscious, would we remember tales of wonder? What happens when we die?

These were not academic questions for me. As a pastor, one never gets too far away from illness, surgery, and death. Freddie's journey, in particular, was weighing heavily on me. So I decided to speak to my boss, Ron.

RON AND HIS DAUGHTER

Ron Naylor was the senior pastor at the church in Muncie. It was Ron who had called me up unexpectedly when I was graduating from seminary and all my options had run out. It was Ron who had suggested that Jacquie and I hop into our van and drive for fourteen hours, with Jacquie dangerously pregnant, to visit Muncie and to meet the search committee, as if it were just a crosstown trip. It was Ron who knew the first time we met that I was the right person for the job. And it was Ron who broke every church rule in the book to bring me on as his associate.

We could talk about anything. Though I was his associate, implying a secondary status, Ron treated me as an equal in every respect.

One day, I shared with him my anguish over Freddie's illness. Seeing such suffering firsthand was more than I could take. My grief welled up into tears.

Ron sat and listened. I could see that something was stirring in him. He seemed to be struggling over whether to tell me.

At last, he began to speak to me about his daughter, Jennifer, for the first time. She was his oldest child, unusually bright, talented, and alive. Early in her life, Ron and his wife, Susan, discovered that Jennifer was having great difficulty breathing. When they took her to the doctor, the worst was realized. She was diagnosed with cystic fibrosis.

It's a devastating disease. Fluid and mucus gather in the lungs, causing a condition much like drowning. One treatment is to literally beat on the child's back while she's stretched over the bed, face down, to break up the congestion. To strike painfully at an already desperately sick child in the name of healing seemed bizarre. But there was no choice, if the child was to survive. The grief had to be swallowed.

Usually it was Ron's wife, Susan, who administered this regimen. Ron could hear the pounding from the other room.

Despite daily treatments and medications, Jennifer lived only until her eighth birthday. Eventually, they took her to the hospital and watched her life slowly ebb away.

Afterward, Ron and Susan were left with only the silence of a loss they couldn't comprehend. Susan's wailing echoed through the hospital corridor.

The staff came into the room to remove Jennifer's body. Out in the hallway, a nurse turned to Ron and asked, piously, "Was she saved?"

Rage drifted over Ron in a searing flash. In his mind, he wanted to rail at her insensitivity, her nerve of pushing her theology instead of caring for his loss. But he held back the torrent.

"She had a deep and abiding faith in Jesus Christ Superstar," he hissed through clenched teeth.

There simply is no way to get over the loss of a child.

In the years before Jennifer's death, Ron had taken an annual vacation with some friends to the boundary waters of Minnesota. After the funeral, he debated about going, but finally decided it might help with his healing.

The fishing was uneventful. Jennifer's memory loomed large the whole time.

On the way back, one of his friends was driving while Ron, propped up in the back seat, drifted in and out of sleep. He was teetering on that strange edge of consciousness.

Suddenly, Jennifer appeared to him.

Ron paused as he was telling the story. "It was as if I were in another dimension altogether. She was standing in front of me just as clear as I'm seeing you now. We had a long conversation. She started saying, 'Daddy! It's so wonderful here! I'm not sick anymore! Everything is so beautiful! I can think so clearly!'

"We spoke for a while about my life and hers. She told me so many secrets, but I just couldn't remember them later. Finally, she ended up by saying, 'Daddy, wouldn't you love to be here with me?'

"After thinking about it for a while, I said to her, 'Oh, honey, I want to be with you more than anything. But somehow I feel that there is more for me still to do on earth.'

"It was clear that if I had wanted to stay, I could have passed over to the other side. But no sooner were the words out of my mouth than the whole vision faded. It was like water seeping between my fingers. I wanted to grasp it, but couldn't. Suddenly, I was awake in the back seat again.

"Right at that moment, we were coming to a toll booth on the turnpike. My friend rolled down the window to pay the cashier. Out of nowhere, we heard a tremendous roar. A semi had lost its brakes, and the driver was downshifting to try and break his speed. But it was too late.

"He crashed through the turnstile next to us, and his fuel tank hit the guardrail. It was ripped off the cab and came flying at us. The tank lodged under our car, and yet somehow it didn't explode. If I had told Jennifer I wanted to stay, that would have been my ticket."

That's why Ron couldn't live in the middle. He had seen the other side, and he knew too much.

ETC

Ron had teased the spark of my soul into a fire. So, when he urged me to check out a small school that had been formative for him, I decided to give it a try. The Ecumenical Theological Center (ETC) in Detroit, Michigan, was on the cutting edge of spirituality, drawing from traditions far outside the Christian mainstream. Meditation, spirituality, mysticism, yoga-based exercises, chakras, healing touch, contemplation, and so much more were commonplace. It was like Disney World for spiritual seekers.

At the time, such exploration was considered by the Christian mainstream to be dangerous and even satanic. In the eyes of my Presbyterian colleagues, ETC was a school to be avoided at all costs. So I would slip out of town, making cryptic excuses about going on a retreat.

In those days, ETC was located in one of the buildings at Marygrove College. Approaching the Marygrove campus from any direction was like driving through a war zone. All around was a boarded-up, bombed-out ghetto. Pawnshops dotted every corner; winos and drug dealers wandered the littered landscape. The deafening roar of traffic and construction work seemed to steal the last vestiges of serenity. Making my way toward the campus, I could hardly believe that this was a suitable environment for retreat and meditation.

But Marygrove itself was a jewel, hiding in the thicket. An iron fence marked its edges. Inside was an enclave of tranquility. I walked across the small, serene campus, approached the building that housed the center, and couldn't believe my eyes: the entire center resided in one short dormitory hallway rented from the college. This single corridor housed the administrative offices, the student overnight housing, bathrooms, the library, and the lounges. Space was so cramped that the small rooms each served multiple functions.

It was winter, and plastic had been put over the windows in a futile attempt to reduce the drafts. The heating system droned endlessly, yet seemed to have no capacity for producing any actual warmth. My first impression was underwhelming in the extreme.

The first course I took was Healing as Spiritual Practice. There were only five of us in the group. The instructor was a pastor working in California (where else?) who had a gray goatee (what else?) and spoke in thick, rich, trance-inducing tones (I should have known).

His name was Francis Geddes. I had no idea when I first met him that, within five short days, he would show me the wonders of the universe. Nor did I have any clue that he would stoke the fires of my spiritual hunger to a raging blaze.

The initial exercises were disarmingly simple. They were a series of short meditations, usually five to seven minutes in length. To focus our attention, for instance, we would look at a match held in the palm of our hand or stare at a clover plucked from outside. We trained our eyes on icons (pictures of saints and biblical scenes) for no apparent reason. We sat and focused on the breath coming in and out of our nostrils. We chanted.

It was so foreign to me, and yet somehow strangely familiar. It sounds like the most boring drudgery anyone could imagine. And it was. That was the point.

THE DOOR OF DECEPTION

The mind, says the mystical tradition, is like a teeming hoard of chattering monkeys. As long as it's allowed to spew in endless and aimless commentary, it'll shield the true nature of reality. The mind is the place where we split the world into ever finer gradations of good and evil. Paying attention to its constant stream of criticism, we can begin to see how destructive this monologue is.

The search for the kingdom of heaven begins with an understanding of the thing that is most familiar to us—yet, most often ignored because of that familiarity—the mind. It is like the air we breathe. It's been such a constant part of our lives that we can't imagine it's possible to live outside it. For many people, the mind is life.

I had read Aldous Huxley's *The Doors of Perception*[44] in 1972. As a college student still finding my way after leaving home for the first time, that book had been like a slap in the face. In it, Huxley chronicles his reflections as a test subject studying the effects of LSD (before LSD became illegal).

His thesis was that the brain, rather than being an instrument designed to gather information, actually works in the reverse. Its primary function is not to gather sensory input but to *reduce* it. The world we live in has such a vast number of stimuli that it can be overwhelming. When faced with a life-threatening situation, such an overload can be counterproductive. Focus is essential for survival.

In the Western world—where we're exclusively trained to manipulate our material existence with rational thought—the ability to narrow and focus is considered to be of supreme value. Highly developed concentration skills are thought to be the prerequisite for genuine productivity.

The mind aids this focusing of perception by acting as a screen. Information is compared to past experience, evaluated, and categorized, and then only the data that is essential to survival is allowed to pass through.

WITH OUR OWN EYES

Yet, the information we collect is highly suspect. The human body is subject to serious limitations attending the five senses. Our eyes can only see within a small band of the light spectrum. Our ears are only sensitive to a limited range of frequencies. Our sense of smell is dramatically underdeveloped, as compared to other species.

Beyond that, even the signals we take in are an artificially assembled composite of reality. For instance, our eyes are constructed such that there are no cones or rods in the area of the optic nerve. As a result, we all have a blind spot in the very center of our visual field. To compensate for this, the eye is constantly jiggling, taking thousands of individual snapshots that blend out the dark spot, so that we don't notice it. What we "see" is actually a composite of these individual photos, assembled by our minds.

As Evelyn Underhill says in her path-breaking book *Mysticism:*

> It is immediately apparent, however, that this sense-world, this seemingly real external universe . . . cannot be the external world, but only the Self's projected picture of it. . . . it is a picture whose relation to reality is at best symbolic and approximate, and which would have no meaning for selves whose senses, or channels of communication, happened to be arranged upon a different plan. The evidence of the senses, then, cannot be accepted as evidence of the nature of ultimate reality: useful servants, they are dangerous guides.[45]

In this regard, seeing is not really believing. Rather, believing affects what we call seeing. The old saying, "You get what you expect," is profoundly true.

MALE-PATTERN BLINDNESS

It's a truth that I like to prove over and over for my wife. Recently, I was looking for a dictionary. After going through a halfhearted search, I decided to go to the real authority—Jacquie.

She told me that the dictionary was sitting under the alarm clock that was on the nightstand to the right side of our bed. She spoke very slowly, enunciating each word for clarity.

Knowing that I had looked there only a few minutes before, I was quite confident that she was mistaken. Nonetheless, I traipsed upstairs, did a thorough forensic examination, and headed back downstairs empty-handed.

Jacquie saw me standing by the stairs. "Well, did you find it?"

I couldn't suppress the grin of smugness as I said, "I have to tell you that you're quite mistaken. Sherlock Holmes and I searched every inch of the area, and we've turned up nothing."

"Paul, how many times do we have to go through this? Go back upstairs. I guarantee you; it's there." She repeated the directions, this time even more slowly.

To make things more interesting, I decided to offer a little wager: "I'll bet the universe that the so-called dictionary is nowhere near the nightstand."

"You're on," Jacquie smiled, as she shook my hand.

Just to amuse her, I returned to the scene once again. An even more thorough search produced nothing.

Once again, I came downstairs and announced the results. It was one of those moments when everything hung in the balance. I held tightly to my confidence.

Without a word, Jacquie disappeared into our bedroom and, seconds later, emerged carrying a dictionary. "Hand over the cosmos, buddy," she said.

I looked at the dictionary in her hands. It was red. "Wait a minute! I was looking for a *blue* dictionary. If I had known it was *red*, then I could have found it too. You switched colors on me. Foul! You cheated! I'm keeping the cosmos." Thus the universe was spared on a technicality.

All of which is to say that what we expect to see is what we find. Because I had a different color in my mind from what was actually there, all my sensors were tuned for the wrong information. As a result, that dictionary absolutely, positively, was not there . . . for me.

I know that it's shaky, at best, to prove something on the basis of masculine ineptitude, but that is precisely my point. When operator error is added to our limited sensory capacities, and incoming sensory data is sifted through our skewed experiential filters, our perceptions are much more a product of our internal environment than of the external world. When this data also is run through the make-believe land of "the Knowledge of Good and Evil," it's a wonder that we can even find our nose to scratch it.

A MATCH MADE IN BOREDOM

When we were told to "just look" at a match or a clover during my class at ETC, it was to show us how difficult it is to actually see. No matter how developed our ability to focus, the mind gets bored with sustained, concentrated perception. The aim of "just looking" is to do just that, despite all the impulses to move on to more lively entertainment.

In the effort, we begin to understand how little looking we actually do. Most of what happens when we think we're looking is not looking, but *thinking*. It's entertaining a stream of conversation about the object in hand and, when that gets tiring, shifting to commentary about other entirely unrelated issues. We compare the match to other matches we've seen. We remark to ourselves about its light and shadow. We become fascinated, as the mind starts to make it dance in our palms. We make up stories about it. We're distracted by the droning heater. We think about the furnace in the house we grew up in. Our stomach growls in hunger. A picture of the kid who shoved a jelly sandwich in our face on the bus comes to mind. We feel an itch in an inconvenient place, and we obsess about how to tend to it without attracting attention. We wonder how many minutes this interminable exercise will last. We realize we're no longer "just looking."

To begin a meditation is to become aware of how fleeting our attention and perception are. Slowly, the curse of the Garden of Eden begins to be recognized, perhaps for the first time.

But, sooner or later, the mind will give up its fight. It is then that the world comes out from behind its hiding place.

After the first few days of this purposefully mindless activity, everything began to feel different. It was like slipping between the rapid-fire staccato of flashing thoughts into a luxurious spaciousness. The environment of Marygrove College started to radiate.

HEALING AS SPIRITUAL PRACTICE

It was only after we had gone through this training for a couple of days that we were ready to begin our first steps toward the practice of healing. Each session would begin with one of us volunteering to lie on the floor as the healee. The others in the group would gather around his or her body and calm down to a meditative state.

At the leader's prompting, all hands would be placed on the volunteer's body. This position would be held until the leader signaled that the prayer was over. Everyone in the group had at least one chance to be on the receiving end. Some reported interesting results.

Then came my turn. I was excited to see what the experience of receiving such intentional healing energy from my classmates would be like. Yet, I also fell into a familiar trap. After hearing the previous reports, I wanted something significant to happen, just so I could know for certain that this stuff was real.

Yet, immediately I thought, *What if nothing happens? What if this kind of thing works for everyone but me? How will I ever know?*

I wanted an *experience* desperately. This world had grown so heavy and disheartening that it seemed as if my very survival hinged on discovering that there was more to life than mere material existence. The stakes were high.

I lay down, my mind cluttered with desperation and curiosity. In silence, my classmates gathered around my body. After a few minutes, Fran uttered a short prayer. I could feel the warmth as hands were placed on me. I expected to feel a sense of moving energy, but there was none. I had hoped to see a vision, but all was blank. Maybe a few voices to liven things up. Nothing. With all my senses alert, I was waiting for something—anything—to happen.

Then Fran spoke another soft prayer, signaling the end of the session. I wanted to speak up in protest, "Wait! Wait! Nothing happened! I didn't feel anything!" But I kept silent.

The absolute worst had been realized. No changes, no insights, few sensations. *Maybe this is all imaginary,* I thought. I was crestfallen. My moment had been squandered.

Toward the end of the week, we were introduced to the concept of proxy healing. In this process, one person volunteers to receive the healing energy and then convey it (for lack of a better term) for the benefit of another who isn't present.

When my opportunity came, I immediately thought of being a proxy for Freddie. I approached this with some enthusiasm, because, as I later realized, it was much easier for me to ask for healing for someone else than for myself.

As I lay prone on the floor, my classmates moved into position, with Fran Geddes sitting at my head. By now, we had all learned a process of silently grounding, focusing, and connecting with the healee. Fran began a quiet prayer that was a signal for everyone to place their hands on me. Everything else, except for the concluding prayer, was done in silence.

When their hands made contact, a startling current surged through my body. Instantly, I was transported to a realm of unearthly beauty. Stretched out before me was a mountain range seen in what I can only describe as silhouette. The mountains had an iridescent quality.

Draped around each peak, sparkling against the black background, was a string of pearls. Yet these were not normal pearls; they glowed with a radiance that was painfully beautiful. They seemed to call out. If you can imagine colors that speak, it might get close to what I perceived.

Suddenly, a hand reached down from above and picked the string of pearls from atop the mountains and slowly carried them to one who was waiting. As I looked closer, I could see that the person waiting was Freddie. The purple scar from all his previous brain surgeries was clearly visible.

Carefully, the string was draped around his bald head like a crown, and a tail of pearls was allowed to fall down his neck, directly over his scar. Each pearl began to radiate and pulse. New, brighter colors swarmed in and around his neck and head, seemingly alive.

Then I watched as Freddie was laid out on a table, face up. Standing at the head of the table was a being with wings. Light was streaming forth, as the wings were moved up and down, conducting brilliant energy into Freddie's body. The word *magnificent* doesn't even come close to the glory of that being.

Suddenly, I realized that I was seeing something similar to what the Old Testament prophet Ezekiel tried to describe in one of his visions:

> Their wings were spread out above; each creature had two wings, each of which touched the wings of another, while two covered their bodies. Each moved straight ahead; wherever the spirit would go, they went, without turning as they went. In the middle of the living creatures was something that looked like burning coals of fire, like torches moving to and fro among the living creatures; the fire was bright. The living creatures darted to and fro, like a flash of lightning.[46]

I was stunned. It seemed as if the vision lasted for thirty minutes or more. Then I heard Fran's voice, calling us out of silence, ending the healing. With my eyes closed, I could literally *see,* with internal perception, each hand as it was removed from my body. They looked like glowing balls of white light.

At the end of each healing, it was our custom to have each participant report impressions of their experience. Afterwards, the healee would have a turn.

I have no recollection of what was said by the group. I only know that when it came to my turn, I couldn't speak. Every time I tried, tears would choke my words. I did manage to ask how long the prayer was. Fran replied that it was about two-and-a-half minutes.

When Words Fail

How do you explain the unexplainable? In trying to describe the kingdom of heaven, Jesus too was at a loss for words. Language, designed to depict the material world, has no capacity to explain realms beyond the physical. Because of this, Jesus would frequently resort to analogy:

> With what can we compare the kingdom of God, or what parable will we use for it? It is like a mustard seed, which, when sown upon the ground, is the smallest of all the seeds on

earth; yet when it is sown it grows up and becomes the greatest of all shrubs, and puts forth large branches, so that the
birds of the air can make nests in its shade.[47]

The kingdom of heaven starts with something so apparently insignificant that it can be easily overlooked. A mustard seed is, indeed, tiny. Grab a
handful, and if one seed drops to the ground, it won't be missed at all. Yet,
that one overlooked seed can become, as Jesus said, "the greatest of all
shrubs." The kingdom can't be judged by appearances.

When we began to meditate on a match held in our palms, I had no idea
that it would lead to such a stunning vision. Nothing could have prepared
me for the world that opened up when I stopped my addictive habit of
thinking. Neither did I realize that such inner silence could grow into an
awareness that reached far into the heavens, so that even the "birds" of the
angelic realms could make nests in my perception.

To me, that glimpse into a realm beyond imagination was like rediscov-
ering the pearl of great price. To return to it, to commune with it, I would
have given all that I owned.

When I came home, I tried to tell Jacquie of my experiences. The
shroud of emptiness had suddenly been lifted. That realm that had appeared
in the agony of my fractured hip had come once again into view. I trembled
and wept while attempting to convey the awe-inspiring vista. But words
failed me.

FREDDIE'S FUNERAL

Glimpses of the kingdom can be distressingly fleeting. I had hoped that
this vision would be the sign of a miraculous healing for Freddie. It was not.

Just a few months later, I would be called to his ramshackle trailer in the
middle of the night. Freddie was lying on the couch, his swollen head in his
mother's lap. He knew it was the end.

I, on the other hand, was still hoping for a miracle. Like the family members who dance around impending death, pretending not to see, I was whistling past the graveyard.

I had too much invested in Freddie's recovery. His plight had touched me so deeply that, as soon as we were asked to heal someone, Freddie came to mind—out of all the suffering people I had seen. For such a young boy, he had endured so much, so unfairly. Perhaps some part of me hoped to be the hero, credited with making him whole.

But the road to spiritual insight seldom conforms to our expectations. It cares nothing about creating celebrities. There is only the vision. Then there is the interpretation. The two are not the same. Only later can we connect meaning to what we've seen.

Finally, I was able to accept the unacceptable. In the silence of the evening, his mother and I coaxed Freddie into letting go. Slowly, quietly, his breathing settled, then stopped. His body went limp.

I was hoping for some brilliant display of light, like the vision. But there was only the stillness of a snow-covered night, and then the emptiness of looking into the open cavity—a glass-bottomed boat with no one left to steer it.

I had a difficult time doing his eulogy. A small crowd attended, because Freddie's family didn't belong to our church. Few people knew of their struggle. I had to stop at several points as the words stuck in my throat.

As I thought about it afterwards, I considered the possibility that what I had seen in the healing at ETC was a glimpse of the world Freddie would be traveling to. In that regard, death would be the ultimate healing. As it says in the book of Revelation, Freddie would enter a world where "mourning and crying and pain will be no more."[48]

But this was nothing more than speculation, a feeble attempt to wrap my grief in words of comfort. It didn't work. Sometimes it's best to forgo the interpretation, keep silent, and "just look."

CHAPTER TEN

The Fear Factor

In Muncie, Indiana, our house backed up against apartments owned by Ball State University. If the wind was blowing right, which was most of the time, trash from the student complex Dumpsters would make its way into our backyard.

One evening, after putting our three children to bed, Jacquie and I retired early. We were sleeping soundly, when suddenly there was a flash of light. It woke me up. Instinctively, I turned to the clock to read the time: 1:06 in the morning.

The ceiling light was on in our bedroom. I blinked, trying to understand what was going on.

What I saw next didn't really startle me; it just didn't compute. Standing at the foot of my bed, dressed in full uniform, with his revolver drawn, was a policeman. I didn't have time to get frightened, because he started to speak as soon as I laid eyes on him. His words were quick and to the point.

"Sir, a man has just threatened to kill his wife in the Ball State apartment complex. He has a gun, and we chased him into your neighborhood. He is armed and dangerous.

"Your back door was open, and we think he might be in your house. We are going to bring your children into bed with you, then we are going to search your house, and then we will lock your doors."

Our children have always been very sound sleepers. At the time, they were aged six, five, and two months. None of them woke up as the transfer was made. Then, silently, the officers began to sweep through the house.

My mind started spinning scenarios. What if they searched the house and missed him? What if we were locked inside, with no way to defend ourselves? What if I was walking through the house and stumbled across him? Scenes from murder movies flashed through my head. The psyche apparently needs a story with an ending more than anything else, even if that ending is one of disaster. We waited for what seemed like an eternity.

After the police left, we watched as they searched through the backyard, sweeping flashlights in the darkness. Even though they had pronounced the house safe, there was no comfort. I had stashed too many Easter baskets in hidden nooks and crannies to think the police had exhausted all possibilities.

There is no way to describe the overwhelming dread of such an experience. It means being paralyzed by fear, too terrified even to breathe.

We dared not speak. If the potential killer was in the house, we didn't want to give away our location. I tried to think of weapons we might have that I could use. Where was the baseball bat? Could I get to the kitchen knives? Would I be better off not to struggle? Should I hide and wait, in case he made a move?

Finally, there was a knock on the door. It was the police. They had apprehended the fugitive. We could go back to sleep. The ordeal was over. But even though the news brought a sense of deep relief, there would be no more sleep for us that night. It would take hours to calm down again.

Shortly after his arrest, the fugitive was brought to the courthouse for arraignment. The defendant posted bail, and, within hours, he was released. He immediately found another gun, caught his ex-wife as she was making a quick stop at home, and shot both her and himself.

SURVIVAL INSTINCT

For most of us, we have become so closely identified with our physical bodies that we can't help but equate physical death with personal annihilation.

So, when confronted with a potentially life-threatening situation, we usually find ourselves consumed by dread.

Unlike my brush with death years before in that car tumbling down the pavement of California's Highway 1, this time there was no sense of calm, only mad desperation. There was no fascination with the experience at all, only an overwhelming desire to get beyond it and survive.

The impulse to survive is deeply ingrained in us. This instinct comes from an ancient region of the brain that cares nothing about rational arguments, only self-preservation. It is not the least bit interested in novelty. It only knows what it knows, and its methods of coping with the unexpected are only three: fight, flight, or freeze. As long as we can fight or flee, we can achieve some sense of control. But, if we are immobilized, the psyche reaches new heights of terror, and we freeze.

This raging panic over death can be a formidable obstacle to spiritual inquiry. The reason is that spiritual encounter, by its very nature, implies moving beyond the limits of the physical body. Extrasensory perceptions, out-of-body experiences, near-death experiences, visitations by angelic beings, divine encounters, life-changing illnesses, and even simple meditation can be traumatic precisely because they force us to deal with information that originates from nonphysical realms.

For a mind obsessed with survival, such blurring of the line between physical and nonphysical reality appears to come dangerously close to death. So the psyche reacts by retreating in terror, before our more inquisitive impulses have a chance to kick in. The spiritual encounter is often aborted before there is any chance for significant interaction to develop.

NIGHT TERRORS

When I became interested in mystical studies in general, and in out-of-body experiences in particular, I began reading everything I could get my hands on. For a while, I did exercises designed to promote what was called astral projection—the process of leaving the physical body in order to explore astral realms.

While in the midst of these efforts one night, I was awakened by the distinct feeling that someone was standing at the foot of my bed. It was a presence that I could feel but not see. In fact, I couldn't open my eyes at all.

The presence seemed to have some sort of mysterious energy that I couldn't even begin to put into words. It was far different from a dream. My first reaction was to cry out in fear.

But, for some reason, my vocal chords were unresponsive. My second reaction was to run, but my muscles seemed paralyzed.

Now, this had happened to me in dreams before. Often I had found myself chased by a dark figure so menacing that I didn't even dare turn around to identify it. In trying to escape, I felt like I was running through a sea of Jell-O that prevented me from moving my arms and legs, except in the most excruciatingly slow manner.

The real terror of the figure standing at the end of my bed was that I knew this was no dream. I was wide awake. And, still, there was no moving my body. I was immobilized, and blind with terror.

You'd think that, given my interest in spiritual worlds, it would have occurred to me to initiate communication with this entity. But, no. I lay there and struggled until finally I was able to wrest control of my body from the unexplained force, and I called out to Jacquie. The being disappeared, and I soon was back to normal.

But then I couldn't help but kick myself as the magnitude of the lost opportunity swept over me. It was then that I began to realize how difficult it is to master the impulse of fear.

FEAR OF BIBLICAL PROPORTIONS

Throughout the Bible, whenever an angelic intruder makes contact, the first words are invariably, "Have no fear." We tend to idealize those encounters because, well, they're happening to biblical folk, aren't they? And biblical people aren't like us. They're in the Bible!

We're so used to thinking of them in this unearthly way that we don't consider the traumatic nature of a divine visitation. In fact, the reason the intruder says "Have no fear" is because the people being visited are usually stricken with terror.

If we can take their terror seriously, then we can begin to understand that the biblical characters aren't at all different from us. And if they're not different from us, then their experiences are also open to us. Oddly enough, our common fear also brings us one step closer to the radical possibility of doing the things Jesus did.

In much of the popular literature concerning spirituality, very little is made of the fear-inducing qualities of the mystical journey. The truth is, such fear is a great barrier. Those who do mention it often characterize it as something designed to keep the uninitiated from prematurely entering angelic realms. Fear acts as a sentry to guard the entrance.

Because of fear, the path to transcendence often takes a very long time. As Jesus said, "The spirit is willing, but the flesh is weak."[49] Though we may tell ourselves, over and over, how much we desire to move into regions of wonder, the need to protect the physical body, at all costs, can be overwhelming.

OUT OF BODY

But it doesn't take a full-blown bout of terror to abort a journey. Sometimes just being startled is enough.

During one afternoon at ETC, Jack Biersdorf, the driving force behind ETC, was leading us through a deceptively simple guided meditation. Starting with the feet, we were instructed to imagine space between the cells of our toes. There would be a pause, and then we would focus on another part of the body and, again, imagine space between our cells. As I did so, I was amazed at how it completely relaxed the body part. Then the body part disappeared from awareness.

It wasn't long before my whole body seemed to be drifting into a new realm of unbounded freedom. Suddenly, I was looking at an orange shag carpet, but the floor was tilted to the left. There was a steel door frame, the kind used in commercial buildings. I could see where it made contact with the carpet on both sides. The walls were painted concrete blocks, and, at the intersection with the floor, there was vinyl baseboard.

I suddenly realized that I was viewing the hallway *outside* of the room I was sitting in! I was looking at that worn-out, orange shag rug we all made fun of. My vantage point was about twelve inches off the floor—while I was in another room!

This realization so startled me that I snapped back into my body in a flash. This time, there was no fear, only the shock of realization. But that realization was well beyond anything my survival instinct was willing to cope with. Fight or flight kicked in, just the same.

Not Ordinary, but Not Unfamiliar

In the course of a normal day, our awareness often drifts in and out of our bodies, though we seldom realize it. When we daydream, we're actually watching another world open up to us while we're still fully awake. We're conscious that our physical body is carrying on, but our whole attention is elsewhere, either imagining something in the past or anticipating something in the future. While we sleep, we leave our bodies every night, though we seldom recognize it as an out-of-body excursion.

Children tend to be much more loosely attached to their bodies. In imaginative play, they're able to casually visit realms inaccessible to adults. What adults call imaginary friends are a firm reality to children. I suspect this is why Jesus said, "Truly I tell you, whoever does not receive the kingdom of God as a little child will never enter it."[50] The boundaries of a child's world are far less rigid and much more open to surprise. For them, spiritual dimensions are familiar territory.

A children's book that was one of my favorites when my kids were young is *The Alligator's Song*[51] by Robert Tallon. No matter how many times my kids would get it down from the shelf, I was delighted to read it to them.

It's the story of Eddie, a young boy who is awakened by lightning in the middle of the night. He goes to the window and can hardly believe his eyes.

There, in the midst of the garden, is an alligator, singing a sad song. It's a cry for someone to help him get back to the sea.

"Ma, Ma!" shouts Eddie. "There's an alligator outside my window. Come look! Quick!"

"Now go back to bed," his mother says. "There is no alligator. You've been reading that scary book again." So Eddie goes back to sleep. But his sleep doesn't keep him from having a wondrous adventure with the alligator.

How different it is with adults. We go back to sleep and learn to forget our adventures. The sad part is that we even continue sleeping while we're awake, unmoved and unaware of the wonder of creation. Even though we leave our bodies all the time, we consign our journeys to figments of our imagination and toss them away as useless.

To recover the golden world of children, we must face our natural fears. It can be a long, disheartening struggle. But the reward of experiencing a profound oneness with creation and finding our true essence is well worth the effort.

THEOLOGICAL FEAR

For many adults and children, there is another kind of fear that can be just as inhibiting to spiritual exploration. It's the fear induced by religion.

For many people on the mystical path, the acceptable limits of their religious tradition are so constricting that they feel compelled to reject all that they have been taught, in order to explore. They have had to make an agonizing choice between listening to their hearts and listening to their preachers' warnings.

Seldom is it realized that popular religion itself is a product of the dualistic mind. Its first order of business is not to view the unity of creation, but to split it into good and evil. Everything flows from that basic distinction.

Thus, for fundamentalism, the first proposition is not God, but the devil. The assertion of Satan is so jealously guarded that it is often said that Satan's greatest ploy is to convince people that he doesn't exist. The implication, then, is that anyone espousing a theology that diminishes the role of Satan is actually acting as one of his agents.

Satan is indispensable to a theology preoccupied with morality. Because most popular religion is concerned with behavior control, rather than spiritual exploration, it's crucial that good behavior be clearly defined. This can be done only by contrasting it with bad behavior. This contrast is the essence of dualism. Therefore, a force opposing God is actually a necessity for many adherents to find their way. Without the devil, the bulk of popular preaching has no teeth. Take away the enemy, and all reason for living is lost.

Practically speaking, for many, there is a much greater belief in the power of the devil than of God. The reason we still have evil in the world, it is sometimes said, is because Satan has yet to realize he has lost the ultimate battle with God. Therefore, he's still active, and we must be on constant guard against his wiles.

In this view, God, apparently, needs a lot of help from us. This is a strange proposition, because this same theology maintains that we're incapable of saving ourselves. To hear them tell it, we need a savior to accomplish what we cannot. But, apparently, that savior can only do so much. The rest is up to us—the very ones who couldn't save themselves in the first place! The inherent contradiction of that logic is rarely acknowledged. How strange that God needs our help, but apparently Satan doesn't.

It's understandable, then, that for many, Satan is more powerful than God. Therefore, they view the world with extreme suspicion. Anything that is unfamiliar is a possible beachhead for the devil's attack.

Unguided or novel spiritual exploration is taboo. Meditation is prohibited, because, if you stop thinking, your defenses are left open for Satan to enter. This theology offers a very fragile kind of salvation.

Certainly, Satan and the Antichrist get far more attention and popular press than does God. Even a cursory examination of popular Christian fiction shows that the real star is the Evil One. No discourse on the End Times would be complete without a blow-by-blow description of the Antichrist and his work.

Without the devil, these fire-and-brimstone religious traditions couldn't exist. Their whole theology would collapse like a house of cards. Their starting point is not love, but fear, a fear that stays with many of them all their lives.

For me, it all comes down to a basic dilemma: If there is a devil, who has the greater power—God or Satan?

I'm utterly convinced that God has the capacity to protect and guide me in all situations. Even when I make terrible mistakes, I can proceed in my explorations with confidence. There is no place where God is not found. With that realization comes a wonderful freedom.

THE DEVIL WITHIN

One way to creatively approach the issue of evil is to recognize, once again, that we carry a pantheon of personalities within us. Some of these, we're quite proud of. Others, we would rather die than reveal.

It's these hidden portions, oddly enough, that hold the greatest potential for wholeness. As I've said earlier, once these rejected parts are not only recovered, but are allowed to speak their message, then tremendous amounts of energy are released. One can then proceed in a direction of purpose and passion.

The danger of fascination with the devil, however, is that the rejected personalities, which are an *inner* phenomenon, get projected onto the *outer* world. Once this happens, we become unconscious of the traits within ourselves. Attributing them to Satan's influence is a convenient way of making sure they remain separate from us.

If we can admit, however, that the very things we condemn in others are part of our own psyches, then the world can become our teacher. When someone enrages us beyond all reason, for instance, we can begin to ask creative questions:

"What aspect of my personality is this person mirroring for me?"

"Is this person reminding me of an experience I wish to forget?"

"When have I felt this before?"

"Is there an issue haunting me that I'm unaware of?"

None of these questions can be entertained if the offending person or situation is dismissed as "the work of the devil." If that's the case, all we can do is react with fear or derision.

But, if we can begin to see the link between our interior world and our external environment, everything changes. It's then that life becomes an excellent adventure, and even the profane world becomes sacred.

A BRIEF HISTORY OF SATAN

A full history of the concept of the devil is beyond the scope of this book. However, I would like to point out several interesting ideas concerning personified evil.

First, in the Old Testament, satan (the name wasn't capitalized, because there are no capital letters in Hebrew) is only mentioned four times outside the book of Job. That's *four times* in the space of more than twelve hundred pages of writing! Unlike popular Christianity, which makes so much of Satan that it couldn't survive without him, the Old Testament wouldn't be changed in the least if he were omitted entirely.

Second, every time the word *satan* appears in the Old Testament, it doesn't signify the incarnation of evil. Instead, the word means "adversary." The function of this individual was to act as a prosecuting attorney *within God's court.* He was certainly not considered to be an enemy of God.

The reason for this is that there can be no opposition to God. Why? Because Judaism is based on the idea that there are no other gods. There is only one. Therefore, competition from another deity isn't possible.

In fact, the word *devil* doesn't appear in the Old Testament at all. The word *devils* (plural) appears, but, again, only four times. Each time the word is mentioned, it's only in connection with sacrifices made to these false entities. This is hardly enough to base a theology of evil on.

Third, the word *hell* appears nowhere in the Old Testament. The word often translated as "hell" is really the word *sheol.* This is an entirely different concept, for *sheol* is a destination for *everyone* who dies. It's not a place of torment. Neither is it a place of great joy. It's more like limbo.

What popular Christianity swears are the rock-solid foundations of their religion—concerning Satan, the devil, and even hell—have no existence at all in the Old Testament. In fact, these ideas drifted into Judaism during periods when the Jews were living in foreign countries. As such, they are very late additions to their theology.

JESUS AND SATAN

Jesus himself mentioned Satan only twelve times. Three incidents are replicated in Matthew, Mark, and Luke, leaving only three other unique usages. In each of these cases, it appears that Jesus was using the Old Testament conception of Satan as the prosecuting attorney. Satan is clearly subject to Jesus' bidding.

Jesus used the word that we translate as "hell" on eight separate occasions. In some of these, he was using the Old Testament word *sheol.* In other occasions, he was using the word *Gehenna,* which means the "Valley of Hinnom." This was a place on the outskirts of Jerusalem where people burned their garbage. It's only later in the Christian tradition that these terms were developed into a full theology of hell as a place of eternal punishment.

Contrast this with the fact that Jesus made reference to the kingdom of God, or the kingdom of heaven, more than *one hundred times* in Matthew, Mark, Luke, and John. It's apparent that Jesus was far more concerned with illuminating this idea of the kingdom than he was in nurturing fears of damnation.

Why is this point crucial? Because it flies in the face of the vast majority of preaching, which is based on fear. The picture that appears upon close examination is not anything like the religion that is held in popular conceptions.

The tragedy is that this fear is so pervasive that it virtually chokes out any desire to explore different and life-giving spiritualities. The devil has been blown so far out of proportion that the real emphasis of Jesus' teaching has been all but lost.

It need not be so. When the Bible is examined from a fresh perspective, it's not the story of Satan's grip on a trembling world that comes to the fore. It is, instead, the chronicle of a Jewish and Christian tradition wrestling with the experience of God's presence in a variety of forms.

Theological fear need not inhibit the spiritual path. If we can stop our ears to the constant barrage of negativity and fascination with the devil streaming from contemporary pulpits, and simply read for ourselves, we'll discover a marvelous freedom. A closer examination reveals that the primary foundation of the biblical narrative lies in an unsettling, yet wondrous, encounter with unity.

CHAPTER ELEVEN

Lazarus's Excellent Adventure

Somewhere over the rainbow way up high
There's a land that I've heard of once in a lullaby[52]

It has always intrigued me that in the movie *The Wizard of Oz*, the scenes in Kansas were shot in black and white. Those dull shades of gray stood in stark contrast to the vibrant Technicolor of Oz.

But even more fascinating was that such color, and the fantastic world from which it sprang, only became visible to Dorothy when she lost consciousness. It was her coma that gave her the eyes to see.

The implication is hard to miss. "Somewhere over the rainbow" is a land of splendor that makes our usual world pale into dusty shades. In that place of radiant color, it's not only bluebirds that can fly, but also humans. Without limits or gravity to shackle our dreams, we are able to soar as high as our imaginations can take us. Adventures untold await those who are willing to risk journeys outside the normal confines of awareness.

What makes this idea so poignant is that each of us longs to touch such a world, yet it seems so far out of reach. In lamenting our loss, our hearts ache with Dorothy as she compares her life to that of the birds soaring above and wonders, "Why then, oh why can't I?" In that moment, her song becomes ours.

It's easy to dismiss Oz as a fairy tale. One way of coping is to tell ourselves that if dull shades of gray are all that life has to offer, it's best to ignore the rainbow.

Another way of coping is to try to construct our own Oz with alcohol, drugs, or other addictions. (Ironically, Judy Garland, the singer of that beautiful song, did exactly that.)

A few of us will look, instead, in the direction the movie points us—to exploring the unconscious realm.

We are so used to discounting dreams and visions as nothing more than overactive imagination that we can overlook the fact that Dorothy came back from Oz profoundly changed.

But, even if we do discover that the doorway to Oz lies in our willingness to become conscious of our unconscious, we usually turn away. Not only do we recoil from facing the "lions and tigers and bears, oh my!" that live there, but we tremble at the thought of giving up control over our mundane world. Shades of gray may not be nearly as engaging as Technicolor, but at least we can take comfort in the familiar.

The yellow brick road, on the other hand, leads to unsettling destinations lying deep within the unknown. To embark on its path is to brave the tornado that smashes life as we've known it. That's why Jesus said:

> For those who want to save their life will lose it, and those who lose their life for my sake will save it. What does it profit them if they gain the whole world, but lose or forfeit themselves?[53]

Our "normal" state of awareness is dominated by an ego desperate to preserve its identity. Because the ego truly believes that image is everything, it'll stop at nothing to prove itself in the everyday physical world of the five senses. To lose awareness of the material world, as far as the ego is concerned, is to risk annihilation of the life we have so painstakingly assembled. The nonphysical and the unconscious, then, are fraught with danger. They hold the power to undermine everything we hold dear.

Knowing this instinctively, we gladly trade the adventure of the yellow brick road for the safety of the treadmill. While striving to "gain the whole world," we train ourselves not to notice that we have "forfeited" our true selves.

CARPET STAINS

There are many ways to kill off the true self. My weapon of choice was the ministry.

The pastoral image is designed to give the impression that clergy are on intimate terms with the great and wonderful Oz. In the minds of our parishioners, we skip gaily along a brightly colored path that sidesteps the usual traumas endured by lesser mortals.

Newspapers know this, so they like to do stories on us around Christmastime. It's a way of reclaiming the myth of a perfect family.

I wasn't aware of this dynamic early in my career. So it was quite a surprise when, out of the blue, a reporter from the Muncie newspaper phoned, wanting to do a piece on how my family celebrated Christmas. The article was to include a full-color photo of all of us gathered around our perfectly decorated Christmas tree, dressed in our casual but neatly pressed "school clothes," smiling contently for the camera in that "don't you wish you were us" kind of way.

It should have been a real honor.

Instead, it produced utter panic at our house. We hadn't even had time to look for a Christmas tree yet, much less decorate it. And the house itself was a disaster. The walls in the hall were covered with black smudges from hundreds of tiny, greasy handprints. Surrounding the back door was an obstacle course of mismatched boots, book bags, coats, smelly laundry, and mysterious brown bags, most likely harboring banana peels from last week's lunches.

And then there was *The Stain*.

Why is it that when children have to throw up, they can never make it to the toilet? Most adults have learned through experience that when they feel nauseated, it's best to head directly for the bathroom. Children, on the other hand, head directly for their parents' bedroom. You're sleeping soundly, when suddenly a weak little voice shatters your bliss: "My stomach hurts . . ."

Your eyes blink in the twilight to make out the trembling form of a half-awake, three-foot-tall zombie dressed in Superman Underoos, holding its midsection.

"Go to the bathroom!" you cry out. Those words have been shouted out hundreds of times before, but, for some reason, a child's brain always greets them like a completely novel idea. The zombie hesitates. "Go *now!*" you shout, jumping out of bed.

The frail little form turns toward the bathroom then struggles, sways . . . and unloads on the carpet.

It's an impressive display of projectile vomiting. How the entire contents of that stomach can be unleashed in one quick burp is truly one of nature's miracles.

In our house, this place of the perennial unloading was known simply as The Stain. Nothing could get it out. It was a fermented combination of Fruity Pebbles, Count Chocula, ketchup fries, and funnel cakes. Carpet cleaners would come to our house, offer their condolences, and then leave as if in mourning.

We dreaded the thought of having to explain it to a reporter from Muncie. But fortunately, there were still a few days left before the interview. We ran out, bought a tree, borrowed decorations from neighbors, and crammed the debris by the back door into a closet. I even slapped some paint on the wall to cover up the greasy handprints.

But The Stain would not yield. Though I tried every cleaner known to humanity, it was undaunted. The harder I scrubbed, the more it grew in size and density. It mocked my efforts.

As a last resort, we boarded off that section of the house and prayed for a reporter with a strong bladder.

It worked.

And after it was all over, the reporter strung together our incoherent mutterings into a story that actually made us sound pretty good. The picture by the Christmas tree appeared in full color, and my family looked so perfect that it made me wonder who those people were and wish our family could be more like them!

And The Stain? Over the years, it continued to marinate, becoming more full-bodied with each new layer. Eventually, we began to look upon it fondly as something that added character and charm to our home. But we never spoke of it to outsiders. The myth of the pastor's picture-perfect family wouldn't allow it.

THE PERFECT PASTOR

The myth of the perfect family has its roots in the larger myth of the perfect pastor.

One never-ending duty of the pastor is to visit those facing major difficulties in their lives. For me, this was a constant source of anxiety and stress—not because I didn't want to comfort people, but because the job was never done. Whether it was keeping up with members in the hospital, tending to those in nursing homes, or staying in touch with parishioners who were recently bereaved, the demands were relentless.

Most of my older members were gracious in the extreme. A few, however, were amazingly talented in wielding the bludgeon of shame.

"So nice to see you! It's been so long that I thought you forgot all about me!"

"I can't remember the last time you were here!"

"I thought you'd forgotten where I lived!"

It's amazing how much you can sweat in a three-piece suit. What was so bizarre was that I could never respond. I was trapped in the myth. And the myth demands that the pastor be infinitely patient and kind.

Early in my career, I'd made the mistake of confronting several members in a truthful, straightforward manner. It was a way of communicating that I had learned in the construction industry. There, such straight talk was effective. In the pastoral role, however, it was disastrous. I was never forgiven, and all communication was cut off. A few parishioners left the church.

Because the pastor can never respond truthfully, those who are harboring a hidden rage can launch their darts without fear of retribution, as long as they never speak of their anger directly. Blood is spilled, but decorum is preserved.

The game cannot work, though, unless the pastor is heavily invested in a false image of perfection, which I was. I would sit through such disguised disapproval and pretend not to have heard the rage behind the words.

Make no mistake, the pastorate *was* my choice. I have no regrets. It was a path that was deadening and painful. But it was necessary for me, because it taught me much about myself.

In the end, I found out why Carl Jung said of his father, who was a pastor, "He did a great deal of good—far too much—and as a result was usually irritable."[54] When I first read that as a young man, it seemed absurd. How could anyone do "far too much" good? Wasn't that the whole goal of life—to be good and to do good?

It would take years for me to understand that devoting my life to only doing good could be fatal in more ways than one. Not only did it slowly wear me out, but it also perpetuated a false image, leaving no time for my true self to emerge. As I would eventually discover, the true self is made up of both light and darkness.

TOO LITTLE, TOO LATE

As a rabbi, Jesus too had a pastoral role to fill. But, for some reason, he wasn't driven to play a false role by the unrealistic expectations of others. There was the case of his good friend Lazarus.

Lazarus had been clinging to life for days. Martha and Mary had sent word to Jesus that their brother was near death.

Now, most pastors, upon hearing the urgency of this message, would have left immediately to help—if for no other reason than to be spared being gored in the bullring of public opinion. Jesus, instead, waited two more days.

Clearly he was wasting precious time. It was incomprehensible to everyone around him. Didn't he care? Was he afraid he wouldn't have the power?

Had he become too important in his own eyes to remember the little people? Was he afraid he'd be arrested?

Finally, after two days, Jesus announced that he was going to see his friend. Some were glad for the news. But others were terrified, knowing that this trip would take them deep into enemy territory. That Thomas knew it was suicidal was evident as he announced, "Let us also go, that we may die with him."[55]

But the danger to Jesus didn't matter to Mary and Martha. All they wanted was for their brother to be well. However, because of the delay, it was too late. By the time Jesus was spotted coming over the crest of a hill, Lazarus had already been placed in the grave.

Martha ran out to meet him. Suddenly, all of her pent-up emotions poured forth as she screamed in her rage and grief, "Lord, if you had been here, my brother would not have died!"[56] Then, remembering the need for decorum when speaking to members of the clergy, she gathered herself and smoothed over her anger. "But even now I know that God will give you whatever you ask of him."[57]

Jesus replied tersely, "Your brother will rise again."[58] It was a simple statement, very matter of fact, but clearly impossible.

DEALING WITH THE IMPOSSIBLE

There is a powerful bias in the human psyche against anything that is impossible. While we say we long for the miraculous, in fact, we avoid it at all costs. To be confronted with the unexplainable is to be ripped out of the comfort of the familiar and to be cast into the terror of uncertainty. It's to embark on the yellow brick road, with all of its twists, turns, and unwelcome surprises.

One of the great tools we've developed for avoiding the miraculous is theology. This is *thinking about God,* which is radically different from enduring the trauma of a personal encounter. Theology allows us to calm our nerves and to retreat into the safety of our own heads. It trades the awesome confrontational power of divinity for intellectual propositions over which we can argue.

Why would we want to be so thoroughly known? To be revealed in this way is to have our carefully constructed personas shattered. Such shattering is worse than physical death.

THE TRAUMA OF SEEING GOD

In the Hindu sacred text the Bhagavad Gita, the hero, Arjuna, is being taught by Lord Krishna the secrets of transcendence. In order to accommodate Arjuna's frailty, Krishna has been appearing to him in a form that is able to shield his supernatural splendor.

Realizing this, Arjuna asks to see the Lord in all his glory. To do this, Krishna must first give to Arjuna a supernatural eye that is capable of withstanding the shock of what he's about to witness, for Arjuna has no idea of the magnitude of his request. After giving this gift of higher sight, Krishna then reveals himself.

The vision is too much to bear. So Arjuna cries out:

> Seeing thy great form, of thy many mouths and eyes, O Mighty-armed, of many arms, thighs and feet, of many bellies, terrible with many tusks, the worlds tremble and so do I.
>
> When I see Thee touching the sky, blazing with many hues, with Thy mouth opened wide, and large glowing eyes, my inmost soul trembles in fear and I find neither steadiness nor peace, O Vishnu!
>
> When I see Thy mouths, terrible with their tusks, like Time's devouring flames, I lose sense of the directions, and find no peace. Be gracious, O Lord of gods, Refuge of the worlds![59]

In the end, Arjuna can't sustain the vision and pleads that Krishna morph into a form that is less threatening:

I wish to see thee even as before with thy crown, mace, and disc in thy hand. Assume thy four-armed shape, O Thou of a thousand arms and of universal form.[60]

Complying with Arjuna's request, Krishna returns to a more accommodating appearance.

In the book of Isaiah, the author too suffered the same terror as Arjuna when he was transported into ethereal realms:

The pivots of the thresholds shook at the voices of those who called, and the house filled with smoke. And I said: "Woe is me! I am lost, for I am a man of unclean lips, and I live among a people of unclean lips; yet my eyes have seen the Lord of Hosts![61]

We live with a suspicion that, in viewing the majesty of the godhead, we'll be undone. So we run for the shelter of a mind that will distract us from truly seeing. We retreat from perception and run to interpretation.

Interpretation is the domain of the mind. It brings us comfort, but, being the mind, it also splits the world and even the very nature of God. The Creator becomes not Lord of the Universe, but a weapon to be used against those of other faiths. Suddenly, we no longer have a God who fashions outrageous variety in the world, yet has no favorites, but instead one who creates winners at the expense of losers.

We argue about the correctness of our theology. We insist that our interpretation is closer to the deity. The words provide refuge from the direct encounter.

MARTHA'S HEAD GAMES

When Jesus said, "Your brother will rise again," Martha couldn't take it in. Like all of us, Martha was so good at thinking about God that she couldn't experience the divine in front of her. Her mind jumped to what she'd been taught: "I know that he will rise again in the resurrection on the last day."[62]

What Martha was alluding to was the common belief that the Messiah would come sometime in the future. At this event, all history, even time itself, would come to an end. The Messiah would call the dead out of their graves. Those who had died in martyrdom would be given back their lost wholeness.

Martha had already pushed down her anger and grief for the sake of decorum. Now she was distancing herself from the miracle by playing head games. Looking to the future, she could perhaps find relief from the intolerable present.

Lest we be too hard on Martha, it's vital to understand that hers was a tactic sadly familiar to us all. From the bright glare of grief, we all crave shelter. We deny what we're feeling because we fear the pain. We stuff our emotions, because we're terrified of their raw power. While we would like to think that we identify mostly with her sister Mary, it's Martha who is most like us.

Jesus, recognizing her unconscious ploy, brought her back into the present. "I am the resurrection and the life."[63] No more words needed to be spoken.

AUTHENTIC GRIEF

Martha went to call Mary. In the midst of her mourning, Mary quickly gathered up her robes and hurried to Jesus. When their eyes met, she fell down on her knees and cried. Hers were the same words as Martha: "Lord, if you had been here, my brother would not have died."[64]

But for Mary there was no retreat from the grief. There was no debate. She knelt before Jesus in the vulnerability of her shattered life. Mary had the courage not to go numb to the pain. She dared to feel all that was surging through her, and yet not turn away. Seeing this moved Jesus deeply. The two of them wept together. In their grief, Jesus and Mary shared a deep communion.

Even as they embraced, the onlookers were whispering their disgust. "Could not he who opened the eyes of the blind man have kept this man from dying?"[65]

Turning toward the tomb, Jesus commanded that the stone at the mouth of the cave be rolled away. Martha was dismayed. She tried to remind him that the body, now dead for four days, was already emitting a terrible stench.

But the stone was removed anyway. Peering into the depths of the darkness, he called out, "Lazarus, come forth!"[66]

To the shock of everyone there, the dead man came stumbling out, his eyes blinking from the piercing brightness of the sun.

"Unbind him and let him go,"[67] Jesus commanded.

Because of this unusual event, many who had previously been skeptical began to believe. Others were threatened by this display of power, and sought all the more to destroy him.

But what of Lazarus? What would he have said about his extraordinary journey? Did he have tales to tell about traversing beyond the bounds of the material world? Would he have returned, like Dorothy in *The Wizard of Oz*, deeply changed?

Sadly, we'll never know. However, the journey must have convinced him that the dividing line between life and death is far more permeable than most think. In itself, that would have had a great impact on his life.

DOCTOR GREEN EYES

In my work as a pastor, I learned over time that what people needed from me was simpler than I knew. They just needed me to be present. Listening to their story was a healing act. This was true especially for the dying.

I met Sally only once. Yet, during the short time we were together, she confided in me this remarkable experience.

Years before, while still in her early twenties, Sally had been struggling with the direction of her life. Every job she landed turned out badly. One after another, her employers found reasons to let her go. The more jobs she lost, the more difficult she found it to get hired. She began to feel severely depressed, as the prospects for her future seemed to close off.

Throughout most of her life, she had struggled with a heart condition that severely reduced her stamina. Many employers were reluctant to take on someone with a preexisting condition. It seemed as if everything was against her.

One evening, she collapsed in a restaurant with a massive coronary. The ambulance rushed her to the emergency room. After stabilizing her in the emergency room, she was taken to ICU. Once there, she suffered yet another heart attack.

A code red was called, but it was too late. They tried several times to shock her, but her heart refused to restart. The monitor showed nothing but a flat green line. Her breathing stopped. The last few nurses began cleaning up and putting away the crash cart. One stopped to raise the sheet over the corpse's face. A doctor from another floor came into the room almost unnoticed.

By this time, Sally remembers hovering above her body. There was no sense of anguish. In fact, the feeling was euphoric. At last, she was freed from all the pain of her heart. Finally, she was released from the constant worry of making a living. She felt herself drifting toward a path that wound its way into the distance.

She followed it until she came to some kind of a border. On the other side was a green pasture stretching to foothills. In the distance was a snow-capped mountain range. There was a sense of peace and calm unlike anything she had ever experienced. With every fiber of her being, she longed to move toward something in the distance.

Looking down, she realized that the border was actually a white fence with a gate. Feeling a great surge of energy and joy, she started to move toward the gate. No sooner did she approach it than a hand reached out and prevented her entry.

For some reason, she couldn't turn around to see the person whose hand was blocking her way. No words were exchanged, but she was made to understand that there would come a day when she could pass through this gate, but not now. There was still work she had to accomplish back in her body.

With this, she broke down into tears; torrents of grief swept over her. The news was crushing. She fought going back with everything she had, but it was useless. With a painful snap, she was back in her body.

Opening her eyes to the agony of the ICU, Sally looked up to see the face of a doctor she had never met before standing over her. His eyes were ablaze with an emerald green color. She could feel his strength as he held her hand, as if he were infusing her with a strange form of energy.

Slowly, she calmed down, and he began speaking to her. For three hours, he sat by her bedside and began to tell her all that would happen in her lifetime to come.

When he was finished, he said, "You won't consciously remember any of the details that I have spoken to you, but you will recall the fact that we conversed. Just know that some part of you has understood all that I've said." With that, the doctor got up and left the room.

After he went out, a nurse came in and said, rather nonchalantly, "You're number forty."

"What do you mean by number forty?"

"This is the fortieth time I've seen this happen. If you see that doctor again, he won't have any remembrance of your conversation with him. He'll look at you as if you had never met."

Sure enough, several days later, Sally chanced to see the doctor passing by in the corridor. He was the same person, only this time his eyes were radically different. Gone was the brilliant emerald color. Sally stopped him and asked about what he had told her. He seemed quite perplexed and embarrassed, saying that she must be mistaking him for someone else.

Sally told me that the experience of her own death radically changed her life. No longer could she get excited about the trivial things. No longer did she carry the same debilitating fear that had kept her back for so long. Her heart condition had improved dramatically.

"Once you've seen for yourself that there is a life beyond, you can never look at this world in the same way. I now know that every person is of infinite worth. I know that my life matters and that I am not alone."

Dorothy could not have said it better herself. No one can visit Oz without being profoundly changed.

Death can be the greatest of teachers. And great teachers use the time of death to communicate their most life-giving lessons.

CHAPTER TWELVE

Sacred Profanity

In his book *Working,* Studs Terkel interviewed people from a variety of occupations. From spot welders to hookers to corporate CEOs, each one gave intimate details on what it was like to live their lives and do the work they each had chosen.

Mike Lefevre was a laborer in a Chicago steel mill. He describes the start of his day this way:

> The first thing happens at work: when the arms start moving, the brain stops. I punch in about ten minutes to seven in the morning. I say hello to a couple of guys I like, I kid around with them. One guy says good morning to you and you say good morning. To another guy you say fuck you. The guy you say fuck you to is your friend.[68]

I laughed out loud when I read that, because it's so true. In the blue-collar world, profanity is a way to cut through all the baloney of etiquette and get to something more basic. It's a way of saying, "Look, you and I are on the same level here. So don't give me any B.S." The people you say "fuck you" to are your real friends.

The passage was so perfect that I decided one day to use it as a devotional for a class I was taking at ETC in the mid-1980s. It was a small group of pastors, about eight students and one faculty member. We would rotate responsibility for bringing something to open our meetings that would introduce a note of sacredness to our gathering, to remind us all that we were embarking on a holy quest. After that, we would begin with prayer.

After reading that little vignette, I reflected on the fact that, as pastors, we're seldom privy to the off-color inside jokes that true friends can share freely. More often than not, we come across a group of people huddled in the delightful conspiracy of a bawdy story, only to have the laughter stop when we come up and hear someone say, "Oops! Better not say that. He's a pastor."

I told the class that I'd begun to wonder what the possibilities were for genuine friendship in our profession. I finished by saying, "I just wanted you all to know that you are my friends . . . so, fuck you!"

There was a roar of laughter. A series of wholehearted "fuck yous" were offered in return. The phrase quickly became the theme for our meeting.

One pastor, though, was appalled. He was so deeply offended that he left and never came back.

That's the risk of daring to mingle the sacred and the profane. The categories of good and evil are so dear to us that when someone seems to mix them up, we recoil in disgust and even rage. God is "up there" and good. We're "down here" and hopeless. Blurring the lines is taboo.

MASTER OR SERVANT?

Oddly enough, it wasn't taboo for Jesus. He too was well aware of the gap that separated him, as a representative of God, from ordinary people. It wasn't a gap perpetuated by Jesus, but one that persisted in the minds of his followers. It had to be broken in order for there to be any hope of genuine friendship.

In the Gospel according to John, the night before his arrest, Jesus was gathered with his disciples for a supper. He knew that his time was drawing to an end, so he chose to offer his most important teachings to his disciples. This would be the last opportunity.

It was an extraordinary session that challenged everything they thought they knew about friendship, their relation to God, and even their very self-understanding. It began with a simple but surprising act.

It's not hard to imagine that the gathering had turned into a raucous party. Wine was flowing. There was singing and dancing. Loud voices competed over who could tell the most ridiculous story.

No doubt, a few tales were so raunchy that they could only be whispered in private—with heads leaned together and hands shielding lips, lest the master should hear—and the listeners burst out laughing.

Lazarus was the guest of honor. Friends being what they are, there were the inevitable remarks about how natural he looked for a dead man, how the embalmers had done a fine job.

Mary and Martha brought out an endless supply of food and drink, serving it all up with unbridled joy. Their brother was alive, and nothing could dampen their euphoria.

In the midst of the frivolity, Jesus slowly rose from the table. Without any explanation, he took water and poured it into a basin and tied a towel around himself. Methodically, he began washing the feet of everyone in the room.

Washing feet was a job for the servants. Stooping to such a menial task was hardly the place for one so highly esteemed, a man so holy, a man who had just brought another man back from the dead. But Jesus was about to turn all of their ideas upside down.

> Do you know what I have done to you? You call me Teacher and Lord—and you are right, for that is what I am. So if I, your Lord and Teacher, have washed your feet, you also ought to wash one another's feet. For I have set an example that you also should do as I have done to you.
>
> Very truly I tell you, servants are not greater than their master, nor are messengers greater than the one who sent them. If you know these things, blessed are you if you do them. . . . Very truly, I tell you, whoever receives one whom I

send receives me; and whoever receives me receives him who sent me.[69]

Upon hearing this, the disciples looked at one another and said, "Huh?" Who, then, is the master and who is the slave? There were blank stares all around.

As if to blur the distinction even more, Jesus commented later on,

> I do not call you servants any longer, because the servant does not know what the master is doing; but I have called you friends, because I have made known to you everything that I have heard from my Father.[70]

Those words must have unleashed a slew of questions in their minds. A friend with Jesus? Can we be that close as to be on equal footing? Could we possibly reach the kind of playful, easy familiarity that characterizes true friendship, even with all the raunchy exchanges and off-color inside jokes? Where nothing is held back? Where we don't have to be on our best behavior? What, then, is holiness? What does it mean to be a friend, when there seems to be such a big gap between our abilities and those of Jesus?

But those questions were nothing compared to their astonishment when Jesus announced, "Very truly, I tell you, one of you will betray me."[71] It was unthinkable! One of us?

Cryptically, Jesus announced who it was when, after dipping a piece of bread, he handed it to Judas. "Do quickly what you are going to do,"[72] he told him. And Judas immediately went out.

Now, eating from the Tree of the Knowledge of Good and Evil as we do, which demands that we be very clear about who the heroes and villains are, we can't help but heap scorn upon Judas. After all, Jesus was God and, therefore, all good. Anything or anyone who deliberately causes harm to come to a good person must be, by definition, a bad person. The obvious flannel board lesson is that we must not be like Judas.

Much has been made of the fact that Judas was a lover of money, which, according to Jesus, was the root of all evil. When Mary took a costly perfume and anointed Jesus' feet with it in gratitude, it was Judas who objected.

"Why was this perfume not sold for three hundred denarii and the money given to the poor?"[73] he challenged.

Those who heard him scoffed under their breath, knowing that Judas, as keeper of the common purse, used to steal from it. The obvious lesson: don't steal, don't love money, and don't be like Judas. But most of all, don't betray Jesus. Be a good friend.

The implication is also that we should be like the other disciples. Yet, when we look at their track records, there's not much to commend any of them. Peter practically came to blows with Jesus when Jesus spoke too specifically about his own death. And when that death drew near, it was Peter who denied, not once, but three times, that he even knew the man.

Thomas refused to believe his fellow disciples when they all stated that they had seen the risen Christ. James and John argued about who was the greatest. Time and again, the disciples would hear Jesus' words and come away scratching their heads, unable to fathom the inner truth of his parables.

When we can move beyond the stylized, idealistic picture of this group of followers, they all come off as quite ordinary, even a little dull-witted. It's not that we should try to be more like these other disciples. We don't need to. We're already like them. And they're like us.

Yet Judas has, through the centuries, been singled out as the supremely bad egg. We seem to need heroes and villains more than we need insight. The fruit of the tree demands it. Good and evil. White hats and black.

JUDAS IN ANOTHER LIGHT

One of the more interesting treatments of Judas looks at him through a different lens altogether. According to this perspective, Judas was not the one who was the most faithless. Instead, it was Judas who believed most fully in Jesus as the Messiah.

Traveling so closely in Jesus' company, Judas had seen many displays of power. In Judas's mind, it was clear that Jesus was demonstrating all the qualifications of the long-hoped-for Messiah.

The Messiah was expected to be a great military leader. Israel had been under the domination of foreign intruders for hundreds of years. Around 167 BC, the nationalistic fervor of the people had erupted in the Maccabean revolt. Against all odds, the revolution had been successful in overthrowing the Syrian occupation and gaining religious freedom. The temple was cleansed and rededicated, an event that is still commemorated today in the celebration of Hanukkah.

The liberation didn't last long, however. In 63 BC, Pompey took control of Jerusalem, and Roman rule was established.

Yet the temporary success of this, the Maccabean revolt, had fanned the flames of hope. Over the years, it had become a common assumption that the Messiah would bring that hope to realization by liberating Israel, and so restore it to its rightful preeminence among the nations.

When Judas saw the power of the teacher from Galilee, he and others suspected that the wait for the Messiah was over. When the crowds gathered to line the streets to Jerusalem to herald Jesus' entry, laying down palm branches and singing, "Hosanna! Hosanna in the highest!" they were not just acknowledging Jesus as a spiritual leader. They were naming him as the military leader they'd all been looking for.

Judas would've been delighted by this. After coming into the city in such a prominent way, Jesus would surely confront the political leaders and be swept into power by the masses.

How disillusioning it must have been when Jesus left the political center of Jerusalem to stay in a little town near the wilderness. The people had literally laid his destiny at his feet. Was this the way the ruler of Israel should behave?

It must've been disconcerting—especially for Judas—that Jesus always seemed to move away from his power. After he would heal someone, he would demand that the person tell no one. He spent the bulk of his ministry in the far reaches of Israel, rather than building coalitions in Jerusalem's halls of power. He associated with lowlifes and outsiders, offending and shunning the very movers and shakers who could clearly aid his rise to power.

Judas knew he had to do something to force Jesus' hand. After all, a true friend seeks to bring out the best in those he cares about. Judas may have loved money, but he also understood the ways of power. If Jesus didn't assume the power that was his destiny, a whole nation would suffer.

Instead of jumping to the conclusion that Judas was a duplicitous traitor, let's consider, for a moment, the possibility that Judas simply wanted to force a showdown. What if Judas believed in Jesus' powers so completely that he never considered for a moment that Jesus' enemies would be able to take him away? What if he believed that, given a little push, Jesus would have no choice but to summon the powers he had displayed outside the walls of Jerusalem.

And when the political leaders saw what he had to offer, they couldn't help but recognize that here was the one who was even greater than Moses. The entire nation would be bound together, once they realized that the Messiah had finally arrived. It was the perfect plan.

The best way to force a showdown was to see that Jesus was arrested and placed in the hands of those who held real political power. Making it look as if he were betraying Jesus for money, so as not to arouse suspicion of his real intent, Judas struck a deal for thirty pieces of silver. In his heart, he was putting his own reputation on the line, so that the world would finally see the glory of the Messiah.

Of course, the plan didn't work. At least not as Judas expected. His horror at watching the whole thing go miserably wrong was devastating. There was one opportunity after another for a miracle. Yet, inexplicably, there was no flash of power. No angels came to the rescue. No invisible armies. God himself seemed to turn away, as Judas's Messiah was flogged and crucified.

Stunned and uncomprehending, Judas watched the lifeblood drain from his hopes as the impossible happened. Inexplicably, his dreams came to nothing more than a corpse on a cross. In a state of distraction, Judas tried to return the money. Then, overcome with resignation and despair, he hung himself. The depth of his miscalculation was more than he could bear.

I mention this treatment of Judas to underscore the fact that our initial and habitual assessments of good and evil are not necessarily accurate. Even in a case where a man's name has become a synonym for betrayal, our assumptions may be comfortable, but they also might be wrong. There is always more than one way to look at a story.

Yet we prefer to rush to judgment. It makes life simpler. We're not interested in new ways of seeing old stories. Little do we realize the heavy price we pay for our ironclad assumptions.

CONTEMPORARY DUALISM

When we split the world into good and evil, the natural tendency is to place a huge gulf between God and us. We assume that we must keep some distance between the sacred and the profane. If they were allowed to intermingle, they would become mutually polluting.

For some in the early church, the earth, because of its gross, material nature, was considered to be evil. (Notice how radically different this perspective is from the "very good" earth presented in Genesis.) At some unspecified distance from the material world was God. Because God was essentially spirit, the divine being represented all that was good. Humans were barred from entry into the holy realm precisely because they carried with them the taint of physical matter. Thus, there was placed a huge gulf between good and evil, between the spiritual and material worlds, and hence between God and mere mortals.

Much of conservative Christian theology is built precisely upon this foundation. Because we're not holy and have no access to God, we deserve death. The only way to regain divine acceptance is to have someone die for us, in order to pay our debt. We have screwed up so badly that we have no chance of repairing the breach. Only if a perfect person steps in for our sake and offers himself or herself on our behalf will the debt be paid. The only one who can qualify for the standard of perfect holiness is God. Therefore, only God can die for us. That's why Jesus was fully God, and that's why only Jesus' sacrifice would do.

Check out any Bible tract left in a public restroom, and you will find the same message. Tune in to any TV evangelist, and you'll hear this preached endlessly. As Billy Graham has said, "I really have only one sermon."

So, at one end of an impassable chasm we have God: totally good, infinitely wise, holy beyond comparison. At the other end, we have humans: depraved, foolish, and crappy.

Actually, the whole issue of crap, in itself, is pertinent to our discussion, for nowhere is the dividing line between sacred and profane more pronounced. Bowl cleaners, air fresheners, perfumes, soaps, deodorants, and scented toilet paper all speak of our fetish for covering up the most basic characteristic of the human condition—we stink.

Recall that when Jesus came to the tomb, the one thing that most concerned Martha was that the body had a stench. Even in death, we seek to distance ourselves from the truth. To stink is to be mortal. Cleanliness, on the other hand, is next to Godliness.

FREUDIAN SLIP

When I first came into the pastorate, I was terrified of public speaking. To calm my fears, my boss, Ron Naylor, told me about one of his own experiences as an intern. It set the bar so high for embarrassment that I never felt quite as nervous again.

The Sunday service in the Presbyterian tradition usually begins with a flourish—the Call to Worship. It's intended to bring the congregation to attention and to set a mood of expectation. It's usually intoned with booming voice and great enthusiasm.

On this particular day, Ron, the student pastor, was assigned the Call to Worship. The words he was supposed to read were, "AND MAY THE SPIRIT OF GOD LIGHT OUR HEARTS ON FIRE!" after which, the organ and choir were supposed to immediately launch into the first hymn.

What came out of his mouth instead was "AND MAY THE SPIRIT OF GOD LIGHT OUR *FARTS* ON FIRE!" The senior pastor fell out of his chair laughing. The whole congregation was rolling in the aisles. The hymn didn't start for a very, very long time.

A DIVINE MOONING

Sacred and profane. The Bible doesn't necessarily maintain this split. Much of what we read in English has been sanitized, without our knowing it. If the Old Testament is read in its original language, Hebrew, a much more earthy quality often emerges.

Take, for instance, one of the encounters Moses had with God. As a result of their increasingly frequent contact, Moses began to feel a deep desire to see God visually. And so he asked to see God in all of the divine glory. God's response was, "I will make all my goodness pass before you, and will proclaim before you the name 'The Lord'; and I will be gracious to whom I will be gracious, and will show mercy on whom I will show mercy. But you cannot see my face; for no one shall see me and live."[74] God then put Moses in the cleft of a rock to protect him. While the glorious spectacle moved past, God placed his hand upon Moses to keep him from seeing. Once past, the hand was removed so that Moses could see only the Lord's "back."

Now, the interesting thing is that, in Hebrew, words are not only singular or plural, as in English, but there is also a third ending, which gives a dual designation. This dual ending appears on the word translated as "back." In fact, a more accurate rendering would be, "and I will cover you with my hand until I have passed by; then I will take away my hand, and you shall see my two backsides; but my face shall not be seen."[75]

In seminary, my Hebrew teacher made note of this fact. In pointing out the dual ending, he said, "When you think about it, it's very difficult to escape the notion that the writer here is referring to God's buttocks."

Upon hearing that, it became very hard for all of us to escape the notion that, in the most sacred revelation of the divine being, God was actually mooning Moses.

SHREDDING TIME AND SPACE

Jesus too shredded our treasured division between God and humanity. "The Father and I are one,"[76] he says in the Gospel of John. "Very truly, I tell you, the Son can do nothing on his own, but only what he sees the Father doing; for what the Father does, the son does likewise. . . ."[77] Before Abraham was, I am."[78]

These were bold claims. At the last supper, according to the Gospel of John, Jesus emphasized this again. Philip pleaded with him, "Lord, show us the Father and we will be satisfied."[79]

Jesus said, "Have I been with you all this time, Philip, and you still do not know me? Whoever has seen me has seen the Father. How can you say, 'Show us the Father'? Do you not believe that I am in the Father and the Father is in me?"[80]

As these words are read in church services, heads nod, smiles come out, tinged with the comfort of familiarity. Once again, we're reassured of the supremacy of Jesus. It's so familiar that the passage is hardly even heard. Seldom, if ever, is it even noticed that Jesus has just shredded time and space.

He is telling us that two separate and distinct entities, the Father and Jesus himself, are not only occupying the same space, but they are interpenetrating in such a way that one is in the other. And, even more, the other is in the one.

Most of us can picture something nestled inside something else. The chick inside the shell. The hand inside a mitten. But can the shell be in the chick too? The mitten in the hand while the hand is in the mitten?

That Jesus could be in the Father is easy to grasp. After all, Jesus is God's Mini-Me. So Jesus could make his way through the world uniquely contained in a cloud that was the essence of God. He was the boy in the bubble, breathing purified air, different from the rest of us. We can accept that. We *expect* that.

But the flip side of his statement is that "the Father is in me." Time out! If the Father is the creator of all that is, then the Father must be bigger than the universe. How could the totality of God be confined in the human body of Jesus? How can the bubble be in the boy? The shell in the chick?

For the person nodding off in the pew, this is no real problem. Jesus is God. God knows about things we don't, so let's just let God be God and not worry about it. After all, we're only human.

DOING WHAT JESUS DID

But in his discussion with Philip, Jesus doesn't leave it at that. He goes on to say something that's truly astounding: "The one who believes in me will also do the works that I do and, in fact, will do greater works than these, because I am going to the Father."[81] Now think about that statement for just a moment. If we take that statement seriously, human potential becomes virtually unlimited. The separation between Jesus and us that has been based on our widely differing capabilities has been removed. The old apology for our bumbling frailty—"Well, I'm only human, you know!"—suddenly makes no sense when we realize we've been *squandering the wonder* that is our birthright.

From this perspective, Jesus becomes a model for human potential, rather than a savior for a lost humanity. It's an idea that has been utterly missed by the popular church obsessed with categories of good and evil.

THE TWO FUNCTIONS OF CHURCH

During one of my classes at ETC, I was puzzling over the way church people keep their distance from anything that gets too close to God, including the pastor. The sanctuary itself is designed with this in mind. The clergy, who are assumed to be closest to God, are separated from the pews and elevated in the chancel area.

They are the only ones dressed in robes, most often black. All seating is focused in the direction of the pastor, and laypeople are offered the protection of the pews. Those who need the most protection from the divine sit in the back or in the balcony. Those who can't imagine themselves as good enough to approach the holy never even enter.

As I was musing over this, I commented in class one day that "holiness seems to be like kryptonite to Superman. People seem to be interested in it, but they really are terrified to even come close. It's like the pastor's robe is really a radiation suit, and so they push the pastor to connect with God in their place.

"Like the old Life cereal commercial with the kid brothers pushing the full bowl back and forth between them: 'You eat it!'

"'I'm not gonna eat it! You eat it!'

"The irony is that the one place where people should be able to come to get close to God is the one place where they turn away and ask someone else to do it for them."

Jack Biersdorf, the teacher of the class, responded with a comment that has stayed with me ever since.

"Historically, the church has served two different functions. One function is to pave the way for connection with the divine. But it has also been recognized, through the ages, that this connection can carry great danger for those who are not properly prepared. So the other function of the church has been to guard against premature contact with holiness."

Unfortunately, what has happened is that, much of the time, the church has forgotten how to prepare people and now is able only to act as a shield to the spirit.

I AND THE FATHER ARE ONE

As he spoke with his disciples, however, Jesus was in the process of knocking down the last vestiges of the dividing wall. Not only was Jesus connected in an intimate and mysterious way with the Father, but he also said flatly that his disciples would do the impossible. They would exceed his works.

What is astounding is that those who classify themselves as followers of Jesus seem to be so oblivious to this promise. The reason is that we have never been able to stop eating from the Tree of the Knowledge of Good and

Evil. We can't resist the urge to judge the world according to categories that place God at one end of the spectrum and humans at the other.

In his final prayer with the disciples, Jesus singled out this persistent desire to split the world and to wall off humanity from God:

> I ask not only on behalf of these, but on behalf of those who will believe in me through their word, that they may all be one. As you, Father, are in me and I am in you, may they also be in us, so that the world may believe that you have sent me. The glory that you have given to me I have given to them, so that they may be one, as we are one. I in them and you in me, that they may be completely one so that the world may believe that you have sent me and have loved them even as you have loved me. Father, I desire that those also whom you have given me, may be with me where I am, to see my glory, which you have given me because you have loved me before the foundation of the world.[82]

Now, it might be argued that Jesus was only speaking this prayer for his disciples, and that this unity is only for those who fall within the sphere of Jesus' influence.

Yet, if this is the case, it flies in the face of the most famous verses in Christian scripture:

> For God so loved the world that he gave his only son, so that everyone who believes in him may not perish but may have eternal life. Indeed God did not send the Son to condemn the world, but that the world might be saved through him.[83]

The emphasis in this passage is on the world, not on a specified, individual few. Yet, even if Jesus were speaking only about his disciples, it was an amazing thing to say. It's a rare Christian who would dare to proclaim, "I am one with God. God is in me and I am in God."

We can accept it on the lips of Jesus, because we're accustomed to placing the same gap between Jesus and ourselves as between God and all humanity. We're so used to safeguarding the holiness of the deity that those words would seem like pure blasphemy if spoken by a mere mortal.

And yet that was exactly the direction of Jesus' prayer. There is an essential oneness that is the cornerstone of the kingdom of heaven.

MADNESS OR INSIGHT?

Recently, I saw on television a program probing the mysteries of the mind. One segment dealt with an epileptic young man. During his bouts with epilepsy, he would have fantastic visions where he considered himself to be God. In fact, one time he went running down the street screaming, "I am God! I am God!" loudly enough for all the neighbors to hear.

His father yelled from the front door, "Get back in here before they call the police!"

To appease his father, the young man came back in the house, saying, "It's all right. They won't arrest me." In his mind, he was thinking, *They won't arrest me. I'm God! They wouldn't arrest God!*

Of course, he's wrong about that. Anyone who goes around saying that they're God is assumed to be delusional, perhaps even dangerous.

We would like to think that if Jesus came back and made the same claims, we would be able to tell the difference. After all, who could mistake the Son of God? But Jesus probably looked just as delusional to the authorities of his day as the epileptic young man looks to us today.

Yet, what if the young man was actually seeing reality as it is? What if we're the ones who are blind? Just because we all agree that we're not God, does that mean we're right? What if viewing the kingdom of heaven requires giving up our cherished ideas about who we are and who God is, and accepting the oneness that Jesus was speaking of?

The implications are so radical that, to believe them, we would need a direct experience of traversing the split between heaven and earth. And we all know such things never happen.

CHAPTER THIRTEEN

Straddling the Split

In 1978, Jacquie and I had been married for three years, and we began discussing the idea of having children. Because we were fundamentalist Christians at the time, we thought it important to consult God.

The way we figured it, we'd find out God's will by having Jacquie discontinue birth control. If she got pregnant, then it was God's will for us to be parents. If she didn't, then God was saying no.

It never occurred to us to ask whether it was God's will for us to stop using birth control. That would have been complicating things.

So Jacquie went pill-less, and within a few months, much to our delight, she became pregnant. We waited awhile before telling our friends and relatives—just to be sure. But we couldn't keep the secret for long. Soon we were being celebrated by friends and family. Even strangers were giving us pats on the back.

In those days, Jacquie and I were working with the youth group at our church. We would take the high school kids for an annual trip to the beach. That entailed a grueling, ten-hour trip from Pennsylvania to South Carolina in an old school bus with straight-backed, cardboard-cushioned seats with no air conditioning. But we were game.

Several weeks before the trip, though, Jacquie had begun spotting. Not a good sign when you're pregnant.

We went to the obstetrician, who told her to rest and take it easy—everything would be fine. We wrestled about whether or not Jacquie should go on the trip.

Ultimately, she decided to risk it. After all, God had already given us the thumbs up for parenthood. We would be traveling under divine protection.

And so, after loading up countless suitcases, sleeping bags, pillows, and rumpled high schoolers into an old school bus, we hit the bumpy road and headed for Ocean Isle Beach.

At rest stops along the way, Jacquie continued bleeding. She handled it with her characteristic optimism. Besides, there was nothing we could do about it now.

Finally, we arrived at the beach house, exhausted, sweaty, and ready to run off pent-up energy. It was nonstop volleyball games, swimming, sunbathing, meal preparation, and Bible studies that the kids mostly slept through.

Several days into the trip, I was taking a walk on the beach with a few of the kids, when suddenly I glimpsed Jacquie walking briskly toward us. When we met, she grabbed my elbow, spun me around, and pulled me away from the group without so much as a word. One look at her face and I knew that something was tragically wrong.

She started sobbing uncontrollably.

"What? What is it?" I pleaded.

She couldn't answer for the longest time. Her words kept getting stuck in her throat, lost in the torrent of tears.

Finally, she blurted out, "I lost the baby!"

"When? How?" I sputtered, having no idea what to say.

"Just now while I was going to the bathroom!" she sobbed, leaning her head against my chest.

All at once, the whole world went silent. All I could do was hold her, trying helplessly to ease the pain of a would-be mother who had lost the most precious thing she could imagine.

I was a stranger to such profound grief. Thinking it was my job to be the strong one, I focused on Jacquie's feelings. She was the one who had carried the baby. She was the one who had formed a relationship with it. Of course, she would be the one to feel the grief.

But me? Our baby was a stranger to me. I hadn't had time to become attached to anything other than a wispy dream. From my point of view, we would try again soon enough. There would be other opportunities for us to become parents. Oh, sure, there was a surging emptiness in me, but it was nothing compared to what Jacquie was feeling. "Really, I'm fine," I would tell everyone.

Jacquie too eventually became "fine." She was a labor-and-delivery nurse during those years, and she knew full well that many first pregnancies end up as involuntary abortions. "It's nature's way of preparing the womb," she would soon be reminding me and anyone else who asked. Everyone marveled at our faith.

We gave little more thought to the unnamed child who had been born into the watery grave of a swirling toilet. Though I had never laid eyes on my first baby, I convinced myself it didn't matter.

WAKING UP SLOWLY

It takes a while to open up a man's heart. We're so hell-bent on making our mark in the external world that we can become oblivious to things that seem to come more easily to women. Things like relationships, love, caring, and compassion are often acquired tastes for men. I was no exception.

Indeed, we did try again to have a baby. Once again, we waited to hear God's will spoken. It took longer this time. Many months passed, while we monitored Jacquie's every period. Finally, in 1979, Sean Paul Rademacher made his blond-haired, blue-eyed entry into this world.

To prepare for his birth, Jacquie and I dutifully attended Lamaze classes, detailing everything we could expect about childbirth. I felt thoroughly prepared and was convinced I knew it all.

Nothing could have been further from the truth. No amount of classroom instruction could have prepared me for the carnage of extracting a human being from my wife's womb.

During labor, I played my well-rehearsed role of coach, directing Jacquie's breathing, helping her to focus, rubbing her back with tennis balls wrapped up in an old sweat sock. I was proud of myself. Her cervix was dilating nicely. We were making good progress.

Eventually, the nurse indicated that she was a full ten centimeters. It was time to move Jacquie to the delivery room. I clapped my hands in joy, offering high fives to the nursing staff. We were just about finished up, I figured. Nothing more to do now but squeeze the little bugger out. In a couple more minutes, we'd be Mom and Dad.

Little did I know that it would take two more hours of Jacquie pushing to bring Sean into the world. "Pushing" is a genteel way of saying that she would go through a torment that can only be described as a living hell. It was horrifying to watch the woman I loved enduring such torture. To me, it seemed like endless hours of sweat, tears, panting, and pain.

Then, in a flash, it was over. With one final push, Jacquie let out a bloodcurdling cry that somehow morphed into a song of wonder: "AUUGGGGHHHRROOOLOOK, Paul! It's a boy!"

And with that, the nurse plopped Sean onto Jacquie's stomach. He lay there, blinking and wide-eyed, awed by the world of light that he had just entered, while Jacquie cooed in delight.

They say that childbirth is a pain that a mother forgets. Not so for a man.

After Sean was born, I went out into the waiting room. There was my extended family gathered in anticipation of the great news. As soon as I stepped through the doors, it seemed like a hundred hands were outstretched to congratulate me. Hugs and kisses from everyone.

But I was horrified, white as a sheet. I wanted to shout, "You wouldn't be smiling, if you saw what Jacquie just went through! They turned my wife inside out . . . You wouldn't believe the pain!"

I couldn't stay very long. The cheerful dissonance was too much to bear. It's no wonder they used to keep men out of the delivery room.

Though I went back to work on the construction site the day after Sean's birth, I stumbled around, reliving the anguish of what I had witnessed. I was so shocked by Jacquie's torment that it took me three days before I could decide that having a baby was a good thing.

THE WAITING GAME

It amazed me that Jacquie was willing to go through it all again, but fifteen months later, we welcomed Sean's brother, Jesse, into the world.

It would be hard to imagine two more different people. While Sean was laid back, playful, and happy, Jesse was hopping mad, wanting to be fed *now!* Intensity was his middle name. But within him, there was always a heart of stunning compassion.

And so there they were: Dirt One and Dirt Two. Different as night and day. So different, in fact, that we often wondered if they could have possibly come from the same parents.

The thing about babies is that they like to wake up in the middle of the night. Jacquie and I worked out a schedule where we would trade off nights for going and getting the baby when he cried. The first night I did my turn without much hesitation or fanfare. It was a new experience, and I was thrilled about being a new dad.

But it didn't take long before my enthusiasm began to wane. After long days of hauling concrete, I would come home bone weary. When I heard the baby in the middle of the night, my body refused to move. Then it hit me. Maybe if I pretended to be sleeping, Jacquie would get up for me!

Now, there is a fine art to fake sleeping. You don't want to snore right out loud. That's overkill. By the same token, you don't want to leave any doubt that you're dead to the world. So the best technique I've found is slow, deep, heavy breathing. It takes an actor's deft touch to pull it off.

And pull it off I did. At first, when Jacquie heard the baby and then my slow, deep breathing, she assessed right away that I was too tired to even be awakened by the baby's crying. Knowing how hard I work, she chose not to disturb me. Quietly, she would slip out of bed and into the baby's room.

But soon Jacquie was on to me. After a few weeks, whenever the baby's cries came from the other bedroom, there was slow, deep, heavy breathing coming from the other side of our bed.

Each night became a test of wills to see who was going to outlast the other. Eventually, Jacquie started to shake me to wake me up. When that didn't work, she started to kick me. As a last resort, she would push me out of bed. So much for the romance of child rearing.

It can take a long time to open up a man's heart. Especially when he's sleeping.

A Change of Heart

So it came as a complete surprise to find my experience of our third child was radically different.

Stacy was born two weeks before I started my job as an associate pastor in Muncie, Indiana. It was a time filled with tension and anxiety. So many changes were facing us: a new career as a pastor, a new job, a new place to live, a new house, new neighbors, a new church family, and now a third child.

But something happened when Stacy was born. For some reason, this birth was totally different. The minute I looked at her face, even before I knew if she was a boy or a girl, I blurted out in breathless wonder, "She's beautiful!"

I gathered her up in my arms and walked to the corner of the delivery room and looked up. I don't know who it was, but someone was in that room, invisible, yet unmistakably present. All I could do was to say over and over, "Thank you. Thank you. Thank you."

Stacy was a gift. No, she was more than that. She was a sign to me that, for all the changes we were facing, everything would be all right. As I held her, a comforting peace settled over us.

That's why when Stacy cried in the middle of the night, I didn't try to fake sleep. Jacquie didn't have to shake me, or even kick.

It got to the point where I would look forward to the melody of Stacy's voice. For when I heard her, I would go to her crib and take her out into the family room. There I would sit in the rocker and pat her back, listening to the gentle rhythm of her heartbeat. In the silence of those morning hours, the angels would come to visit, hovering on the fringes of my perception. In those precious moments, I became one with creation.

But, at the same time, I grieved for what I had missed with Sean and Jesse. How blind I had been in my haste to conquer! Little did I realize that the unspeakable glory of creation was waiting to dawn on us.

THE PRIORITY OF EXPERIENCE

The idea of oneness is terribly important. Pastors, priests, and rabbis can speak to us of the moral necessity of looking upon others as if they were our brothers and sisters. They can encourage us to share our wealth. They can touch our hearts with stories of need. But in the end, the idea of oneness is only an abstraction; what really changes us is experience.

Once I left concrete contracting and entered the ministry, I would often lead my churches on mission trips to the Yucatan peninsula of Mexico. In most people's minds, the reason we would go there was to "help the poor Mexicans." They had seen photos of the devastation from hurricanes or the poverty of an economic system near collapse. As Americans, they were used to accepting the fact that we are world economic leaders and that we have some obligation to "help the less fortunate."

I would advertise the trip by talking about a spiritual awakening. But people preferred to hear that they were "helping the poor Mexicans." On my first trip down, that's what I thought too.

It was early in my stay in Muncie. The senior pastor, Ron, organized the trip. I was put, along with three teenaged boys, on a crew that was constructing a roof for one of the new buildings in a clinic. In the Yucatan, wood for construction is rather scarce. There is a severe termite problem, so most buildings are made of cement block and concrete roofs.

Everything about a concrete roof is heavy. Concrete T-beams, weighing three hundred to four hundred pounds each, are wrestled by hand into position to span the walls. Between the beams, countless concrete blocks are lifted, one after another, to fill the gaps. On top of the blocks and beams, three layers of concrete are poured. And any way you lift it, concrete will inevitably extract its pound of flesh.

In the Yucatan, we carried it by hand in plastic five-gallon buckets. A bucket is hoisted onto the head or shoulder and then carried up a rickety ladder made of twisted branches lashed together with hemp. Of all the ways I had ever handled concrete, this was the worst. Sun and the heat multiplied the usual agonies. Caustic concrete got in our shoes, down into our shirts, and in our gloves, so that calcium burns became a full-body experience.

The boss on our crew was Daniel. He spoke no English. We spoke no Spanish. Gradually, we picked up a word here and there, but mostly we communicated by sign language, whistles—to get one another's attention—and visual demonstrations. At break time, we would sit around in the shade sharing Coca-Colas.

At first, there were long silences, but soon we became inventive in finding ways to tell our stories and elicit Daniel's. We showed pictures of our families. We drew pictures in the ground. We made comical gestures. After work, we dragged ourselves down to the public square and played basketball—gringos against Mexicanos.

It's an odd thing for Americans to be in a position where we're the outsiders. When we encounter someone who doesn't speak English, we become uncomfortable, fidgety, and even embarrassed. Sometimes we even assume that foreigners are stupid.

Daniel displayed none of that. His patience and interest gradually put us at ease. We learned, over time, to settle into a slower pace of communion. We even grew comfortable in silence. Our times sitting in the shade together became precious.

Before we knew it, the roof was finished, and it was time to say good-bye. Our trip was to be concluded with a joint worship service and communion.

I still remember walking across the grounds of the clinic that day, strangely upset. The day was bright with sunshine, yet cooler than before. Beautiful flowers were in bloom in shades of yellow and orange under swaying palm trees. Still, an emptiness refused to go away. I had come to the Yucatan looking for something, but I had no idea what. I only knew that something was terribly incomplete.

Music from loudspeakers drifted over the breeze. It was a recording of a choir singing one of my favorite hymns.

It stopped me dead in my tracks. In that moment, the world opened up again. The precious oneness of creation broke over me, with everything around me taking on the aura of holiness.

In the worship service, I spoke of the miracle of the human spirit, amazed at how it can break through barriers of language, economics, and culture. I described the unity we had discovered in our relationship with Daniel and remarked on what a gift he had been to me and the three teenaged boys from our church. The interpreter translated my words into Spanish.

As I looked in the back, I could see Daniel. His round face was covered with tears. I then saw the three teenagers sitting beside him, weeping without shame.

After the worship service, we all came together, and we hoisted Daniel on our shoulders, chanting, "Daniel! Daniel! Daniel!" He was laughing and crying at the same time. So were we.

It may sound a bit sappy to claim that we were the ones who benefited from our time in the Yucatan, but it's true. Only when we experienced for ourselves an unexpected unity with total strangers could we see how much we had to learn about relationships. Only by stepping out of our comfortable lifestyles could we see our own spiritual poverty.

I went on to organize many more such trips. Inevitably, at the end, someone would always say, "Why didn't you tell us this would be such a spiritual experience?"

"I just forgot to," I'd reply.

The Way of the Mystic

Even after my experiences while rocking my infant daughter or working alongside Mexicans in the Yucatan, it took many years before I could begin to realize what these momentary experiences of oneness really meant.

Within the literature of the mystics, this state of union with God is well understood and documented. Underhill quotes Teresa of Avila:

> The soul neither sees, hears, nor understands anything while this [mystical] state lasts; but this is usually a very short time, and seems to the soul even shorter than it really is. God visits the soul in a way that prevents it doubting when it comes to itself that it has been in God and God in it; and so firmly is it convinced of this truth that, though years may pass before this state recurs, the soul can never forget it nor doubt its reality.[84]

Teresa uses virtually the same words to describe the union of soul with God as did Jesus in speaking of his identification with God at the last supper: "I am in the Father and the Father is in me."

Little do we realize that this experience of oneness is near at hand in every moment. But it usually takes slowing down our minds before we can contact it.

Abigail

At ETC, stilling the mind in order to perceive nonphysical impressions was at the very center of all our activities.

During one seminar called Body as a Means of Grace, Jack Biersdorf led us in a meditation focused on the heart. The energy of our hearts was expanded gradually until it encompassed the universe. The point was for us to understand that the energy that flows through us has no limits.

As we were doing the exercise, suddenly I saw the profile of a beautiful young woman. Her hair was dark, long, and flowing, her eyes alive and vibrant. She appeared to be in her early teens, playful and confident.

Slowly, she turned toward me. I was struck by the curve of her neck and the purity of her skin.

"Do you know who I am?" she asked.

"No, should I?"

"I'm your daughter, the one you never met."

At once, I was overcome with emotions I never knew were in me.

"You mean, you're the one we lost in that first pregnancy?"

"Yes, Daddy."

It was so hard to believe. I had given her so little thought through the years, convinced that she was just a blob of tissue flushed down a toilet. Yet, now the child I had never met was standing before me, the same age she would have been had she lived.

The idea that I actually had four children, rather than three, was disorienting. Old, buried emotions swept over me: feelings of joy, mixed with shame and guilt for having ignored her all these years, feelings of grief that I had never acknowledged.

I wanted so much to take her in my arms, but I didn't know how. I longed just to touch her, but I was afraid her image would melt away if I tried. There was so much I wanted to say, yet I had no idea how to begin.

As she looked at me with those penetrating, loving eyes, I became lost in the wonder of our meeting. All my anxiety softened into a peaceful inner quiet.

"It's OK, Dad. I've been watching you. You don't have to explain anything. You may not understand this, but I've been quite involved in your life. I guess you could say that I'm helping with your ability to see the other world. The things you've been encountering are no accident."

"You mean you were there when I fell off the roof?"

She giggled. "Oh, yeah. And I've been a part of most of the things you never tell your congregation. I guess it's sort of our little secret."

Then she did a pirouette and laughed out loud. "There's so much I haven't showed you yet! But I've come to you today so you will know that nothing is ever lost. See? I'm still alive, even when you had no idea! That's pretty cool, don't you think?"

I had to agree. "But wait! What's your name? I never had a chance to give you a name!"

"That's OK. I gave myself one anyway. It's Abigail."

Abigail.

Only years later would I find out that *Abigail* is a Hebrew name that means "my father rejoices."

"Daddy, I just want you to know that I'm always with you and that I will continue to show you things beyond your imagination. I love you, and we have so much to discover together. There's magic everywhere you look."

With that, a great sea turtle came swimming through the air and floated beside Abigail. Abigail's eyes twinkled as she said, "See? All you have to do is climb on and go for a ride."

Then Abigail reached for the edge of the turtle's shell, grasping it just where the head pops out. With a brush of its great flippers, the turtle and Abigail were off, floating silently away from me. My daughter's legs stretched out and above the tortoise shell, and she laughed as I looked on in awe.

When I came out of the meditation, I couldn't speak. All I could do was to find my bed and lie down, utterly exhausted. The thought that my daughter was alive was more than I could take in. The idea that she had been a guide for me to nonphysical worlds was astounding.

Later, I found out that, in the myths of ancient China, a turtle's shell had formed the vault of the heavens.

And in legends of Hawaii, there was a green sea turtle that could turn herself into a little girl. The turtle's name was Kauila, and she watched over the children playing on the beach of the Big Island. She also brought fresh water to the island, nurturing all who lived there.

And so my Abigail clutches the vault of the heavens and brings fresh water of spirit to her rejoicing father.

It can take a long time to open a man's heart. But as I watched my lost daughter floating away in lightness and laughter, I could still feel our connection in love. It was a connection even death could not sever.

CHAPTER FOURTEEN

Three Mysteries

No matter what activity we engage in, the vast majority of our efforts are tied to the body. So much so that we, in Western culture, tend to equate *body* with *life*.

Of all our bodily experiences, the themes of birth, death, and sex seem to capture our imagination the most. It is because we know instinctively that they are portals to transcendence, intimate reminders of the fact that we both enter and exit this physical form.

And if we come and go from this bodily existence, then it's a short jump to consider that there *must* be some nonphysical existence from which we come and to which we return. Birth, death, and sex, then, draw us into the mystery of the unseen world, for they lead us beyond ourselves.

ADDY AND EVE

I am the son of an engineer. Despite my best efforts, from time to time, my father's structured ways of seeing the world ooze to the surface.

When we were kids, my siblings and I wanted a puppy. No matter how many times we pleaded, my dad's reasons always won the day: "What would we do with the dog on vacation? . . . Dogs need to be fed . . . They need to be cleaned up after . . . There will be veterinarian bills . . . It's just too expensive . . . They're a nuisance." We never got our dog.

So when Jacquie mentioned to me one day the idea of our getting a puppy, the sound, rational, studied arguments of my father spewed forth. Common sense would tell any clear-thinking, dispassionate observer that it was not the least bit prudent.

Jacquie listened to all of my thoughtful objections and then proceeded to ignore them entirely. She didn't even give me the benefit of an argument. It was as if I were totally inconsequential to the decision.

Besides, she had that look of Eve in her eye—one I'd seen before. It was the look of the "mother of all life," the queen bee, bent on bringing little beelets into this world, with or without the cooperation of her drone.

I had first seen that look when she decided that we needed to have three children instead of the two boys we already had. Any sane, reasonable person would be content with two children.

At that time, too, I had an abundance of rational arguments against a third addition—arguments ranging from the expenses of braces and college educations to global overpopulation.

None of that mattered. Eve was going to give birth, and nothing would stop her.

Give the queen bee credit—she knew the weaknesses of her drone. She was well aware that I'm allergic to pain.

So she offered a bargain: "Either we have no more children, in which case you get a *v-a-s-e-c-t-o-m-y*"—she stretched the word out in long sinister tones—"or we have one more baby, after which I'll have my tubes tied."

Our bargain's name is Stacy.

But what amazed me was the vehemence of her intent once that bargain was struck. In the past, I had always been the one who wanted to have sex—coaxing and coddling, offering back rubs to gain her favor. But after the bargain, suddenly I was married to an insatiable vixen! Night after night after night of coitus continuous.

At first, like a dullard drone, I thought it was because she found me suddenly irresistible. Gradually, though, I realized that she was on a mission. Eve had a timetable. I was but a small ingredient in her recipe of creation.

It hurt. I felt cheap and used, loved only for my body. A mere plaything.

Slowly, it became clear: my lot in life was always going to put me on the losing end in disagreements over expanding our family—with human or not-quite-human additions. This was Jacquie's domain.

Against my best wishes, she brought home a rabbit one day. Over my dead body, she presented our family with a kitten. And the *coup de grâce*—even though I had strictly forbidden it—she persisted in bringing home library books about dogs. She would leave the books open in strategic places and invite our children to think up names.

The list of possible species gradually narrowed to poodles. And then to toy poodles. It was a conspiracy, and I was a drone outnumbered.

The poodle was named Addy, which was short for *adenocarcinoma*. Jacquie chose the name in a fit of gallows humor after the doctors had discovered cervical cancer on her womb. In a few days, my Eve would have a hysterectomy.

In Hebrew, the name *Eve* is derived from the verb "to live." True to her mission, my Eve has, indeed, taught me how to live.

If left to my own structured ways, my life would have been one of convenience. No more uncontrollable beings would have been part of it than were absolutely necessary.

Expenses would have been low in order to save for early retirement. There would have been an abundance of free time for Jacquie and me to chase after the world's fascinations together, unfettered by demands of home fires burning.

But her womb changed all that. I came to know the orthodontist on a first-name basis. Our tires were perpetually balding from swim practice carpooling. The house always needed a paint job that I could never seem to find the time to do. My life has been one of perpetual disrepair and debt.

But it has also been a life of unexpected joy. Against my better judgment, these beings Jacquie has hatched into my world have made me rich beyond imagination. Amid the constant distractions and inconveniences, life has wriggled its way into my heart.

But, inevitably, there comes a symbolic end to birthing. As such, it signals a time for bidding farewell to the wonder of carrying creation in the belly, stepping aside so that those more youthful might discover Eve's message for themselves.

That is why I was a beaten man from the moment she started talking about getting a dog. I played my dutiful role of the curmudgeon, dragging my feet for heightened dramatic effect.

But there was no real desire to win this argument, even if I could. It *must* end with a tiny fur ball being placed on my chest, a tongue licking my earlobe, and this strange pain in my heart. Eve would have it no other way. It was her swan song.

The first night Addy stayed with us, my sixteen-year-old son came home late, screeching the tires, revving the engine before shutting it down. He slammed the car door shut and ambled into the kitchen, adrenaline and testosterone coursing through his veins.

Throwing the keys on the counter with a flourish, he suddenly discovered the cardboard box that was Addy's temporary den. With tough-as-nails hands, he reached down to cup the trembling fur ball.

Jacquie and I had long since retired for the evening when Jesse burst through our bedroom door. His voice echoed the breathless whisper of wonder reserved for those who gather newborns into their arms for the first time. Another drone-in-the-making stopped dead in his tracks. He gasped, "She's so fragile!"

It's true. Life is fragile, so delicate, so helpless. And so we cling to it in an attempt to grasp its fleeting wonder.

As I considered Jacquie's upcoming surgery, that fragility haunted me. What if something happened to her? What if they discovered contaminated lymph nodes? What if I had to face the future without my Eve?

Such is the nature of this unpredictable, inconvenient life.

A Wicked Landing

In the end, we were fortunate. The surgery was a success and, some twelve years later, there has been no reoccurrence of cancer.

But the lesson has not been lost. We stand at a very mysterious threshold. The themes of birth, death, and sex have a way of bringing us to the edge of awe. Like children drawn to the railing overlooking Niagara Falls or the Grand Canyon, we are captivated by something of immensity, and we feel dwarfed by comparison. These themes invite us to peer beyond the confines of the physical body, and the view is both mesmerizing and terrifying.

Yet we do it all the time without noticing. When we enter domains of the imagination, our attention leaves the body and drifts into realms that have no material existence. The extent of that shift can be, at times, astonishing:

While waiting for my plane to New York City one day, I had picked up a copy of *Wicked*, by Gregory Maguire. It is the story of *The Wizard of Oz*, told from the point of view of the Wicked Witch of the West. It is a brilliant tale that casts the usual heroes as villains and, so, turns all our assumptions about the characters and their motivations upside down.

When it came time for boarding, I clumsily wrestled with my baggage and ticket while staying glued to the book. I barely noticed the flight attendant droning on about flotation devices and oxygen masks and, before I knew it, we were airborne.

After an hour, or a week, or a month (I really had no idea, because time had stopped in this head that was so firmly planted in the Land of Oz), the attendant came on the speaker to point out that the Statute of Liberty could be seen out the left side of the aircraft. *Good, we'll be landing at LaGuardia soon,* I thought.

But after another long stretch of time (a decade perhaps?), I glanced out the window to see, not New York City, but pasture land. A lady across the aisle had her head in her hands as if in distress. *Must be airsick,* I thought. *Poor baby.*

Chapter after chapter, the story of *Wicked* unfolded, to the point where even *I* began wondering why we had not yet landed. Finally, I could feel us beginning our descent. The plane touched down with the pilot leaning on the brakes in an oddly aggressive manner.

When we came to a stop, the entire cabin erupted into cheers. And then . . . I kid you not . . . the flight attendant came on the intercom and said, "Welcome to Oz."

I tapped the person in front of me, asking, "Where *are* we?"

"We're at JFK."

"What in the world are we doing here? We're supposed to land at LaGuardia."

"Didn't you hear? They couldn't get the flaps down and had to go to the longer runway at JFK. We've been flying around for hours trying to burn off jet fuel in case we crashed. Didn't you see all the fire trucks lined up when we came in?"

All that time, I had been in the middle of a life-or-death drama without any awareness whatsoever. Where had I been? Though my body was present, this thing I call "me" was nowhere to be found.

SENSORY DEPRIVATION

What is the nature of this "me" when it is not defined by the physical body? That has been the domain of philosophy from time immemorial.

Mystery schools from Egypt, Greece, and Tibet, to name just a few, researched and taught methods for separating the soul from the body so that these mysterious domains hinted at by birth, death, and sex might be explored firsthand. It was a method of inquiry that seems to have been fairly well accepted throughout the ancient world.

Even the Apostle Paul indicated a familiarity with this type of initiation. In II Corinthians, he recounts a remarkable experience, attributed to an unnamed third person (though most commentators suspect he is really speaking of himself):

> I know a person in Christ who fourteen years ago was caught up to the third heaven—whether in the body or out of the body I do not know; God knows. And I know that such a person—whether in the body or out of the body I do not know; God knows—was caught up into paradise and heard things that are not to be told, that no mortal is permitted to repeat.[85]

Contemporary readers gloss over this passage. Yet it is startling that Paul so casually speaks of being "in the body or out of the body." There is no attempt to explain what he means by the phrase, as if this were common knowledge to the recipients of his letter.

Because this concept is utterly foreign to most twenty-first century Christians, few people are ever motivated to try and understand what Paul is speaking about.

But if it *is* possible to move beyond the confines of the physical body, are there methods that can work today? Are we limited only to the faint mysteries of birth, death, and sex to inform us? Or is there more?

There is a memory I have from the 1960s. It was a TV documentary that showed a very unusual scene:

> A woman lies in a white box. Her arms and legs are covered with gauze. On her head is something that looks like a football helmet with a translucent shield over her eyes. Her ears are plugged to deaden all ambient noise. The air has been filtered to eliminate any lingering odors. She lies motionless for hours at a time, and all she can see is a world of white haze.

As I remember it, this vignette was from a university experiment in psychology. At that time, people were beginning to investigate very odd things. The woman was lying in what was called a sensory deprivation chamber. The purpose of the study was to investigate what happens to people when the normal stimuli of life have been dramatically reduced.

When I saw that, a feeling of revulsion swept over me. Being trapped in a noiseless, gauze-covered, white-fog environment seemed like a prison. I was sure I would have died from boredom, or at least have been driven mad by the urge to itch. The closest thing I could compare it to would be confinement in a full body cast.

What they discovered in this strange experiment was this: when deprived of sensory input, human beings begin to hallucinate.

Back then, hallucinating wasn't considered to be a good thing. That was what people did when they were on drugs.

And how did they know that the test subjects were hallucinating? Because they were seeing and hearing things that sane, rational people didn't see or hear. Therefore, what they were reporting couldn't possibly be real.

While viewing that scene as a child, it never occurred to me that such isolation could lead to anything but misery. Beyond that, it was just flat-out bizarre.

But in fact, we go through a similar process of sensory deprivation every night: sleep.

ZOMBIES

When my boys were teenagers, every morning was like waking the dead. There was no point in talking to the zombies as they slithered out of bed and stumbled about while getting ready for school. They would look at us as if we were from another planet.

Indeed, we were! Only moments before, these semiconscious bipeds had been cavorting in realms that were absolutely enthralling. Without warning, they had been jerked out of their "dream" world and dumped into this one by an alarm clock with the tone of a circular saw cutting up an aluminum ladder. And a "good morning" to you too!

The point is that every night our awareness goes through a natural process of separating from the physical body. We then go on extraordinary journeys, and our only memory is something we call a dream.

The difference between this separation of our awareness and the ancient mystery schools is that, in sleep, we cease to be conscious, at least of the physical world. It's as if one movie ends and another movie begins. There is no continuity between them, and no memory of having viewed the first movie while watching the second one.

But in ancient rituals of initiation, the intent was to move into nonphysical environments while still retaining normal waking consciousness. When understood from this perspective, mystery schools can be viewed as merely enhancing an already quite natural human ability. It's simply a process of extending the range of normal human awareness. The trick is to remember the continuity of this physical life, while simultaneously hitching a ride into the ether.

Is such a thing possible?

During my years as a pastor, I kept wondering why only extreme experiences brought the experience of heaven close to daily life. Did we have to come perilously near to physical death before the heavens would reveal their secrets? My own first glimpse had come after I fell off the roof. Since then, those secret realms had been revealed in experiences that came about through being close to someone's death, like Freddie's, or through experiences of childbirth, or through meditations that were spectacular in their healing effects, like meeting Abigail.

Yet how could I sustain these visions on a daily basis? I read book upon book, practiced meditation, took workshops, kept a journal of my dreams, and bought audiotapes and videos.

I wanted so much, yet I couldn't decide on any one thing. By nature, I was far too undisciplined to engage any particular practice for an extended period. No sooner would I seize upon one approach than my attention would dart to another, more tantalizing possibility.

Making my efforts even more sporadic were the pressures of day-to-day life. Aside from the necessity of making a living, having children was also a built-in assurance that any attempts to meditate would be shattered by sibling fights, questions about homework, or someone knocking on the bedroom door because "it was quiet in there."

If I tried to meditate at night, I fell asleep. If I tried to meditate after lunch, I fell asleep. If I even thought about meditating, I fell asleep.

If I did manage to get into a meditation, the phone would ring, the dog next door would bark, or the furnace would blow up. Caroline Myss's assertion that we are entering a time when we are called to be "mystics without monasteries" seemed like a nice idea, but, in practice, it failed miserably.

During the child-rearing years, Jacquie and I considered it a victory if we were able to hang on to a modicum of sanity. Moving into ethereal realms was out of the question.

The most brilliant thing we did as parents was to buy a dehumidifier. It wasn't that the air in our house was humid. In fact, it generally was quite dry.

We ran the dehumidifier in our bedroom because the droning compressor would drown out the noise from our children.

It was a lifesaver. Our nasal passages were blocked and bleeding from the dryness, but it was a small price to pay for an island in the storm.

But even the dehumidifier couldn't preserve my meditation time. Time itself was in short supply, as every waking moment was spoken for. Sporting events, school plays, carpooling, and awards banquets kept us on the run constantly. My work was loaded with committee meetings, appointments, and gatherings. All I could catch during those years were fleeting glimpses of the world beyond. It was frustrating and disheartening. The thing I wanted most in life was slipping through my fingers.

ANOTHER BOOK

In 1987, Jacquie and I had borrowed a camper and made a tour of New England, Cape Cod, and Canada. In Toronto at that time, there was something called The World's Biggest Bookstore. Nowadays, it would be considered average in size, but back then, it was like a gold mine. Everywhere there were stacks upon stacks as far as the eye could see.

We had been inside for just a few minutes when one book practically grabbed me by the scruff of my neck. I picked it up, and my hands started shaking. I couldn't put it down.

It was titled *Far Journeys*.[86] It was the story of Robert Monroe, who, when he was in his forties, began having spontaneous out-of-body experiences, or, as they later became known, OBEs.

I had never heard of such a thing, but after reading what he wrote, it made perfect sense. Here was one writer who could connect with my personal experience.

After reading that book, if I could have gone to The Monroe Institute at that very moment, I would have done it. It would, however, be ten years before I would get the chance.

PART III

The Kingdom Rediscovered

*I tell you, many will come from east and west and will eat with
Abraham, Isaac and Jacob in the kingdom of heaven.*
—Matthew 8:11

CHAPTER FIFTEEN

Lifting the Veil

The year was 1997. By that time, I had been a pastor for twelve years. They were twelve long years of trying desperately to keep my spiritual quest alive.

The only thing harder than finding time to meditate was keeping my spiritual quest a secret from the churches I served as pastor. At best, my search would be misinterpreted. At worst, it would be labeled demonic. People would think I was crazy. Because my experiences were as precious to me as life itself—because they *were* life, a taste of heaven in an often-dreary world—I simply couldn't risk having them treated roughly by people who didn't understand.

Yet the distance between the heaven I'd glimpsed and the life I was living every day continually weighed on me. I longed to collapse that distance, to find the exquisite joy of meeting Abigail or the beauty of the world beyond pain on a regular basis, in daily life. Yet I didn't know how. More important, I couldn't talk to anyone except Jacquie and a few close friends about what I was seeking. I was the pastor, after all. I was the one others looked to for help in their own quests.

A Lifesaving Gift

Then one day, out of the blue, someone offered to pay my way to The Monroe Institute. It was a dream come true. The Monroe Institute would provide me the gift of being surrounded by kindred spirits for the first time in years. What a relief it would be to speak openly about my quest!

I signed up that same day and then waited, like a kid on Christmas Eve, trying to pass the time.

I left for Virginia a day early and booked a room in an inn nearby. The next morning, my whole body was trembling in anticipation.

It was fall and the leaves were radiating a panorama of color. Turning into the driveway that was marked The Monroe Institute, I felt as if I were entering hallowed ground. Coming through the front door, I was flanked on the right by a portrait of Bob Monroe and, on the left, by a painting of his wife, Nancy Penn. I felt welcomed into a family that was both mysterious and thrilling.

Everything was silent. The morning sun was peeking through a skylight. In my enthusiasm, I had arrived so early that I woke the leaders out of bed. Bleary-eyed and blinking in the light, they told me in a perfunctory manner where I could find my room. Then they went back to sleep.

The program wouldn't start for another twelve hours. It didn't matter. At some core level, I was home.

My room was anything but ordinary. There were no beds in sight. In an otherwise rectangular space, two cubicles, large enough to lie down in, were tucked into the corners. Their exteriors were covered in pine tongue-and-groove paneling. There was a square hole in one of the walls, just large enough to crawl through. Pulled to one side was a curtain so heavy it felt as if it were lined with lead.

Peering inside the opening, I could see a neatly made bed, a set of stereo headphones, and a control panel full of buttons and knobs just begging to be fiddled with. I pushed one knob and blue light flooded the chamber. Another one gave red light. Another gold. There were speaker volume controls, toggle lights, and a few other controls. I had no idea what they did.

This setup was what Bob Monroe called a CHEC unit, short for Controlled Holistic Environmental Chamber. I crawled inside and lay down, pulling the curtain closed, so I was in total darkness. I played with the lighting and finally opted for the blue color. I tried on the headphones and adjusted my pillows. The silence was delicious.

This CHEC unit would be the place where I slept and listened to the tape exercises that comprised the bulk of the course. Lying there, I could hardly stay still, as a thrill of energy rippled through my body. It seemed like forever before the first activity would begin. But I had waited ten years for that moment. I told myself I could wait a few more hours.

I wondered if the trainers would be able to read my aura. Or if they could peer into my past history. Secretly, I hoped this experience would show me that maybe I wasn't crazy after all. Maybe there really were unique ranges of perception hovering just out of my view.

Table Communion

Dinner came. We gathered and had introductions. The air was buzzing with anticipation. I met kindred spirits, people from around the world who, like me, had felt a strange hunger for years. At dinner that night I experienced true communion, the unity of our shared desire for mystical experience. In this place, there was a refreshing freedom to express all of my deeply held longings. In that group, the spiritual domain seemed less distant, perhaps even within grasp. How much within my grasp I could have never guessed.

Logistics were followed by a short lecture. When they finally asked us if we were ready for our first tape, there was a gasp of relief and exhilaration as we all shouted in unison, "*Yes!*"

Little did I know that the kingdom of heaven was about to explode into my awareness.

Mind Awake, Body Asleep

The Monroe Institute seemed like the modern version of the ancient mystery school. In my room, I was able to crawl inside my very own personal crypt, specially designed to quiet external annoyances. It was all so strange and yet so luxurious. Sensory deprivation can be a true joy in a world that is relentless with noise.

The process at the Institute consisted of climbing onto our bed, placing the headphones around our ears, and listening to a recorded meditation. The sounds on the tapes would lead us to certain meditative states.

Our initial destination was a state that Monroe called *Focus 10*. The numbers associated with the focus levels were somewhat arbitrary; they didn't indicate higher or lower states, but were simply different destination points.

Focus 10 was described as "mind awake, body asleep." Years before, I had ordered some Monroe audiotapes to try at home. A friend I'd once shared a Focus 10 tape with had reported, "You know, Paul, it was the strangest thing. I was listening to the tape and I was really disappointed, because nothing was happening. I was about to rip off the headphones, when suddenly I heard someone snoring. It was loud and annoying. I couldn't figure out how that person had gotten into my bedroom. Finally, I realized that the snoring was on the tape. I had gotten a bad copy. Some technician had fallen asleep while making mine and hit the record button! I was pissed! But I listened a bit longer and was shocked to find out that the snoring was coming from me!" Such are the strange experiences of the mind awake, body asleep state.

Another friend was quite amazed at how relaxed she could get in Focus 10. She told me that as much as she enjoyed the tape, what she really wanted was a tape for "mind asleep, body awake . . . and cleaning."

Although I had become somewhat familiar with Focus 10, now the experience was different, more vivid. Once my body quieted down, a parade of clear images started across my field of vision. It was exciting, but also frustrating.

These images seemed to be shy. I could see them on the periphery, but the moment I turned my attention toward them, they vanished. I felt I was chasing butterflies.

To make matters worse, the parade flitted by so quickly that I barely had time to register the individual vignettes. As if I were awakening from a dream, the images would simply melt away by the end of the tape, or they would quickly be displaced by the next vision.

Soon, however, the images began to slow down. Gradually, they took on a lifelike quality that was distinctly different from daydreaming. As I think about it now, they seemed to have the power to draw me into the action, so that I could interact with what was happening. I could do this while still remembering that my body was quietly resting in CHEC unit #1 in the Nancy Penn Center.

MEMORY AND THE BODY

Early in the week, I had signed up for a massage. Because our bodies hold memories, working with a therapist can release issues that have been blocked for a long time.

The therapist asked what I wanted to focus on and laid out options for different kinds of massage. Because at the time I believed in "no pain, no gain," I asked, "Which one hurts the most?"

She replied, "Postural integration."

In truth, it was only a little uncomfortable, at least physically. The real surprise was when I began to cry, for no apparent reason, while she worked deeply into the hip I had fractured in the fall from the roof. I suddenly began feeling sad about my father.

The truth was, I had never really processed the shock of my dad's death. He had suffered from Alzheimer's disease for twelve years.

Six months before he died, when I was still in Muncie, I visited my parents in Arizona to see how things were going. It was clear that caring for Dad was becoming more than Mom could handle. He was agitated all the time, wanting to know what he should be doing. The only peace came when he would finally go to sleep. But even then, he could wake up in the middle of the night, shouting out our names, calling for help. The nights became a maddening procession of catnaps and sleeplessness. *How has Mom been able to do this alone for eleven and a half years?* I wondered to myself.

Finally, we decided he had to go into a nursing home. Taking Dad there was the blackest day of my life. Feelings of betrayal swirled like a tornado through my mind. Watching him thrash and struggle in his new and confusing environment was like watching a caught fish flopping around in the bottom of a boat.

I tried desperately to think of another way. Maybe I could bring him home with me. Maybe I could add on another room. Maybe . . . Maybe . . . Maybe . . . Finally, the orderly looked at me and said kindly, "It's OK. Let it go. You've done everything you can."

Six months later, I would be standing at my father's bedside watching him breathe his last breath. Once we moved him there, his deterioration was shocking. It was hard to escape the notion that our decision to place him there had ultimately killed him.

A PARTING REQUEST

On the night of his death, I stood over his bed, watching his breaths grow ever more shallow and far apart. As my eyes drifted to his uncovered legs, I was surprised to see they weren't the legs of an old man at all. They were muscled and firm. What's more, they looked a lot like mine. His hands too were my hands; his arms, so similar to mine that I did a double take.

Suddenly the space between us collapsed. With a shudder, I wondered for a split second which one of us was in the bed. What is the dividing line between parent and child?

The ancient Hebrews didn't believe in life after death in the way we've come to see it. If a person were to survive physical death, it would be through his or her offspring. The ancestor was literally brought to life each time a descendant spoke the ancestor's name. Musing over the connection between my father and me, I couldn't help but wonder if the Hebrews didn't have a deeper understanding of death than we do.

Having read the literature on near-death, I was convinced that Dad would be going into a world of great wonder. I leaned in close and began to tell him what he might see. Finally, I whispered, "When you get there, will you promise to come back and let me know what it's like?"

He opened his eyes for just a moment, glanced in my direction, and nodded in the affirmative. He then drifted into unconsciousness. Those were the last words I spoke to my father.

After he died, I'd gone through the usual stages of grief—surprised at odd moments when the line of a song or a snippet of memory would dig an aching hole in my belly. Occasionally, I would let loose in a torrent of tears. Eventually, time had covered over the sharpness of the pain, and my grief lay in the past.

Now, as my massage session continued, I was caught up once again in feelings that had been long buried. "Ah! So it's still there! And it still hurts!"

Apparently, I was getting my money's worth from the massage session. I had been presented with sufficient pain.

A MASSAGE AND A DEAD MAN

Back in my CHEC unit for the next tape and once again in Focus 10, images flowed past me, many of them having to do with eating. In the Old Testament, eating was often associated with the idea of knowing. To ingest food is very much like incorporating experience. It's only when we take something in experientially that we truly understand it. It then becomes a part of our being.

Suddenly the scene of my previous massage came into view. Only this time, I was watching it from an upper corner in the room. I could see my body and the therapist working on me. But to my amazement, there were other hands working on me at the same time. In fact, there was a whole circle of figures gathered around me.

Who *they* were, I couldn't really tell. There was only one person I could make out clearly, and even then, I could only see his torso and arms, not his face. His chest was hairy and strangely familiar. It was the same chest that had swung me back and forth through the waters of Lake Erie as a child, laughing, almost dancing on the water's surface. Then—on the count of three—that same chest would launch me or my friends high into the air, as if we were astronauts blasting off, our arms and legs flailing as we screamed in delight just before splashing down.

It was the same chest that I remember, as if it were yesterday, hanging on to the edge of our ski boat, after diving for a swim in the cool waters. The sunlight would glisten off his balding, sunburned head as he swam out to teach yet another of his children to get up on one ski.

When I saw that chest, I knew that my father had kept his promise to come back. There were no words; there was no acknowledgment of recognition. He was just there working.

To say that my father's presence was disconcerting is an understatement. Now that I was embarking on one of the most wondrous adventures of my life, I wasn't at all sure I wanted to invite him along for the ride. This was my time, not his.

THE VISE OF ALZHEIMER'S DISEASE

I felt lingering hurts and resentments from earlier years with my father. There was the time when Jacquie and I were preparing to leave for seminary and were trying desperately to finish the house we had begun building. Even at that time, early in his journey with Alzheimer's disease, Dad was having a great deal of trouble staying on track. He wanted to help with the house, so I'd give him simple things to do—things that he couldn't screw up too badly.

At one point, I wanted to cut a hole in an overhang for a light. Dad wanted to cut the hole, so I went over it with him several times, to be sure that he understood where to cut it. Then I walked away for a moment, and when I returned, he was cutting random holes all over the brand new plywood. Whole sheets were ruined.

I was furious. I wanted to scream and curse him. Just as he would've done when I was a child, I wanted to shout, "I STOOD HERE—NOT FIVE MINUTES AGO—AND TOLD YOU NOT TO DO THE VERY THING YOU'RE DOING! WHAT ARE YOU THINKING? WHAT'S WRONG WITH YOU?"

It all bubbled up—all the times he had screamed at me for making a mistake. All the times he had spanked me for "my own good" as a child. Seething with a white-hot rage, I prepared to say things I would regret for the rest of my life.

But there was another emotion—just as strong as my anger—that kept me from saying them. There, standing before me, was not the able man I once knew, but some shadow figure, staring back at me, haunted and confused. If I lost it in a rage, whom would I be angry with? Alzheimer's disease had stripped him of so much that there was nothing left. I knew, deep down, it wasn't his fault.

And so I bit down hard. With every muscle tensed to the breaking point, I turned and walked away.

And yet at other times, he was able to express a tenderness that was unbelievably compassionate. Like the evening I announced to my parents that I was taking my family and going to seminary.

We had been living together with them on a farm we mutually owned. It had been my mother's dream that she would spend her later years surrounded by children and grandchildren. Our going to seminary meant that we'd be leaving the farm and moving away. The shattering of her dream was more than she could bear. She left the room, sobbing.

My father and I sat at the kitchen table in silence. We could hear Mom's muffled cries coming from the bedroom. Slowly, he reached over to my hand and cupped it in his.

Gently he said, "She'll be OK. Give her time. It's an honorable thing you're doing." It was the closest I had ever come to receiving a blessing.

When I finally graduated from seminary, I was ordained in my new church in Muncie. My parents came from Pennsylvania for the occasion. When the service was over, he came up to me. There were no words between us. He just looked into my eyes, took me into a hug, and sobbed on my shoulder. We stood there for the longest time, holding one another. In that moment, I knew that the man I had wanted to please all my life was finally intensely proud of me. No one could have given me a greater gift.

When I realized, after the vision during my massage, that Dad was still involved in my life in some unseen way, even after he had died, all of my conflicting emotions surged to the surface. Suddenly, I was thrown back into a turmoil that I had earnestly wanted to leave behind. I had come to The Monroe Institute to explore heavenly realms—not be locked into the hopeless morass of emotions connected to my father.

WELCOMING ON THE OTHER SIDE

It wasn't long, however, before there was a new twist. Soon we were introduced to Focus 12. This is the state of expanded awareness in which you can perceive beyond the limits of the five senses. As so often happens when you move into different states of awareness, the images can be very fleeting.

It's like running along a roadside. There's a hidden world of insects, vegetation, and animals right at your feet, yet you can see it only if you stop and intentionally look.

One day I was, more or less, jogging along in Focus 12 when suddenly I saw beings of light. They barely made an impression on me at first. But something inside me called out, "*Wait!* Weren't those beings of light? That's not something you see every day. Let's stop and have a look." They were working with someone who had just died and was beginning the journey into the afterlife. Having read Robert Monroe's books, I was familiar with the concept of rescue-and-retrieval work.

In some of his forays out of his body, Monroe occasionally would encounter people who had recently, or even long ago, expired. Some of these "newgoners" weren't aware they had passed away and, so, were locked into make-believe worlds that mimicked the physical world in which they had lived. Sometimes it was very difficult to convince them of their own demise. If it could be accomplished, then Robert would lead them toward new afterlife destinations. Over time, he came to understand that he had been doing this kind of work for a long time in his sleep, though he hadn't been conscious of it.

Having read about this far-fetched idea in advance, I wasn't startled to see beings of light engaged in the same kind of work. They motioned for me to come over. When their circle parted, I saw a man who was obviously stressed so much by the journey that he was barely conscious. His body sagged under its own weight like a wet dishrag. There didn't seem to be an ounce of energy left in him, and he could barely hold up his head. He was far too weak even to speak. His skin was ashen.

Then I looked at his face. I could barely believe my eyes. It was my father, who had died six years before.

TIME WARP

I knew instinctively what I had to do. I scooped his frail body up into my arms and began walking with him. Speaking words of assurance, I explained to him that he had just come over from dying and that he was entering into a wonderful new environment. There were many here to help him in his transition, and they would bring him to a place of healing and refreshment.

As I spoke, he nodded weakly, still unable to say anything. After a while, the beings of light came back to me. They said, "We can take him now. His relatives are coming to meet him. They will take him to the next place. You have done a great service."

It didn't seem like such a great service to me. It had just seemed natural, even though I wasn't aware of ever having done anything remotely like it before.

Then it hit me. Years before, I had been at my father's bedside, coaching him into the next world. In the intervening years, I had wondered, with regret, if I weren't somehow to blame for his death by putting him in the nursing home. Now, as if to heal impossible wounds, I found myself on the far side of death, welcoming him into the very place I had told him about on his dying day.

THE COMMUNION OF SAINTS

The images of eating that kept recurring as I listened to the first few tapes began to take on a new depth of meaning. Eating is about the knowledge that comes from personal experience. But even more, it's about an intimate communion that happens when we're sitting at a table with those we love.

Jesus often spoke of the kingdom of heaven as a great banquet that would gather together those spread all over the world. Could it be that this gathering reaches even beyond the bounds of death? Is the veil separating us from the deceased so ethereal that it has no power other than what we give to it?

In the Presbyterian tradition, we have a wonderful celebration that bears witness to this idea. It's called All Saints' Day. During this service, we call out the names of loved ones who have recently died. It's a ceremony of remembrance. It's a way of bringing them back to life for a time.

We also share communion. But on this day, the emphasis is on the gathering of the "church above with the church below." It's recognition that those who have passed on to another life are still very much with us, and we're nourished in countless ways by their presence.

When I was working with Ron Naylor in the Muncie church, we would sit behind the communion table together. During the All Saints' service, he would often lean over to me and whisper, "I can feel Jennifer here." He would then name other people who had recently died whose presence he sensed.

During those first days at The Monroe Institute, as I held my newly deceased father in my arms, six years after his death, and helped to birth him into a new world, for the first time, I began to sense how vast is this table, this banquet, of the kingdom of heaven.

If the workshop had ended there, I would have been satisfied. Little did I know that things would get "curiouser and curiouser" still.

CHAPTER SIXTEEN

Piercing Time

Both Focus 10 and Focus 12 had been somewhat familiar to me, but Focus 15 was entirely new territory.

Instead of the dizzying procession of images and the sense of activity found in the other states, Focus 15 was profoundly still. It wasn't an empty stillness, but rather one that seemed charged with all possibility, as if this were the realm out of which all was manifested. Monroe had called this the State of No Time.

An Alien Object

On one of my first runs to Focus 15, I saw something that looked like a great horn. The best way I can describe it is to say that it was a cross between an Easter lily and the speaker horn from an old Victrola.

The main difference was that it was huge. I found myself floating beside it. Its rim stretched up and away from me, as if I were standing at the foot of one of the legs of the St. Louis Arch.

But it didn't have a solid quality. Instead, its skin was thin, like that of a flower petal, and it glowed with subtle, iridescent, pastel hues of blue, indigo, orange, and yellow.

This strange object was a study in paradox. It seemed to be alive, and yet strangely inert. There was a sense that it was very old, and yet constantly renewed. It was similar in shape to a vortex, and yet there was nothing swirling. It emitted a quiet hum, as if it vibrated with the wisdom of the ages, and, yet, when I listened closely, there was no sound.

Whatever it was, it was eerily beautiful. I wanted to stay in its presence for a very long time. While I was there, everything seemed complete. There was no need to hurry off in search of anything else.

Into the Quantum World

When I was growing up, we were taught that the universe is made up of building blocks. The smallest blocks known, at that time, were electrons, protons, and neutrons. We were told that, although smaller objects might some day be discovered, they would be fundamentally like these small particles—solid, with mass and weight that could be measured.

We had no way of knowing that deep in the recesses of particle accelerators, a whole new way of imagining creation was unfolding. Perplexed by the inability to measure both position and velocity of electrons at the same time, physicists had already begun to theorize that the building blocks of our world were anything but stable. In fact, what we had assumed to be solid and tangible was, in reality, nothing more than a cloud of infinite possibilities.

What's more, this cloud could not be perceived in any objective way. On the contrary—the very thing that collapsed the cloud of all possibilities into one singular position that could be measured, either for its speed or its position, but never both—was the act of observation itself.

At the core of the universe, subject and observer were locked in a dance of perpetual creativity. It would seem that the child's cry, "Mom! Look at me! Watch me!" is built into the world itself. To watch is to bring it into being.

This gives a new meaning to the concept of being created in the image of God. The fundamental nature of God is to create. The very first mention of the deity is inextricably linked to the fashioning of the world: "In the beginning, God created the heavens and the earth."[87] God is known in the making of all that is.

VERBALIZING GOD

Rabbi David Cooper captures this idea in the title of his wonderful book *God Is a Verb*.[88] For most of us, the idea of God is static, a series of nouns and adjectives: Creator, Holy Spirit, Lord, and so on. Cooper says instead that God is a verb, continually creating, always dynamic. Creating is fundamental to the divine nature. Only when our nouns disappear can the dynamic, creating quality of the divine be perceived.

To illustrate, Cooper draws on traditional tales of the rabbis, like the story of "The Snuff Box." A beggar in town approaches Rabbi Baal Shem Tav. The beggar is railing at the injustice of his having once been a wealthy man and now finding himself in rags.

The rabbi, who is able to see into the past and the future, leads the beggar to remember a time when he refused to offer snuff to a man who had been fasting for three days. (The snuff used in those days was an aromatic mix that served to revive anyone undertaking an extended fast.)

When the beggar remembers the event, the rabbi explains that just at the time of the refusal, the heavens were opening up to the fasting man. Because he, a rich man, had failed to offer this small comfort at such a pivotal moment, the angels had closed the book on him and decided that the man fasting should get all his wealth.

However, the rabbi tells him, all is not lost. If the beggar can catch the wealthy man in a position where he, in turn, will refuse to offer snuff, then his wealth will be restored.

Time and again, the beggar tries and fails. Every time he approaches the rich man, without fail, the rich man stops what he is doing and offers him snuff, even at the most inconvenient times.

Finally, the beggar gives up his quest and tells his rich opponent the story of how he had lost his wealth. The man is so moved by what he hears that he offers to share half of all he has. In the years that follow, the town's two wealthiest men become renowned for their extraordinary generosity.

The old rabbis knew that we are intimately linked with creation. The smallest act carries enormous consequences. Though we may not realize it, we're continually creating the world by what we think and do and perceive. There is no world "out there," separate from us. There is no subject and object. No rich and poor. All is one.

THE I AM

Moses shared this kind of intimacy with God. The two of them would speak face-to-face in the Tent of Meeting far from the camp. When Moses entered that tent, everyone could see the cloud of the divine presence descending upon it.

It was while standing in front of the burning bush that Moses had been first introduced to God. In that initial meeting, Moses had had the audacity to ask the name of the one who was addressing him.

What he received has been an enigma ever since. For it wasn't a name like Bill, Johnny, or Sue; it was instead a pronouncement—simple, and yet maddeningly difficult to comprehend. Depending on how it is translated, the name is "I am who I am," or "I will be who I will be," or "I cause to be what I cause to be," or simply, "I am."

The implications of this name weren't lost on Jesus. In one of his many confrontations with the Jewish leaders of his day, he was accused of being a Samaritan (who were considered to be imposters in their claim to be the real inheritors of the divine mantle).

He gave them an answer that was meant to provoke a response: "I tell you, whoever keeps my word will never see death."[89]

This was utterly absurd, as far as his listeners were concerned. Then, as now, death and taxes were the two basic realities you could always count on. They responded, "Abraham died, and so did the prophets; yet you say, 'Whoever keeps my word will never taste death.' Are you greater than our father Abraham who died?" they scoffed. "Who do you claim to be?[90]

"You are not yet fifty years old and have you seen Abraham?"[91]

"Very truly, I tell you, before Abraham was, I am."[92] So they picked up stones to throw at him.

These words of Jesus struck at the very heart of their dearly held assumptions about the nature of God. It assaulted two major cornerstones of Jewish speculation.

The first, as I have mentioned previously, was the idea that, as a person inhabiting this present space and time, Jesus was also alive before the birth of Abraham. What's more, that relationship with Abraham was something apparently ongoing, even in the present. He didn't say, "Before Abraham was, I was," but rather, "Before Abraham was, I *am.*"

Perhaps even more offensive to his audience was the fact that Jesus managed to invoke the divine name for himself. It was the name that had been revealed to Moses—the unpronounceable, most sacred I AM. Everyone listening was very much aware that Jesus was claiming to be God. That was indisputably a sin punishable by death.

If ordinary people claimed the same thing today, most Christians would write them off as being crazy. To most Christians, there is only one man who can claim divinity, and that is Jesus. There is only one who can transcend the limits of space and time and still be present even after death, and that, again, is Jesus.

But the supremely radical notion of the Gospel of John is that, for Jesus, there was no separation between himself and his followers. In his final prayer, he asks the unthinkable:

> As you, Father, are in me, and I am in you, may they also
> be in us. The glory that you have given me I have given them,
> so that they may be one even as we are one, I in them and you
> in me, so that they may become completely one.[93]

In this prayer, Jesus did not stop with claiming divinity for himself. He also proposed that ordinary, beer-belching, nose-picking slackers and buttheads, like you and me, are one with God. No separation.

The Now

The power of the divine name I AM—especially when we dare to make it our own—is that it brings us smack-dab into the now. In the present, all plans for the future drop away, all regrets about the past fall into oblivion.

In the present, all is one. It's the entry point to what Jesus called the kingdom of heaven. Only when we're fully present does the world come out to greet us in all its glory. Only in the present can we be aware of the manna of opportunity surrounding us at every moment. Only in the present can we enter into the abundant life Jesus tried to show us.

For me, the defining attribute of Focus 15 was the overwhelming sense of the present moment. As I floated beside that huge, alien, Easter lily/Victrola horn, it immersed me in the essence of being. It was the state of "no time," as Monroe called it. But that state was so different from anything I expected. Contained in the present was the potential of all creation.

No Time, No Tape

In the discussion following our first time to Focus 15, I asked a question. "We've been listening to a lot of tapes up to this point. I'm wondering if we'll become dependent on them to achieve these states of consciousness?"

The trainers looked at one another smiling, as if knowing something we didn't. Then one of them explained, "Well, as a matter of fact, the next experience is a non-tape."

They told us we would go into our CHEC units as usual, put on the headphones, and music would be played. Gradually, the music would fade out and there would be nothing but silence. We were to go to Focus 15 on our own, and when the time was up, we would know that we were to return when the music would be gradually faded back in.

It sounded simple enough, but I knew that it would never work. After all, it was the signals on the tapes that had made everything happen, right? Maybe you could get to these states on your own after years of training, but we'd only been there a few days at that point. That would hardly qualify us to be yogis in our own right. No pain, no gain. And we hadn't had nearly enough pain to justify real progress.

But, by nature, I'm fairly open-minded, so I returned to my CHEC unit to see what would happen. They had advised us that it would be a good idea to have some purpose for our journey. Intention is a key ingredient for focusing energy in a profitable manner. Of course, I wanted it to be profitable, so I quickly decided to explore a conversation that I'd had with one of the participants over lunch.

MULTIPLE PERSONALITIES, MULTIPLE LIVES

He was telling me about going to a seminar where they did explorations of past lives. I wasn't at all sure that I believed in past lives. My Christian training was adamantly opposed to the idea.

If we do, in fact, have multiple lives, then the whole idea of burning in hell for eternity goes out the window. Only if you believe that we have but one life to get things right does hell have any teeth to it. The fear of never-ending punishment is not nearly so compelling if you get a do-over.

With reincarnation, everything starts to unravel: no hell, no way to keep the adherents on track. No eternal damnation, no way to sell the idea of evangelism. No fire and brimstone, and people just might get up and walk out of church on a Sunday morning. I wasn't at all sure how I felt about it.

But one of my character flaws is the need to see for myself. So I decided to explore one of my past lives, if there was such a thing.

My lunch mate had advised that a good way to get oriented to the time and place of a past-life experience was to look down at your feet. If nothing else, the type of shoes you're wearing in a vision can give you an important clue to the era and culture you're in. So, with this in mind, I decided to go on a quest for footwear, just to see where I'd end up. It was like shoe shopping, without the mall.

The music drifted seductively over the headphones. Playfully, I pretended to be an astronaut entering his space capsule as I closed the heavy curtain and adjusted my pillows.

All systems go, I thought to myself. *Roger that, Houston. Ready for liftoff. Let's just see how high this bird can fly. Let's light this candle!*

Before I knew it, the music started to fade.

I went through my checklist. Focus 10. Yep. Mind is awake; body, pretty much asleep. Focus 12. Rising higher and higher now. There's the roof of the Nancy Penn Center. All of Virginia is coming into view. There's the curve of the horizon. The arc closing into circle, the blue-green of planet Earth. I guess we're at Focus 12, the state of expanded awareness. Cool.

Coming into Focus 15 now. Firing retrorockets. Not too fast now . . . I see some trees . . . There's a body of water with some sort of viaduct leading to it . . . Roman arches of stone appeared. I looked down, expecting to find the laced boots of a Roman soldier. But instead, what I saw was a pair of canvas deck shoes on my feet. *What a rip-off!* I thought to myself. *I come here looking for a past life, and what do I get? Something out of a JC Penney catalogue! I want a do-over!*

Suddenly, I realized that I was staring at my shoes over what looked like a huge rounded belly. A dress was draped over the belly.

Then, almost as if the words drifted down from somewhere outside of myself, something said, "I am the pregnant woman." All at once I was the pregnant woman. This wasn't some distant and forgotten life; this was me, right here and right now.

There was an ache in my lower back. I felt the overwhelming fatigue of pregnancy, and yet the expectation, the thrill of life moving within.

Suddenly, I moved inside the womb. I could feel the pressure of the uterine walls pressing in, crushing me, and restraining my every movement. I could feel the first flickering of awareness, a new entity about to move through the trauma of birth. It was life in all of its raw potential.

Then the words came: "I am the baby." In that moment, time came to a standstill, as all the possibilities for that one life hovered, waiting to collapse into the trail of experience that would be uniquely its own.

Then the scene shifted. In the living room sat the father reading a newspaper. The words echoed in my awareness: "I am the mother and the father of the baby." There is no way to adequately explain this, but somehow I became both of them simultaneously.

Before long, my awareness shifted to the condominium in which they were living. The words came once again, "I am the condo."

I became the structure that contained their lives. As a builder, I had never thought of the houses I created as being living things. And yet, not only was this condo alive with intelligence, but I was living its life in that very moment.

In quick succession, I then became the earth and the solar system. At each point came the words "I am the earth," "I am the solar system."

When I found myself staring into the unending star-studded blackness of space, I saw the divine name scrawled across the heavens, *I AM*. Was this the name Moses had seen so long ago?

What utterly shocked me was the matter-of-fact nature of each new revelation. There was no jolt of surprise in seeing the name of God. There was no sense of awe, as I would have expected, from the realization that the great I AM is me. It had much more the quality of, "Oh, yeah . . . That. This kind of thing crops up every now and then. . . . It's just God."

The very simplicity was almost disturbing. Is the universe really that mundane? When we finally get to peer behind the curtain, after all the hoopla, is it all just a big letdown? Is there nothing more than the discovery of some worn-out phony wizard, frantically tugging on impressive-looking levers and dials to foster some grand illusion?

REENTRY

The music started to fade back in. Time to return. Leaving Focus 15 now. Beginning reentry. So strange . . . So devoid of emotion . . . So businesslike, this universe, this sacred place. Fourteen . . . thirteen . . . twelve . . . Still no emotion. I had just viewed the key to the universe, and all I could feel was the disappointment of, "Well, of course, it's that way! What were you expecting? To find out that you really *weren't* God?"

Now the earth coming into view . . . Scudding silently over the trees . . . There's the Nancy Penn Center . . . Coming back into the CHEC unit.

Eleven . . . Approaching Focus 10 now, "mind awake, body asleep." OK, ready for linkup with the body. Easy . . . easy . . .

In a sudden flash, everything exploded.

The moment I entered my body, I became a bug smashed on a windshield, splattered in every direction. I didn't even have the awareness to think, *I'm the bug on the windshield.*

Everything was shattered. My psyche came unraveled. Waves of emotion poured over me. My chest heaved, gasping for air amidst the sobbing. Breakers of joy and grief and awe and wonder came crashing over me. I couldn't contain it all.

I stumbled downstairs, my face white with shock. I listened as others reported on their trips. But I couldn't say anything. There were no words.

I knew I was in no condition to go into another tape. I went to one of the facilitators to tell him. He took one look at my face and said, "I think we need to go outside." Once outside, I sputtered through the tale of what had happened.

He said, "Some people meditate for twenty years to achieve what you saw."

"That's great," I said. "But I've got this blinding headache right now. Is that what enlightenment is? A migraine?"

IT'S ALL GOOD

He led me out to the lawn, where I could contact the earth, and we took off our shoes. He showed me how to breathe, and then we sat down.

Immediately, a ball of bounding energy came rushing toward us. The dog knocked me over and began licking my face with abandon.

The trainer said, "Yoda! It's Yoda! Yoda's function around here is to ground people when they need it. He does a good job."

When Yoda trotted off, the sun was setting behind the Virginia mountains. Orange and magenta streaked through the clouds. A grasshopper nearby radiated yellow and green. Its beauty took my breath away.

A silence settled over us, punctuated only by the chirping of birds. All of creation shined forth in its outrageous variety. As I looked, it was good, very good. All of it. In that moment, the wonder of life dawned on me like a new beginning.

I thought of Jacquie and my children and thrilled to the unspeakable gift of sharing our lives together. Everything was just as it should be. Then I realized that the awe I had been seeking was to be found right here and now. The present reality of the kingdom of heaven was in full view.

That night my headache didn't go away. One participant, who was a physician and was also studying acupuncture, gave me a treatment. It didn't help. My muscles trembled from exhaustion. The pounding in my head grew into nausea. I tried to go to bed, but couldn't sleep.

In the middle of the night, I went to the bathroom and tried to vomit up my pain. But there was nothing in my stomach, as I retched through the dry heaves.

Yet, even in my most miserable state, I would not have traded what I had seen for anything. It was a small price to pay.

The next morning I was much better, but the vision of the day before still inspired feelings of awe. What more could I hope for? My life was strangely complete. I had seen the kingdom with my own eyes.

A UNIVERSAL LEGACY

The vision of the kingdom is a legacy for us all. Each of us is divine. Each of us is called to our own understanding of our unity with God.

It has often been noted that the very stuff that spews forth from the stars is the same material that comprises our bodies. We're crafted from stardust. As Peter Russell has remarked, "We are a star's way of exploring the stars."[94]

The I AM is us. In all of our shame and guilt, in spite of all the voices that harp over and over the worn-out tale of our failures, still we're the very essence of divinity.

The apostle Paul captured this idea when he looked upon the emerging church as "the body of Christ." We are that body. We are the Christ. Each and every one of us.

CHAPTER SEVENTEEN

Touring the City of Light

Biblical interpretation is always risky business. Television preachers would have us believe that there is only one way to look at the Bible—theirs. Many of them speak with thundering authority on how the Bible must be taken literally, how each and every word is absolute truth.

The problem with this approach is that it only stands up to a casual reading of the Bible. When we look more closely, there are many things that don't fit very neatly.

For instance, the sanctity of the nuclear family is often hammered home relentlessly. It's based on the idea of one husband per wife, one from each sex.

Yet the Bible was written in a Middle Eastern environment. Hence, many of the patriarchs had multiple wives. If the Bible is to be taken literally, then polygamy, obviously, should be an option for us today.

And then there's the variation on that story of Abraham and his half sister, Sarah, who became his wife. But the fact that they were related is not the most troubling part of the story.

A PIMP AS A HERO?

Several years ago, I listened to Terry Gross interviewing Rabbi Burton Visotzky on the NPR show *Fresh Air*.[95] Rabbi Visotzky had gathered people from all walks of life simply to read, and then discuss, the first book of the Bible. It was quite surprising to the rabbi to see the radically new interpretations these people came up with because they were not hampered by tradition and its preconceived notions.

His own awakening came when Visotzky studied the story of Abraham. Before they went into Egypt, Abraham asked Sarah, his wife, not to tell anyone that they were married. Instead, he insisted that she tell them she was his sister.

The reason Abraham gave was that Sarah was very beautiful, and he was afraid they would kill him in order to get her. "Say you are my sister, so that it may go well with me because of you and that my life may be spared on your account."[96]

It was a half-truth because both Abraham and Sarah had the same father, though different mothers. Abraham used this white lie on at least two occasions, once when going to Egypt and once when traveling to the region of the Negeb. In both instances, Abraham came away with great wealth.

As Visotzky and his group read the story, it became apparent that this white lie not only dramatically increased Abraham's wealth, but it elevated his social standing to the point where he was rubbing elbows with heads of state. The rewards were so great that it became very difficult to ignore the possibility that Abraham had been, in fact, pimping his wife for personal profit.

The idea was shocking. It dramatically changed the way Visotzky viewed Abraham. The realization spawned spirited debate within his reading group. But on a deeper level, it also confronted him with the limitations of traditional methods of interpretation.

BATTLE FOR THE BIBLE

Faced with puzzling challenges in the biblical texts, many believers simply poke their heads in the sand, more than happy to turn off their God-given intellect and insist that we all just need to "take these things on faith." Billy Graham, for instance, once said that a watershed in his early career came when he had to decide, once and for all, whether or not the Bible was God's inerrant word. He opted for inerrancy and never looked back.

The real disadvantage of seeing the Bible as pristine is that the characters within it become distressingly boring and one-dimensional. They all become either saints or instruments of the devil. Good guys and bad guys. Either way, they become radically different from us, and their stories never really get into our guts. They're mere abstractions, flannel board cutouts who teach us lessons about how to be good people.

Gone are the craftiness and guile that many of them lived by. Gone are the politics. Gone is the raw sexuality. Gone is the self-interested opportunism that carried them through tough times.

All we see is that they are heroes we should learn from. Because they're not like us, we can never be contacted by God, as they were. The Bible and its characters are reduced to a one-dimensional morality play.

Knowing all too well that the proposition of a Bible without error is a house of cards, more liberal scholars have chosen instead to embrace the intellect fully. The pitfall with this approach is that these scholars are greatly influenced by the leading myth of our time: scientific materialism. Nothing is real that can't be perceived by the five senses.

For liberal scholars, there is no separation between the biblical characters and us. They were motivated by the same things we are. They were every bit as flawed and out of touch. But because most Western people have lost touch with the transcendent realm, then, obviously, the fantastic experiences of biblical characters can't literally be true. Such things don't exist; otherwise, we'd know of them today.

Half a century ago, this view culminated in an effort to demythologize the Bible. Everything was seen in the light of a rational perspective. Anything that smacked of mystery was to be overlooked as being the product of fanciful imaginations. The real story, the genuine history, was everything that was left after the mythological was cut out.

THE NEW JERUSALEM

The odd thing is that both of these methods of interpretation—the school of biblical inerrancy and the school of demythologizing—for all their differences, shared one important element. Neither of them was able to make any room for the transcendent in everyday life. The fundamentalists couldn't grasp it because, for them, there is too big a gap between the biblical characters and us. Liberal scholars dismissed mystical encounters because they saw biblical characters as being too much like us. Both have stripped the spiritual journey of its wonder and mystery.

So when confronted with a vision brimming with mystical overtones, both camps dismiss it. Take, for instance, one of the most enduring images in all of biblical literature: the New Jerusalem. It's presented as the culmination of the human journey, the ultimate restoration of the Garden of Eden. As John describes the New Jerusalem, it is a place where God will "wipe away every tear from their eyes. Death will be no more; mourning and crying and pain will be no more, for the first things have passed away."[97] It seems to glow with its own light: "And the city has no need of sun or moon to shine on it, for the glory of God is its light, and its lamp is the lamb."[98]

For conservative Christians, the New Jerusalem is a depiction of the afterlife. It's a place where all the ravages of this world are healed and the separation between human beings and God is breached. It will never be discovered in this world. In fact, it will come into being only when all of creation is consumed in the end times.

For liberal scholars, the city is a metaphor for hope. It's a symbol, perhaps the product of our collective imaginations. It's a pictorial representation of an illusive peace on earth to be achieved sometime in the future when we've all evolved sufficiently.

Neither believes that such a place exists in the present. And at one time, I would have agreed with them.

A PLACE OF WONDER

When it came time for our introduction to Focus 21, the trainers said very little to us in preparation. Preferring not to prejudice our explorations, the only information they offered was that Focus 21 was some sort of bridge state between physical and nonphysical worlds. Other than describing the mechanics of the tape, that was it.

Moving back to the CHEC unit, I was quite sure that nothing could possibly top what I had already witnessed. I was simply going along out of curiosity. *I'll just keep an open mind*, I thought to myself.

Once in the unit, I went through the usual preparations. I tried, somewhat unsuccessfully, to arrange the pillows to take some of the pressure off my tailbone, which by now was aching from the "stress" of lying down so much.

Finally, the music faded and the familiar ocean surf at the beginning of each tape cued in. I settled down, scratched the last of my itches, and relaxed into Focus 10, then 12, then 15, as the signals took me easily through the now familiar states of consciousness.

As Monroe counted us to Focus 21, I had the sense of moving upward, as if in a glass elevator going up the outside of a skyscraper. Monroe used colors to delineate the different focus levels above 15. "Now move through the red of 16, through the red of 16 . . . Now move through the yellow of 17, through the yellow of 17 . . ." until finally, "Now move into the white of 21 . . . into the white of 21 . . ."

I was shocked. There I was, with no effort on my part at all, suddenly standing in a white cloud. It wasn't an imaginary white, but had the vivid quality of standing in dense fog brightly lit from the sun just above. I turned around in the fog, marveling at how quickly it had materialized and how completely real it seemed to be.

Normally, if I'm imagining something in my mind, I have to go through a process of recalling a similar object or situation. Because I carry within me a rather large data bank of experience, I often have trouble settling on one specific image I want to bring into focus. If I'm successful in bringing this to mind, the image often has a jittery or temporary quality, and I have to work fairly hard to steady it.

This wasn't at all the case with the fog. Boom! It was there. There was no difference in my perception of it from the waking experience of walking into a real fog.

Then turning 180 degrees from my original orientation, I was flabbergasted to see—"Well, would you look at that! A real bridge! I thought that it was a metaphor! God! It's a real bridge!"

Only it wasn't a type of bridge I had ever seen before. Its railing was made of timbers delicately lashed together, and it had an almost Oriental feeling. There was an elegant upward arch to its shape. It looked like a footbridge one might find in the land of Oz.

But the surprising thing was that where you would normally walk, there were two rows of flowers stretching its length. Viewing it, I couldn't decide whether you could walk across it or float across it. The arch disappeared into the fog, so I wasn't able to see where it went or what was on the other side.

No sooner did I wonder what was hidden from view than I found myself flying over a city. But again, it wasn't like any city I had ever seen before. It wasn't lit up with points of light as our cities are in the evening. It glowed from within. The stones of the buildings carried a soft, luminescent sheen.

The city itself sat on a shoreline next to a body of water that stretched off into the darkness. Lights glistened off the calm surface.

Three huge arches dominated the skyline, very similar in shape to the St. Louis Arch. These arches, though, were made of stone. They too glowed faintly against the darkness.

Drawing near to one of the arches, I was awed by the texture and beauty of the stone. It was a combination of ancient building techniques and advanced technology. I had the impression that they were almost alive. Indeed, the whole city seemed to be teeming with a living essence, though at first I saw nothing that would resemble human life.

Moving closer down into one of the streets, I couldn't contain myself any longer. Like a kid on a snow day home from school, I went racing through the thoroughfares, wanting to see as much as I possibly could.

Every building, every stone, was radiant. The architecture actually elicited emotional responses from me, as I was overawed by the sheer glory of the surroundings. Each structure was alive with intelligence, elegance, and wonder.

So I ran through the streets, worried that we would be called back before I had a chance to see everything. Suddenly, I made a left turn into something that looked like a cathedral. Through two arched doors, I made my way into a huge Gothic sanctuary.

Hustling down the center aisle, I could see the pews rushing by in a blur. In a flash, I was standing at the chancel area with a being who radiated light in all directions. It carried an unmistakable sense of power and authority.

There was a communion table. All around was sacred space, precious woodwork. The sanctuary ceiling arched high overhead. I knew instinctively that this was a defining moment for me.

Standing there, I was enveloped in warmth and love. Maybe I would be told the course of my life from that moment on. Maybe I would be given the secrets of the universe.

I wanted to stay within the radiance. Yet I heard myself saying, "I know I really should stay here with you . . . but . . . but . . . I really want to see the city!" I didn't give the being time to respond. Like some hyperactive kid, as quick as I could, I turned and rushed outside.

The sights of that city were so astounding that I wanted to take it all in any way possible. Who knew if I would ever be able to return?

I turned into another building. This one was a dome inscribed with hieroglyphics of the most intricate and wonderful kind. These too had the power to elicit emotional responses.

It was a library of some sort, and I sensed that this was where the records of all history were kept. I suspected that if I pulled one of the books off the shelf, it would give me a three-dimensional depiction of whatever event I wanted.

I was tempted to take one down, but I didn't. The reason was that I didn't want to be disappointed. At some level, I was afraid that it wouldn't be what I hoped it to be. Everything else was so wondrous that I didn't want to spoil the fun if the books turned out to be ordinary ones that I'd have to read. I was in the market for adventure, not literature.

So once again, I ran outside. Coming yet to another building, I suddenly found myself in the midst of a huge gathering of "light people" similar to the ones who had been working with my father after he died.

The room itself was much like a concert hall with an upper and lower tier. Like all the other buildings, everything was extraordinarily ornate, beautiful beyond description.

It seemed that I had barged into a very important affair. I couldn't make out the faces of those present, except for one person to my right who seemed to be ordinary. She was a woman I didn't recognize. She looked at me and nodded.

Suddenly, one of the beings of light came to me and said rather matter-of-factly, "Welcome . . . We've been waiting for you."

"You've been waiting for me? Why would you be doing that?"

"Because what you're doing is very important to us."

"Well, you know . . . I would really like to stay with you and discuss this whole thing . . . but . . . ummm . . . I really want to see the city!" Once again, I rushed outside to take in what I feared might be my last view of the most wonderful thing I had ever seen.

The Revelation of Revelation

In the twenty-first chapter of Revelation, there is a description of an awe-inspiring city:

> And in the spirit, he carried me away to a great, high mountain and showed me the holy city Jerusalem coming down out of heaven from God. It has the glory of God, and a radiance like a very rare jewel, like jasper, clear as crystal. . . . The wall is built of jasper, while the city is pure gold, clear as glass. The foundations of the wall of the city are adorned with every jewel . . . and the city had no need of sun or moon to shine on it, for the glory of God is its light.[99]

Apart from the magnificence of the vision, one thing that is striking about the description is that although John is telling the story in the past tense, when it comes to the city, he suddenly shifts to the present tense. He doesn't say, "The city was . . . ," but rather, "The city is . . ." or "It has . . ." In John's mind, what he saw wasn't something reserved for the future, nor was it something that could only be recalled from past experience. It is, in fact, a present and enduring reality.

Was it his city that I stumbled into? I have no idea. Many of the details don't match up with his descriptions.

What is most vital to me, however, is the notion that such an image as the New Jerusalem may have some solid basis outside of human longing or imagination. I had always thought that John was speaking in very clever, metaphorical language in order to get his message across. That his description might actually have begun with a direct perception gives it new meaning and life.

TAKING ALONG A HITCHHIKER

Far too quickly, we were called back to normal waking consciousness from Focus 21. When it was time to go down to the conference room to share our journeys, I had a hard time sitting still. Before I had a chance to tell my story, another woman spoke first.

"You're not going to believe this, but I went to a city of light! All the buildings were glowing and . . ." She went on to describe virtually everything I had seen! Now I was really curious. I waited to see if anyone else had seen the city. No one mentioned it.

Finally, unable to contain myself anymore, I raised my hand to speak. "I saw the city of light too."

The woman who had first spoken turned to me and said, "I know. I saw you there."

Chills went up and down my spine. There was no hesitation in her voice. No doubt.

I began to wonder if these visions of the city of light might in fact have an objective quality. Was it really possible for two separate people to move into a nonphysical realm and come away with a similar experience?

There was no time to muse on the notion. The next tape was already being introduced. As we were breaking up, another woman in the group came up to me and, half jokingly, whined, "I wanna go to the city of light too!"

To this day, I have no idea why I said it, or where the confidence came from, but I immediately shot back at her, "OK. I'll take you there."

"Great!" she responded, her face lighting up with enthusiasm.

As we moved through the next tape, I became engrossed in what I was doing. Actually, I forgot all about my promise. The images floating by in Focus 10 were quite fascinating.

That's why it caught me off guard when this woman's face appeared suddenly in front of me. "Oh! That's right! I was supposed to take you to the city of light! Let's go!"

Like Tinker Bell escorting Wendy, I grabbed her hand and shot off into the upper regions. The next thing I knew, we were flying over the same city that had so awed me the last time. Not wanting to be hindered in my explorations, I announced, "OK. You're here! You're on your own now. I want to explore."

Flushed with excitement, I continued my tour and never saw her again. When we returned to debrief the experience, I spotted the hitchhiker I'd picked up.

"Well, I took you to the city!"

"Yeah, I know!" she replied. "You practically tore my arm off!"

"When we arrived, I let you go."

"I know. There were some things I wanted to do." My sense exactly.

Is It Just Imagination?

One of the most difficult issues, when proceeding into ethereal realms, is the struggle with the mind. The temptation to chalk it all up to imagination is very strong.

"Oh, I'm just making this all up," is the usual response. So we discount what has been given to us, unwilling to take the risk of believing, lest we be sorely disappointed to find out that it was all an illusion.

I suffer from this tendency as much as anyone else. Over time, I have found that there are several aspects to these experiences that tend to make me trust the perceptions.

The first is the clarity of what comes. It's distinctly different from day-dreaming, as I've said before.

I normally have a high ability to visualize things in my mind. While working on a construction project, I can actually build it first mentally, seeing with surprising precision how the pieces fit together and what the sequence of construction will be.

When I'm doing this type of visualizing, apparently my eyes start to flutter, which is a dead giveaway to Jacquie that my mind is elsewhere. To me, she has an unfair advantage, because at the very moment when I'm trying to foster the illusion that I'm present for her, she can look at me and say, "All right, what are you thinking about now?"

But even when I'm picturing things in that way, what I see doesn't have the depth, clarity, or vibrancy of the scenes that appeared at The Monroe Institute.

This in itself doesn't mean that my perceptions are true. It's merely to note that they're of a different order from mental processes I've honed through the years. It could very well be maintained that I'm simply accessing a different part of my brain, and it's this part that allows me to see more vividly.

But even if the images are coming from another part of my brain, then to me it's still good news. The idea that there is a part of me that is so intensely creative is an exciting thought. If I'm making these things up, then what is this part that holds such creative wonder? How do I get to know it? How do I access it?

It suggests that there is much more to us than we normally admit. The quest to uncover our natural wonder is filled with immense possibilities and is worthy of a study in and of itself.

So the vividness of the explorations may not lead to any objective proof that this is anything other than imagination. But getting in touch with our imagination alone can be endlessly fruitful.

There's a second element that impacts the way we view these experiences. While going through a program, we're encouraged to keep a careful journal of everything that happens, even the things that appear to be the most insignificant.

Over the years, it's been noted that isolated snippets are seldom random. In fact, if one is paying attention, it becomes evident over time that there is something trying to communicate with us.

Miraculously, the most trivial details will often be interwoven with later perceptions to form a tapestry of communication. When this happens persistently, it becomes evident that there is a genius at work.

The question is still open as to whether this genius is of our own making or if it's something outside us. I would like to suggest that, either way, the process is still immensely fascinating.

Again, it's our bias to want to discover something other than our own imagination as the source. But if it *is* us making it all happen, then we're wondrous creatures indeed. And if not, then we live in a universe that is endlessly interesting. We win either way.

A COMMON VISION

A third form of evidence that the mystical realm is genuine comes from the writings of mystics themselves. It has often been remarked that if a Hindu, a Muslim, a Jew, and a Christian could get together, they would argue endlessly about the truth of their respective traditions.

But if a Hindu mystic, a Muslim mystic, a Jewish mystic, and a Christian mystic were to converse, they would all find agreement. The reason is that they all perceive the same reality. This is why the mystical tradition is so important. For if there is ever going to be peace in this world, it will only be when we let go of the illusions of our separation. When we fail to understand the immense role that the mystical encounter has played in shaping the Christian tradition, we're blinded to an entire body of information held in common with other faiths. Whole cultures have been brought to the edge of extermination because of the refusal to see what we hold in common.

A fourth reason these visions may have some objective reality is really an extension of the third. It happens when we compare our personal experience with that of another.

Our experiences will seldom, if ever, be identical, because we all process our impressions differently. Two people sharing lunch, for instance, will recall distinctly different details, though their overall impressions may be similar.

Mystical realms seem to be especially prone to manipulation by our thoughts. So caution in making overly bold pronouncements is in order. It's all too easy to reshape impressions to fit with another person's report.

Yet having mentioned this caveat, the similarities, at times, can be stunning.

CHAPTER EIGHTEEN

Sex beyond the Body

Sex and spirit—the two seem like such a strange combination. After all, the Roman Catholic Church has, for centuries, driven an immovable wedge between them in the interest of promoting "morality" and "holiness." According to Catholic theology, we all suffer the effects of original sin precisely because all of us are born as a result of sexual union.

That's why Mary had to be a virgin and why she herself had to be the product of an immaculate conception. Otherwise, Jesus would have been born in sin just like the rest of us.

Godliness has become synonymous with being asexual. Priests are expected to have thoroughly harnessed their sexual energy and redirected it toward spiritual pursuits.

Protestant traditions, as well, have spent enormous amounts of time and energy in decrying unapproved styles of sexual activity, while limiting legitimate expressions to unions between husband and wife alone. There isn't a television preacher worth his or her salt who hasn't got the congregants frothed up over extramarital sex, homosexuality, and family values.

Sex has gotten such a bad name for so long from the pulpit that we take it for granted that holiness is to be equated with chastity. In many people's minds, to be sexual, especially in forms disapproved of by the church, is to be barred from genuine spirituality.

True saints are able to suppress their sexual urges so thoroughly that, after a while, they're apparently transformed into something less earthy and more palatable to God. Although he's the one who came up with it, God just doesn't like all that dirty sex stuff and, apparently, refuses to have anything to do with those who are so inclined.

But spirit and sex are not so easily separated.

A Delightful Secret

This point was brought home to me one day when I was visiting a woman in the hospital. She was in her early eighties and a staunch member of my church. Hardly a Sunday would go by without her sitting in the pews with her husband. A woman of immense compassion, she was tremendously supportive of the congregation and of me personally.

She had been undergoing chemotherapy and having a rather difficult time. We weren't sure how long she would live.

When I came into her room, her head was covered by a bandana to hide her hair loss. Her face was thin. I looked at her hands, holding a book. Her skin was almost transparent.

As soon as I sat down, she turned to a page in the book and asked me to read it. I wish now that I had written down the title of the book, because what I read struck a chord. The main character was musing about her life and said that she had come closer to God during sex than she ever had by entering a church sanctuary.

Knowing how devout this member was, I fully expected that she would launch into a monologue about how our society was falling apart because there is far too much sexual freedom. This laxity was shredding our moral values. I expected her to say, "Books like this should be banned."

Instead, when I handed the book back to her, she turned her head on the pillow in my direction.

"You know," she said softly, "it's true." She smiled with a twinkle in her eye, as if confessing to a delicious secret.

GUILT, SEX, AND THE CHURCH

Realizing that there was no chance of eliminating the sexual drive, the Christian Church mandated that its only legitimate expression be within marriage. This directive was enforced by a host of proscriptions against other forms of expression. These were buttressed by an endless well of shame and guilt that were proclaimed so frequently, and with such vehemence, that they became part of the human psyche. To be human, almost by definition, was to be guilty about sexuality.

It didn't help when the church looked at the story of the Garden of Eden and interpreted the fruit of the Tree of the Knowledge of Good and Evil as sexuality. It's the ultimate double bind to realize that the very thing that brought us into the world was the source of our downfall.

Sex is not something we do; it is who we are. Is it any wonder, then, that we find ourselves at war with our very essence? Is it any wonder that we live in a ruptured state, as our double mind puts sex in the evil category, making it something to be denied, while the body cries out for union?

I'm convinced that this rending is made even more intolerable because we carry within us a dim, but persistent, memory of some other form of glory. There is a part of us that knows differently, and it cannot be silenced.

Advertisers have known this for a long time. That's why products that are linked to sexual expression are almost irresistible. We fall in love with cars. We caress the soft silkiness of a fabric. We tune in to programs whose trailers flash a woman's bosom in front of us. Obviously, something within us is looking for a type of intimacy that is lacking in our daily lives. In the face of the sexual urge, the pious platitudes of the church can often be meaningless.

Despite all the guilt placed on us, something inside us remembers. Something inside us knows that sexual union is an entry into the sacred. It's not the sacred of a watered-down morality, but it is, instead, a memory of wholeness and freedom we once knew. There is something in us that knows we once lived with a heavenly body.

A RESURRECTION DEBATE

The apostle Paul seemed to have a strong sense of this other type of body when he wrote to the Corinthian church:

> But some will ask, "How are the dead raised? With what kind of body do they come?" Fool! What you sow does not come to life unless it dies. . . . But God gives it a body as he has chosen. . . . Not all flesh is alike, but there is one flesh for human beings, another for animals, another for birds, and another for fish. There are both heavenly bodies and earthly bodies. . . . So it is with the resurrection. What is sown is perishable, what is raised is imperishable. It is sown in dishonor, it is raised in glory. It is sown in weakness, it is raised in power. It is sown a physical body, it is raised a spiritual body.[100]

According to this view, there are two bodies, one physical and one spiritual. For Paul, the first was apparently reserved for the physical world, whereas the enjoyment of the spiritual body had to wait for the resurrection.

In fact, it was the issue of the resurrection that sparked this entire discourse. It was the continuation of a debate that began decades earlier.

At the time of Jesus' ministry, one of many areas of contention between the Sadducees and the Pharisees was the issue of the resurrection. The idea of physical resurrection had gained support during the Maccabean revolt. There was great concern that those who gave their lives for Israel's freedom should have some kind of reward in the afterlife. Speculation was rampant as to what that afterlife would be like.

For some, the idea of a physical resurrection was ghastly. And if you think about it, they had a point. If there was a physical resurrection, would it mean that those who were mangled in battle would come back to life in the same body? Would they continue with the same wounds and disabilities? If so, that hardly seemed an adequate compensation.

It was the Pharisees who advocated the idea of a bodily resurrection. In opposition to them, the Sadducees, ever prudent and concerned with this life, denied the idea altogether.

And so it was that a few Sadducees came to Jesus in order to see where he stood on this most crucial issue. They posed a question to him in such a way that the idea of a bodily resurrection would appear to be patently absurd:

> Now there were seven brothers among us; the first married and died childless, leaving the widow to his brother. The second did the same, so also the third, down to the seventh. Last of all, the woman herself died. In the resurrection, then, whose wife of the seven will she be? For all of them had married her.[101]

It was a good question. Because having children who could carry on the family name was so crucial to the idea of immortality, Hebrew law had stipulated that if a man died without children, it was the duty of the brother of that man to marry the widow. The firstborn male child of this second marriage would be the son of the deceased man, not of his brother. In this way, both the first brother's name and his inheritance would be perpetuated.[102] The tradition was called levirate marriage and was a well-known practice.

If an idea should run counter to the Mosaic law, as far as the Sadducees were concerned, it was a violation of God's sacred covenant and must, by definition, be false. Resurrection, when viewed through the lens of levirate marriage, did exactly that. For this reason, the concept of the resurrection must clearly be mistaken. The Sadducees were convinced they had an airtight case.

Jesus' response was amazingly quick and forceful:

> You are wrong, because you know neither the scriptures, nor the power of God. For in the resurrection, they neither marry nor are given in marriage, but are like the angels in heaven. As for the resurrection of the dead, have you not read

what was said to you by God, "I am the God of Abraham, the God of Isaac, and the God of Jacob?" He is not the God of the dead but of the living.[103]

In making his second point, Jesus was emphasizing that God is still God of the patriarchs, even though, in our eyes, they have long since passed away. But if God is God of the living, then those whom we consider to be dead must still be alive. If they're still alive, there must indeed be some form of resurrection. It's very clever and intricate reasoning.

ECONOMICS AND MARRIAGE

But it's the first point Jesus makes that I would like to explore. The idea that there is a radical difference between earthly marriage and life beyond the physical is not something that Jesus could have learned through the study of the Mosaic law. On this point, the Bible is quite silent.

It could be that Jesus reasoned his way to this conclusion. After all, the institution of marriage had its beginning, not in the idea of love, but rather in the concept of property. It came out of a culture that considered women to be owned by their fathers. Marriages were arranged, usually without consent of the bride, and were often contracted to gain political, economic, or social advantage for the father.

For a man, having a wife was an economic necessity. Only by having children could he be assured of enough hands to tend the farm. Children would ensure that there would be someone to care for the husband in old age. One's lineage could only be perpetuated if there was a male child to whom it could be passed.

If marriage, then, was based on economics, it would only stand to reason that things would be quite different when the physical body no longer existed. For it was the physical body that required an economic system to provide for its maintenance.

So maybe Jesus reached his conclusion via logic. However, the authority with which he spoke would seem to indicate some form of personal experience.

The same can be said with the manner in which Paul responded to the question regarding the resurrection and what form the body takes. There is a qualitative difference in tone when someone is arguing on the basis of rational speculation, as opposed to personal experience. Experience makes all the difference.

Could it be that these two had some direct perception of the form that relationships take on the other side? Could that same perception be available to us today?

A LATIN WOMAN

Such issues were far from my mind when the line was gathering for lunch in the dining room of the Nancy Penn Center. I found myself standing next to a woman from Argentina. She was perhaps in her sixties, and we began a brief conversation. It was the first time we had spoken to one another.

We had barely begun the conversation when she fixed me with a stare and asked pointedly, "Have you ever had a Latin woman?"

I was taken aback by her question. She was attending the program with her husband, and, at the time, I was naive enough to think that married people pretty much remained faithful—at least while their spouses were nearby.

"Why, no! I'm a happily married man!"

"Oh, come on," she said, rolling her eyes. "You have no idea what you're missing. You wouldn't believe the passion!"

It was the first time a woman had so brazenly approached me, and I was flustered. They must do things differently in Argentina.

"No . . . ummm . . . thank you . . . I'm flattered . . . but really . . . thanks anyway, but I truly am happily married," I said, backing up as fast as I could.

After lunch, we started the next tape, proceeding to Focus 21. Moving into Focus 10, the usual images were flitting past my field of vision.

Suddenly, there was the Argentinean woman's face, directly in front of me! It was stable and vivid.

I guess I was in a playful mood, so I thought to myself, *What the heck! I'm out of my body. Let's see what happens.* Besides, I thought it would be fun to suddenly turn the tables on her.

Without any further thought, I reached out to grab her, saying, "Come here, you Latin lover!"

No sooner did I touch her than we came together, and there was an explosion of light. The next thing I knew, I was streaking off into space like a Roman candle, with sparks flying everywhere. All I could do was let out a scream of delight, "YAAAAHOOOOO!"

I had no idea that my playfulness would lead to such a profound and delightful meeting. It wasn't as if we had had intercourse. It was more like the kind of jolt you get when touching a bare electrical wire, only it was ten times more powerful and infinitely more pleasurable. It was an immediate exchange of energies that was far different from sexual encounter in the physical body.

After the tape ended, I went out into the hallway, heading toward the group gathering. As soon as I came through my door, the Argentinean woman emerged from her room directly across the hall.

She seemed staggered and dazed, even confused. Instinctively, I gave her a hug and we proceeded downstairs.

At dinner that evening, I was sitting at a table with some other people. To my surprise, the Argentinean woman made her way to where I was sitting. In a rather secretive tone, she asked, "Did . . . ahhh . . . anything happen for you during that last tape?"

Not quite sure how to respond and not wanting to lead her, I said after a long hesitation, "Why yes . . . I believe there was something."

"And what was that?"

Again, searching for words, I said, "Well, we met during the tape."

"And then what happened?"

How do you describe such a thing? I wasn't even sure of what had happened, and I certainly didn't want to jump to conclusions. I decided to purposely understate the experience.

"Well . . . we . . . sort of . . . uhmmm . . . we sort of came together . . ."

"I'll say we did! And then what happened?"

"Well, there was this flash of light."

"There sure was." She smiled and walked away. I could only guess that it was to go smoke a cigarette.

A Pristine Sexuality

Even at that point, I had no sexual interest in the woman. But what floored me was that our experience had so closely paralleled one another's. Either we were *both* delusional, or a profound exchange of energies had taken place between us that was utterly unlike anything physical.

Just as importantly, it became apparent to me that the way of relating outside the body is radically different from relating in the physical. If, when we die, we're not married or given in marriage, but are like the angels, then, as far as I am concerned, the angels have a pretty good deal. It sure beats hanging around on a cloud all day, strumming on a harp.

If what happened to me is any indication, then it would seem that the drive for sexual intercourse is a pale imitation of a much deeper memory. Before we came into this life, our way of relating must have been far more complete. Unbounded by the skin, we become beings of light or energy. The "heavenly body," as Paul calls it, apparently has a much greater capacity for merging.

The drive for sexual intimacy is immense. The church has long sought to regulate sexuality, because it recognizes that there is tremendous power within it. Endless taboos reinforce the news that sex is profoundly bad. The tragedy is that the glory of sexual union, which is a reflection of the potential for union we have at the spiritual level, has been so thoroughly debased that all we have left are endless debates. Rather than an experience of profound joy, sex has become the source of immense shame.

I don't pretend for a moment to have the answer for dealing with sexuality. But as long as we persist in looking at it only through the lens of morality, we'll be forever sidetracked. As long as we insist that sex has nothing to do with spirit, we will miss perhaps one of the greatest avenues for human expression available to us.

If, on the other hand, we were to look at sexuality from a larger perspective, we might find a way around the logjam of competing ideas. To conceive of humans as beings who simultaneously have both spiritual and physical bodies places the whole discussion in another context entirely. Rather than sex being something that must be strictly regulated as a dark force, it then has the potential for leading us into new forms of communion.

To live without a physical body must be profoundly different. Because such an energy body doesn't need to be cared for in the same way as the physical one, the entire social structure must be radically altered for nonphysical existence.

A FUTURE WORLD

In his second book, *Far Journeys,*[104] Robert Monroe travels into the future. One of the odd things about this world to come is that, according to Monroe, people in it have finally begun to realize that we're spiritual beings first and physical beings second.

Instead of needing to remind themselves that they have a spiritual essence, future humans have the opposite problem: they have trouble remembering that they have a physical body. Visitations to this earth are done by picking up an available body lying around somewhere and putting it on, much like donning a space suit. It's then that the delights of this world can be experienced.

In this future world, the maintenance of this borrowed body is radically different, for it gains its energy not from eating but directly from sunlight. There is no need for the industry that is the basis of our economic system, nor for the pollution we bring to this planet. As a result, the earth has returned to its pristine state, with no signs of scarring by human intruders.

Is this just fanciful imagination? If it is, then the Bible is sadly mistaken in its depiction of just such a world.

The wolf shall live with the lamb,
the leopard shall lie down with
the kid,
the calf and the lion and the
fatling together,
and a little child shall lead them.
The cow and the bear shall graze,
their young shall lie down
together;
and the lion shall eat straw like
the ox.
The nursing child shall play over
the hole of the asp,
and the weaned child shall put
its hand on the adder's den.
They shall not hurt or destroy
on all my holy mountain,
for the earth will be full of the
knowledge of the Lord,
as the waters cover the sea.[105]

See, the home of God is
among mortals,
He will dwell with them;
they will be his peoples,
and God himself will be
with them;
he will wipe away every tear from
their eyes.
Death will be no more;
mourning and crying and pain
will be no more,
for the first things have
passed away.[106]

I consider that the sufferings of this present time are not worth comparing with the glory about to be revealed to us. For the creation waits with eager longing for the revealing of the children of God; for the creation was subjected to futility, not of its own will but by the will of the one who subjected it, in hope that the creation would be set free from its bondage to decay and will obtain the freedom of the glory of the children of God. We know that the whole of creation has been groaning in labor pains until now; and not only the creation, but we ourselves, who have the first fruits of the Spirit, groan inwardly while we wait for adoption, the redemption of our bodies.[107]

The kind of creation described here is not something that we can attain by strengthening our moral resolve. It's not something we can educate ourselves toward. It's not a pristine world that will happen by eradicating evil outside us.

It can only be accomplished as we touch the spiritual domain and remember who we are. Only then can we move beyond the double mind and know firsthand the unity of all creation.

PART IV

The Return

This brings us to the final crisis of the round, to which the whole miraculous excursion has been but a prelude—that, namely, of the paradoxical, supremely difficult threshold-crossing of the hero's return from the mystic realm into the land of common day. Whether rescued from without, driven from within, or gently carried along by the guiding divinities, he has yet to re-enter with his boon the long-forgotten atmosphere where men who are fractions imagine themselves to be complete. He has yet to confront society with his ego-shattering, life-redeeming elixir, and take the return blow of reasonable queries, hard resentment, and good people at a loss to comprehend.[108]
—Joseph Campbell, *The Hero with a Thousand Faces*

CHAPTER NINETEEN

Incarnation

Depending on how it's translated, Jesus either said, "The kingdom of heaven is *within* you" or "The kingdom of heaven is *among* you." The Greek text doesn't distinguish. I'm convinced that both translations are true.

Either way, the kingdom of heaven can't be found if we don't incarnate it in our own lives. But, oh, the obstacles to incarnation!

My favorite movie has long been *Field of Dreams*. In it, Kevin Costner plays a transplanted farmer, Ray Kinsella, who has recently left urban life and moved to the country. While walking through his thriving cornfield one day, he suddenly hears a voice. The words have worked their way into our common conversation: "If you build it, they will come."

He is so perplexed by this persistent voice that, on a trip into town, he begins asking the owner of the feed store if it's common to hear voices while working out in the field. The owner shouts out, "Ray here wants to know if any of you hear voices!" Glances of derision from these crusty old men provide his answer and, immediately, Ray backs down.

Don't speak of the supernatural unless you're willing to be ostracized and ridiculed.

It's difficult to frequent a realm whose very existence is denied by our society. We risk social standing, prestige, and even our livelihood if we become too strident in speaking of our wild excursions.

A GIANT LEAP

Jesus understood this fully, as he demonstrated in the parable of the sower. To most Christians, Jesus is speaking of the fact that some people hear the gospel and are saved from damnation, while others, for various reasons, are not.

This misses his point entirely. He's not speaking of an afterlife judgment. Rather, it's the ability to connect with the divine spirit in the present life. Listen to his words with this in mind and see if the parable doesn't spring to life:

> Listen! A sower went out to sow. And as he sowed, some seed fell on the path and birds came and ate it up. Other seed fell on rocky ground, where it did not have much soil, and it sprang up quickly since it had no depth of soil. And when the sun rose, it was scorched; and since it had no root, it withered away. Other seed fell among thorns, and the thorns grew up and choked it and it yielded no grain. Other seed fell into good soil and brought forth grain, growing up and increasing and yielding thirty and sixty and a hundred fold.[109]

Even Jesus' own disciples didn't understand what he was talking about. Instead of being embarrassed by their ignorance, they asked him in private to explain. He said:

> Do you not understand this parable? Then how will you understand all the parables? The sower sows the word. These are the ones on the path where the word is sown: when they hear the word, Satan immediately comes and takes away the word that is sown in them. And these are the ones on rocky ground: when they hear the word, they immediately receive it with joy. But they have no root, and endure only for a while; then when trouble or persecution arises on account of the word, immediately they fall away. And others are those sown

among the thorns; these are the ones who hear the word, but the cares of the world, and the lure of wealth, and the desire for other things come in and choke out the word, and it yields nothing. And these are the ones sown on the good soil: they hear the word and accept it and bear fruit, thirty and sixty and a hundred fold.[110]

So how is spiritual awareness lost? An *adversary* (the real meaning of *satan*) can steal it from us. This can be anyone who has influence over us who is not sympathetic to our quest—be it a friend, a spouse, a parent, a boss, or a coworker. We seek to please, sometimes to our own detriment.

Despite our initial enthusiasm in perceiving the world beyond, we can also lose the kingdom as we wilt under the glare of public opinion. Like Ray Kinsella, we shy away from ridicule.

We can also become sidetracked by the cares of the world: the need to make a living or the desire for wealth. Most of the people I counseled, when asked why they haven't followed their heart's desire, responded by saying that they were afraid of not making enough money.

GOD'S ONLY SON?

It's no easy task we face—living the reality of the kingdom in our own lives. But it's a challenge we will never accept if we are locked into seeing Jesus as radically different from ourselves. But what if we have at our disposal creative energy that is every bit as potent as Jesus'? In the Gospel according to John, the word, or logos, was the creative force of God.

In the beginning was the word and the word was with God and the word was God. All things came into the world through him, and without him was not one thing came into being. What came into being in him was life, and the life was the light of all people. The light shines in the darkness and the darkness did not overcome it.[111]

With this introduction, John is taking us back once again to the creation story in Genesis: "In the beginning God created the heavens and the earth . . ."

God spoke the universe into existence. It was the word from God that set everything in motion. It is John's contention that this same word went through a miraculous transition and took human form in the person of Jesus:

> And the Word became flesh and lived among us, and we
> have seen his glory, the glory of a father's only son, full of grace
> and truth.[112]

It's important to note that there is much disagreement about how this text is to be translated. The original Greek, in which all of the New Testament was written, had no capitals or punctuation. There wasn't even a separation between the words. It's often difficult to know where one word begins and ends, and determining where the sentences start and finish is even trickier. Simple articles, such as *a*, could be missing and had to be inferred.

To make matters worse, we don't have original manuscripts to examine, but only a series of copies that don't fully agree with one another. The Greek text that is often used for study is actually the result of a series of judgments about which manuscript is the most accurate rendering of any given passage.

Thus, when we come to the prologue in John, it can be read in a variety of ways. Through the years, in order to support the uniqueness of Jesus, the translation most used by the church has been: "We have seen his glory, the glory of the Father's only Son . . ."

The uppercase letters were not in the original Greek; neither is the word *the*. It could just as easily be translated (as the New Revised Standard Version does): "the glory of a father's only son." In this translation, Jesus is not being named as God's *only* son. Instead, the idea is that Jesus' glory was comparable to the esteem and honor that was given to any Middle Eastern male who was an only child. In that society, an only son would inherit the entire estate of his father and would also be the one entrusted to carry on the family name.

This is a radically different interpretation from the view that Jesus was the exclusive child of God. Yet it is much closer to the entire thrust of Jesus' remarks and prayer before going to the cross. In attempting to sum up all that was vital, Jesus made very clear that his intention was not to hog the limelight.

Instead, he was adamant about sharing all that he had. He prayed that, just as he was one with the father, his disciples would be one with him, so they too could be one with the father.

For far too long, this profound connection has been ignored. We are meant to be in intimate communion with God. It's then that we become empowered to do the things Jesus did and more. It's for this spiritual communion that the whole of creation is groaning in travail. When we take on our birthright, it's then that we're revealed as the children of light.

But this idea works against the generations of church teaching that attempts to drive a wedge between God and us, and insists on interposing Jesus as the only mediator. It's a teaching that has been absorbed into the core of our thinking. The double mind treasures this, for the ego is terrified of losing its identity in God.

WIND, EARTHQUAKE, AND FIRE

So when we hear the "word" that comes to us as divine inspiration, we turn away from it in all the ways Jesus outlined in his parable of the sower. In the Old Testament, this word came to Elijah in the form of a still, small voice, as he stood on a mountain:

> Now there was a great wind, so strong that it was splitting mountains and breaking rocks in pieces before the Lord, but the Lord was not in the wind; and after the wind an earthquake, but the Lord was not in the earthquake; and after the earthquake a fire, but the Lord was not in the fire; and after

the fire a sound of sheer silence. When Elijah heard it, he wrapped his face in his mantle and went out and stood at the entrance of the cave. Then there came a voice that said to him, "What are you doing here, Elijah?"[113]

The words that are translated as "a sound of sheer silence" are more literally rendered as "a low whisper." Sometimes this phenomenon was referred to as "the daughter of the voice." It is that speech that comes to us when all has quieted, and we enter into a stillness that is crackling with potential.

Yet we've been trained that the successful life is one that is filled with the activities of great wind, breaking rocks, earthquake, and fire. Movers and shakers are our heroes. We're terrified of silence and seek to cover it over with endless noise. The earsplitting noise of our culture, the ceaseless quest for amusement and entertainment, the premium on "making things happen," the pressure of a society that mistrusts any genuine introspection—all convince us that we can't trust our own instincts.

Still, the kingdom is seeking to reveal itself, if we will only have ears to hear and eyes to see. But we must understand that Jesus' legacy is our own. Only by moving beyond worship of Jesus and seeing him as the example of all that we're meant to be can we find the kingdom.

That divine spirit is seeking entry into this world. It's seeking to come to full expression in us, if we will but awaken to it. The kingdom is at hand.

This is our birthright: to live in the fullness and totality of our being, to know that we don't die, to touch the unity that we share with all of creation, to sense the sacredness of every moment. As we learn to shift awareness, that birthright becomes, more and more, the defining element of our lives.

INCARNATION

For generations, the proposition that Jesus embodied the spirit of God has been central to Christian thought. This spirit took up residence in his body and transformed the physical vehicle. It was the ultimate union of mind, body, and divine inspiration.

Unfortunately, popular Christianity—in its zeal to reinforce the gap between Jesus and the rest of humanity—has long maintained that this incarnation was a onetime event. Jesus, embodying the spirit, came to save us from our sins *precisely because* we couldn't carry the spirit for ourselves. Jesus showed us the potential for humanity when we are intimately connected to God, but this connection was beyond the reach of mere mortals.

But John writes these words: "The true light which enlightens everyone was coming into the world."[114] Note that the light was entering into not just one person, but into the whole world to enlighten *everyone*. This is incarnation, the embodiment of spirit in the population as a whole. Incarnation, then, is something that was demonstrated by Jesus—not to set himself apart as an object of worship, but to show us the potential each of us carries.

And if Jesus carried the spirit to model for us what an enlightened person looks like, then, according to John, it was for the benefit of the whole world. From such a perspective, Jesus is not to be worshiped but emulated.

AN IN-BODY EXPERIENCE

If incarnation is meant for everyone, then those who learn through their bodies, employing the sense of touch, are closer than the rest of us to this goal. When their bodies become the vehicle for perception of the kingdom, it's literally an act of incarnation. It is spirit moving into the physical.

Once I realized this, I attained a whole new respect and admiration for Jacquie's kinesthetic ways. When I look back over our years of marriage, I begin to realize that her touch has been a major influence on our relationship.

Words so often get in the way and can be easily misinterpreted. Touch, on the other hand, sends a message of communion that is unmistakable. It bridges the gap between us, while subtly bringing about emotional and spiritual renewal.

Touch has also changed the manner in which I view the spiritual journey. Throughout the many years of longing for contact with the mystical domain, I had become convinced that the key to access was in somehow leaving the body. Whether it was via near-death experiences, deliberate out-of-body explorations, or meditations that could lead to trance states, it was the limitations of the body that had to be overcome.

I now view these approaches as a few of the many first steps one can take. The real task is not to just perceive these altered states, but to bring them back into everyday awareness, thus aiding in the light coming into the world.

The Monroe Institute has long recognized this paradox. As is often noted, "Many people come here looking for an out-of-body experience. What they don't realize is that they've never had a truly *in-body experience.*"

That's the grand design of this experiment of earth life. Mother Earth is evolving, and we're called to be co-creators in that process. Those who perceive through their bodies are already bringing spirit into matter. It's a pity that this capacity is so undervalued by our society and by those who possess such ability. My kinesthetic wife has made me realize the wisdom of the body.

There is immense value in discovering and honoring the distinctive, sacred gift that each of us has to give to the world. When we disparage that gift, we cheat all of those who follow us. When we muster the courage to tap the riches of our core essence, the world begins to dance in delight.

This union of spirit and matter is the essence of the Lord's Prayer: "Thy kingdom come, thy will be done, on earth as it is in heaven."

CHAPTER TWENTY

Coming Out of the Mystical Closet

I didn't really want to go public with what I had learned. My extracurricular activities had taken this Presbyterian pastor to some pretty strange places. It was best that those activities remained clandestine. Exploring the edge of consciousness took me far beyond acceptable theological limits.

The year was 1998. Six years before, I had graduated from being an associate pastor in Muncie, Indiana, to being a full-fledged, pinstriped-suit-wearin', attaché-carryin', preachin'-ever'-Sunday, boss hog, CEO of my own church in Charlotte, North Carolina.

Well, it wasn't really my own church . . .

I had to share it with twenty-one elders, eighteen deacons, myriad committees, and six hundred members, all of whom had a say in what went on. Other than that, I had pretty much free rein . . . as long as I behaved myself.

Being a senior pastor involves a lot of time keeping up appearances. Since you're supposed to be the epitome of all that is decent, true, trustworthy, and moral, the job necessitates at least tacit agreement with what are known as "essential tenets." These are precepts considered by Presbyterians to be rock-solid, self-evident, don't-even-*think*-about-questioning-them cornerstone beliefs.

It's ironic that, these days, no one can agree on exactly what those essential tenets are. Regardless, I was quite sure I had ventured beyond even the most liberal interpretation of orthodoxy.

Coloring too far outside the lines of the tradition—especially if you're a senior pastor—can often be a one-way ticket to unemployment. With so much to lose, I wasn't overly enthusiastic about coming out of the closet.

But there was also a nagging inner voice telling me that if I didn't share what I had discovered, it would be a betrayal of the gift I had been given and even of the kingdom of heaven itself.

What's more, if I kept this journey secret, I would be condemning myself to a profession that was becoming increasingly meaningless—successful in outward appearances, but devoid of any genuine, life-changing significance.

The inner voice won out. Though it wasn't the least bit prudent, I found myself making plans to share with a few of my church members some of the marvels I had discovered.

A Peek Out of the Closet

My first step was to do a five-day seminar that duplicated the Healing as Spiritual Practice workshop I took at ETC.

Not wanting to attract any more attention than was necessary, I advertised it only once in the church newsletter, sensing that those who had the right hunger would be attracted. A group of thirteen responded.

I rented space and accommodations from a local abbey and made sure I didn't tell my hosts what we were up to.

In many ways, it was a perfect setting.

The abbey had been built in gray-stoned, Gothic architecture and was set in the midst of rolling lawns and shimmering fall foliage. Priests in long robes could be seen going to the chapel for services throughout the day. Their chants drifted over the fall breeze as our group strolled along the neatly trimmed sidewalks.

The fresh young faces of college students, roaming the austere halls, provided a surprising contrast to the stern, imposing architecture. Because the abbey was home to a thriving college, its solemn business of sacred introspection was offset by the irreverence of students, who were more interested in finding a good party than a quiet moment of contemplation.

The priests at this abbey were part monks, part camp counselors, part teachers, and part hall monitors. This mix seemed to bring out a refreshing liveliness and good humor that softened the otherwise imposing sight of their long black robes.

We were welcomed warmly by one priest, then another. They each extended an invitation for us to join them in their services anytime we wanted, even encouraging us to sit up in the chancel area alongside the brothers. We felt at home immediately.

Over the next five days, we stared at matches, looked at icons, chanted, meditated, and laid hands on one another to practice healing. With each new exercise that was introduced, I died a thousand deaths of fear and embarrassment, wondering what these church members must be thinking.

For some reason, they persisted in this curious odyssey. One after another, participants saw that insights and visions they once had thought were unique to saints alone were also possible for them.

They sensed energy radiating from their hands, and they grew comfortable with a process that promoted healing for others. Yet there was also a subtle healing happening for each of us as we prayed for the benefit of someone else. The very act of making contact with the spiritual world, in and of itself, seemed to bring tangible benefit.

In the gentle quiet of our exercises, hearts began to open, and the sense of unity that binds all of us as one was palpable. We even started to reach beyond the bounds of the physical world, as loved ones who had passed away would occasionally pay an unexpected visit.

As in my own experience, new perceptions opened up for everyone. For most, it was the first time they had ever experienced for themselves the reality of something beyond the physical domain. As one person said, "I've been searching for this all my life. This has saved me."

The "saving" he spoke of wasn't a salvation from eternal damnation, but a rescue from a life that made no spiritual sense. It was like discovering a part of himself that he had always yearned for but had never been sure even existed. That sentiment was echoed by almost everyone who attended. They had all but given up the hope of finding spiritual significance in organized religion and were awestruck to discover that it could happen even in this most unlikely context.

In so many ways, it was a breakthrough for them and for me. We all knew we had touched something of profound importance, and we wanted to find a way to continue the process. That group evolved into a monthly gathering where we used meditation, prayer, and healing as a means of deepening our spiritual lives. It also gave rise to a Sunday morning meditation group that would pray in more conventional ways for the benefit of the church, the community, and the world.

The Next Step

I began to suspect that the spiritual pursuit might be possible in the church after all. The following year, I became even bolder. I decided to put together a three-day seminar using Monroe Institute tapes as the vehicle for producing shifts in awareness, while linking those experiences to biblical precedents.

Now, mind you, Bob Monroe was adamant about keeping his system free of any connection to established religion. He wanted his work to be accessible to anyone, regardless of his or her theological perspective. And in fact, to many in Christian circles, his methods would have appeared to be entirely secular. Lacking the Jesus Seal of Approval, they should obviously be rejected as tools for genuine spiritual development. You know how easy it is for Satan to whisper subliminal instructions on audiotape.

Yet for me, and for many others like me, Monroe's approach was far more enlightening, stimulating, and spiritually grounded than anything I had ever encountered in the traditional church. My task, then, was to use this apparently secular material and adapt it to a language that could be understood by those steeped in the Christian tradition. It would be a very fine line to walk.

Again, I advertised sparingly. Before long, a group of twenty had signed up. Many of them were from my previous groups, but we managed to attract a few newcomers as well.

Since I was planning to use audiotapes from The Monroe Institute, it introduced a new logistical problem. The retreat center didn't have individual isolation booths like the ones at the Institute. So everyone would have to gather in one room and listen to the tapes on their own headphones. Chanting, snoring, scratching, coughing, groans, moans, and other disturbing noises would simply have to be part of the group experience. It was far from ideal, but there was no other choice.

To help me with the program, I invited Karen Malik, a long-term facilitator at The Monroe Institute. Over the years, we had become close friends, and it was reassuring to me that Karen would be able to bring such a wealth of experience to the program. She, in turn, was excited about the possibility of integrating consciousness exploration with the Christian tradition and enthusiastic about finding a new application for the Monroe technology.

Karen and I had every intention of finding time to put together the program. We agreed that we'd get the overall structure worked out over the phone. After that, we would fine-tune the details and then spend some extra time really polishing up our plans so that everything would be seamless.

But before we knew it, I was picking Karen up at the airport the night before the workshop was to begin. We hadn't even had one discussion about what we were going to do during the seminar.

I had reserved a lodge in the Appalachian mountains of North Carolina. Each participant had a room to sleep in, but the program had to be conducted with all of us together in one large space that was big enough to spread out an air mattress for everyone. As people arrived, everyone pitched in setting up the sound system, blowing up the air mattresses, and covering the windows with black plastic to keep out the sunlight. I fretted over every detail, sure that this crazy idea was going to cost me my job.

Finally, it was time for the first tape exercise. I wanted to run and hide. Here were twenty Presbyterians, lying down on air mattresses with headphones on, and Bob Monroe was instructing them on the tape to *chant!* Out loud! This was a church group! Good God, what had I done?

But I made it through that first experience, and to my surprise, no one left. Then, gradually, something began to happen. Even though Karen and I didn't have any preconceived agenda, everything fell into place. She provided the technical background, and I helped people to see the connections between what we were doing and the Judeo-Christian tradition.

Even though it was the first time Karen and I had ever worked together, it was as if we had been doing this our whole lives. It soon became obvious that unseen hands were guiding the process from beginning to end. Despite our best efforts to come unprepared, the program unfolded as if it had been handed to us whole. We knew exactly what to do and when to do it. Precisely because it hadn't been planned, we were free to live in the present, open to intuition.

Not only did the participants experience dramatic shifts in consciousness, but for many it was also a major turning point in their lives. As they got in touch with their larger awareness, the guidance that they had always been hungering for suddenly materialized.

Participants began to open up. Many shared deep struggles within the group, and bonds of enduring friendship were formed. In this makeshift slumber party for grownups, old suspicions died away and a beautiful vulnerability allowed us to taste a new sense of unity.

But perhaps the most important change happened for Karen and me. We both began to realize that this process of facilitating the spiritual connection by shifting consciousness is what church was meant to be.

Throughout my inner journeys at The Monroe Institute, I had felt something missing—the presence of a stable community, like the church where I worked, where people went through their life transitions together, and friendships were deep and abiding. What would it look like to live in a community that shared a passion for integrating spirit with ordinary life?

While the participants were listening to tapes, Karen and I dreamed of possibilities. And as the workshop unfolded, we began to see that dream take form before our eyes. As the participants moved ever closer to contact with the ethereal world, not only did they gain spiritual insight, but relationships also took on a new depth that was breathtaking. The spiritual journey was coming to life within the community of my church.

On the last day, we had communion together. Having officiated at the Lord's Supper on numerous occasions, I was very familiar with the words of the ceremony. Yet this time, the language I recited took on new depth and meaning. As part of the Lord's Supper, a prayer is always offered. When it came time to pray, Karen was standing to my right behind the makeshift communion table. Suddenly, something got stuck in my throat. To my surprise, I couldn't say anything at all. I felt like I was going to cough all over the bread and wine, leaving bits of my lung in very unfortunate places. It hit me within a split second and caught me thoroughly unprepared.

I fought it for a few seconds and then gave up. I whispered to Karen that she would have to pray, and then I turned away to cough.

Karen too was unprepared. She had been away from any traditional church for so long that prayer in front of a group was hardly anything she was comfortable doing, especially since her own religious heritage had been so restrictive of the role of women in public worship.

But Karen had no choice. So she started to pray. As she did so, the words were given to her. It was one of the most beautiful prayers I have ever heard. Everything she said was filled with dignity, grace, and love. The spiritual world seemed to be welcoming her back after having been estranged from organized religion for so long, telling her, "You have a place."

As the group was packing up, gentle music was playing over the sound system. Karen and I both looked at each other and hugged. Then we wept for joy. What we had seen was too wonderful for words.

THE BEGINNING OF A TRANSITION

Yet that gift was a two-edged sword. Karen had to go back to California, and I had to go back to being an ordinary pastor. What we'd experienced had been so magnificent that we both longed to find a way to devote our lives to the integration of spirit and community.

For me, the downside was that the group we took to the mountains was a small percentage of my church body. Consequently, the time I could devote to spiritual direction in the pastorate was frustratingly small. It was the one thing I loved, and it was the last thing I could get to. There were just too many other needs.

I knew in my heart that it made little sense to continue in a position that was so at odds with what I knew to be my purpose and passion in life. But I was also terribly concerned about providing for the needs of my family. Considering how chronically consumed by worry I was in those days, it was ironic that one of my favorite passages in the Bible was Jesus' commentary on the uselessness of worry:

> Therefore I tell you, do not worry about your life, what you will eat or what you will drink, or about your body, what you will wear. . . . Look at the birds of the air: they neither sow nor reap, nor gather into barns, and yet your heavenly father feeds them. . . . Consider the lilies of the field, how they grow: they neither toil nor spin; yet I tell you, even Solomon in all his glory was not clothed like one of these. But if God so clothes the grass of the field, which is alive today and tomorrow is thrown into the oven, will he not much more clothe you—you of little faith! . . . So do not worry about tomorrow, for tomorrow will bring worries of its own. Today's trouble is enough for today.[115]

Blah, blah, blah, blah, blah . . .

I knew the words by heart. But what did any of that have to do with my life? By this time, Dirt One and Dirt Two were in college. Money was disappearing so fast that it was like we were shoveling it out the back door. Our daughter, Dirtette Three, was swimming competitively year round. After the swim club dues, the meets, the transportation, the swimming gear, and feeding her, it would have been cheaper if she had been in college as well.

Only a fool would leave a steady job under those circumstances. It would be financial suicide. Lilies of the field don't have tuition and credit card bills to pay! Nice try, Jesus, but I've got to live in the real world. Go bother someone else with your Pollyanna perspective.

A HOLE IN THE WALL

And so I tried hard to forget Jesus' more inconvenient sayings. I needed to forget about idealistic notions that might lead me into careers more in keeping with my heart's desire.

That's the dilemma of midlife. Choices made in the enthusiasm of youth have been outgrown. Yet there seems to be no way to make significant changes without bringing the whole structure of your life crumbling to the ground. And so you pretend not to notice the loss of passion and inspiration. You settle in and try to become comfortably numb.

But, as I have said before, life has a way of always communicating with us, whether we're willing to hear or not. It can be the most insignificant thing that needles and nags us.

For me, that needling and nagging came in the form of a hole in our kitchen wall.

About five feet above the floor, just about shoulder height, the smooth drywall surface was indented in an oblong depression about one foot long and six inches wide, just the size and shape that would be made by a flying elbow. The loose piece of sheetrock hung inside the wall cavity, clinging precariously to the surrounding wall by a flap at the top.

It stayed there for months. I really had no desire to repair it. My heart just wasn't in it. Every time I'd look at it, the memories would come floating back.

The hole had been made by my son Jesse. It had happened when he heard about his friend's father's death, and he launched his elbow in wrenching despair. In times of grief, sometimes all you can do is strike out blindly.

Brad was Gray's dad. Over the past ten years, Gray had grown up in the neighborhood with my two dirt boys. The day after we'd moved in, Gray, Sean, and Jesse had made a maze out of the moving boxes in one of our upper bedrooms. That was the beginning of years of sleepovers, flashlight tag, tanning at the neighborhood pool, fighting over girlfriends, fixing broken-down jalopies, shooting off firecrackers on the Fourth of July. My boys lived at Gray's house as much as he lived at ours.

Brad was one of the first from our new church to welcome us to Charlotte. When we met, he hugged me with such gentleness and warmth that I knew we had come home. There was something about him that went straight to the heart—a genuine caring, a love with no strings attached. I felt it and so did my boys.

Brad and I were almost the same age, though our paths in life had taken quite different routes. When we were teenagers and the Vietnam War was raging, he was drafted and I wasn't. While I went to college, he did a tour of duty in Vietnam. When he came back from the war, Brad and Cyndi settled in the old neighborhood, started a family, and joined the church where I would eventually become pastor.

When we first heard that Brad had leukemia, we all tried to brush it off. The tests had to be mistaken. Then when the tests were confirmed, we all thought that Brad would find a way to fight through it. After all, people recover from leukemia, don't they?

But the leukemia spread. Doctors speculated that it might have been caused by the Agent Orange that Brad had inhaled in Vietnam or by the chemicals he had handled on a daily basis. Naturally, the Veterans Administration denied any such connections.

The succeeding months were a series of heartening victories, followed by progressively worsening news. When Brad spent weeks in the hospital, it meant that we saw one another frequently. Our conversations ranged from everyday questions about how our kids were doing to deep discussions about the nature of life and death.

When I came back from a trip after being away for a few days, I went to visit Brad at his home. He had been released from the hospital, because there was nothing more the doctors could do for him.

I was surprised to see how much his condition had deteriorated. It was clear the end was only hours away. When he saw me, he looked up and said that he had been waiting for me.

We talked for a while, but his speech was slow and slurred. He would be lucid for a moment and then drift away for a while, as if he were making trial runs into another dimension.

Once when he came back to us, he asked if I would say a prayer. His family and friends joined hands around his bed while I searched for words that might bring a measure of comfort. I paused repeatedly, trying to hold back the flood of emotion.

When the prayer was finished, Brad and I hugged one last time. Then we said good-bye. I made my way through the living room to the front door. It was a path littered with pizza boxes, candles burning, and weary friends and relatives talking in hushed tones. The vigil had been going on for days.

The weather outside was a torrent of rain. I sat in my car for the longest time, watching the water cascade down my windshield. The pounding rain on my car roof was deafening, but I barely noticed it. All I could hear was death's approaching silence.

Brad died at home with Cyndi at his side. His name appears nowhere on the Vietnam Memorial in Washington. No one counted his body in the tally to decide who won and who lost the war.

The news hit all of us hard. The hole in my kitchen wall could have been made by anyone in my family, but it was Jesse's way of dealing with the shock of losing Brad.

Every time I looked at that hole, I remembered that a life of quiet dignity and love had slipped away from us. But there was something else.

That battered wall also nagged at me. I couldn't get over the fact that, except for a number drawn randomly by some nameless public official, Brad's fate could have been mine.

It wasn't quite survivor's guilt that I felt, though there was a tinge of that. It was more like Brad's life and death forced me to take a long hard look at the sheer mystery of being. Why should I be allowed to live and not Brad? Why did I act as if I had all the time in the world, when life is so obviously capricious? Where was my life going?

Someone else might have recognized Brad's death as a call to follow the heart's desire, a slap to get on with my purpose, no matter what the cost. But not me. I felt the tug of Brad's life, marveled at the irony of our intertwined fates, and then I did the only thing I knew: I continued to go numb, because I couldn't see any way out.

The funny thing was, it was Jacquie who kept telling me to leave the ministry. She saw how unhappy I was, and she assured me we'd find a way to make it.

But I couldn't believe her. Though I didn't realize it at the time, I needed the excuse of providing for the family. It allowed me to avoid dealing with my own power.

It was Marianne Williamson who noted, ". . . our deepest fear is not that we are inadequate. Our deepest fear is that we are powerful beyond measure. It is our light, not our darkness, that most frightens us."[116] That light that terrifies us so much is our personal genius. It's our birthright, the reason we came into this world.

We'll do almost anything to turn away from it. To embrace our genius means stepping out of the protective shadows of anonymity. If we're true to our calling, we'll no longer blend in with the crowd. Our radiance will expose us to the merciless ridicule reserved for those who dare to be unique.

I certainly wasn't about to do that. And so I nursed secret feelings of resentment that would surge to the surface from time to time. Ironically, it was the very family I was so selflessly providing for that often bore the brunt.

THE ADDY ULTIMATUM

There was the time, for instance, when our still new puppy, Addy, decided to repaint our family room. This was the puppy Jacquie brought home over my dead body. Because I had become outwardly reconciled to Addy, even I wasn't aware of my deep resentment over this family pet. That dog was a constant reminder of how little authority I had in my own household.

One day I had come home for lunch and the house was empty. I didn't see Addy, so I called for her. At the sound of my voice, she came trotting into the kitchen looking very pleased with herself, tail wagging, eyes shining.

Her mouth and face were completely smeared with a brilliant green color. My heart stopped. I couldn't figure out what had happened.

Only a few years before, we had installed new carpeting throughout the house. For the first time since we'd started having vomiting children, The Stain that had been such a part of our lives was nowhere to be found. It was such a change that every morning I would stop in front of the bathroom door, run my fingers through the fibers, and smile with satisfaction. I knew it wouldn't last, but I could dream, couldn't I?

And now, here was Addy, the dog I'd refused to agree to, covered in something that looked like glowing nuclear waste.

I lifted my gaze in the direction from which she had come. There to my horror was a long trail of green spots that emerged from the family room. I followed the evidence and discovered a half-chewed tube of sap-green water-color paint.

White-hot, searing rage billowed in me like a mushroom cloud, incinerating everything in its widening path. I tried to clean Addy up while keeping the paint off my white shirt and my $25.99 tie, but all I managed to do was to work the paint more thoroughly into Addy's beard. I didn't want her roaming the house, spreading the catastrophe, so I put her in the bathroom on the tile and shut the door.

Then I turned my attention to the carpet. I tried every cleaner known to the modern world. But nothing worked. I only succeeded in diluting the stains so that they gobbled up larger and larger sections of the carpet.

I was losing the battle, and time was running out. I had a church meeting to get to. So I did the only thing I knew to do.

Gathering up all my rage, I dialed Jacquie's work number. My fingers were trembling so much that I could hardly hold the phone.

"Hello," she answered cheerfully.

There was no need for introductions. She would know who it was. I started to speak, my voice raspy and dry. My throat was so constricted by my fury that I was wheezing.

"Jacquie . . . *YOUR DOG* . . ." I paused. "*YOUR DOG* . . . has gotten into a tube of *paint!* And now it's *all over our new carpet!*" I was panting for breath between each word.

Then I uttered the fateful words. "*Either the dog goes . . . or I go!*" I slammed the phone down.

This was *exactly* the reason why I never wanted a dog in the first place. Finally, she would see my point and we could get rid of it.

I was a little late getting home from work that day. When I came through the back door, I was surprised to see that Jacquie had called a family meeting that didn't include me. My children eyed me suspiciously. It was a look I had never seen before, as if they were considering alternatives they had never previously entertained.

Then it hit me. They were actually *debating* my ultimatum, "The dog or Dad . . ." I could tell right away that, for my kids, it was anything but a foregone conclusion. My status was slipping dangerously below that of the household pet.

Looking back, I don't suppose I can blame them. I had been so miserable in my work that my frustrations would, at times, boil over at home. Even *I* was tempted to choose the dog over me!

In the end, my family decided to ignore my ultimatum and opted to keep both of us—but only on the condition that I behaved myself. The dog faced no such stipulations.

RAGE OF ANGELS

Rage can be a very telling thing. It has the potential to be one of the greatest teachers, because it lets us know when we're coming dangerously close to an unconscious life theme. And why is it unconscious? Because we're so embarrassed or threatened by it that we don't even want to admit it to ourselves. So we lock it up in the dungeon of our forgotten memories and assign rage to act as a sentry, armed with instructions to shoot first and ask questions never!

If we're aware enough to step back from our rage for just a moment, it can sometimes allow us to see unconscious forces that have been driving us since childhood. Compulsions and motivations that have lingered in the background can snap into focus. New insights can emerge that have the power to set us free—if we're aware.

That's a big *if.* At the time of my Addy ultimatum, I didn't have that kind of insight. So the lesson had to be repeated.

HEAD OF STAFF

As a senior pastor, Head of Staff was my official title. Sounds pretty impressive, doesn't it? You'd think that a title like that would imply some authority to evaluate, hire, and fire employees of the church, but you'd be wrong.

A Presbyterian church is not run by the pastor, but by the session. These are members who are elected to make decisions about the overall direction and mission of the church. Any decision of consequence has to come before this body so the issue can be formally debated. In my congregation, the session was made up of twenty-one elders. That's twenty-one opinions, twenty-one points of view, twenty-one personalities, twenty-one egos.

The problem is that, in the eyes of many members, the success or failure of the church rests squarely on the shoulders of the pastor. If the pastor is a charismatic, engaging, dynamic, entertaining, caring, loving, inspiring, forward-thinking, diplomatic, sexy visionary, then the church thrives. If, on the other hand, the pastor is a run-of-the-mill, will-this-sermon-never-end, why-doesn't-he-ever-visit-me, good-God-I'd-rather-stay-home-in-bed-on-Sunday-morning kind of leader, then the church falls on hard times.

So the pastor has virtually all the responsibility and yet limited ability to make decisions of major consequence. This isn't a problem as long as everyone on the staff is getting along. I was used to this being the case in my churches; I felt extremely fortunate in the number of genuinely dedicated, loving, and competent people I was privileged to work with. But eventually, one staff member's behavior threatened to undermine the spirit of good will.

It didn't happen all at once. At first, our working relationship was quite pleasant. I did notice, however, that even though she was supposed to be working for me, I couldn't actually make any suggestions—much less requests—without encountering an unusual amount of resistance.

Sitting down to talk things out seldom got us anywhere. What started out as passive resistance soon degenerated into outright defiance. The situation deteriorated so rapidly that the tension was taking a toll on the entire staff. I had no choice but to let her go.

I took the matter to the church committee in charge of personnel. They listened attentively and agreed that she should go. Since she had friends in the congregation, the committee wanted to be sure that I didn't take the heat for firing her. So they said they would handle it.

Considering the seriousness of the situation, I assumed that meant they'd handle it right away. But I was wrong.

Weeks passed. Nothing happened. She came to work, as usual, and ignored my instructions, as usual.

I went back to the committee and insisted that something be done right away. They sympathized and assured me that action would be taken. Still nothing happened.

Finally, I delivered an updated version of the Addy ultimatum—"Either she goes or I go."

To my surprise, they heard me but still did nothing.

It was the most bizarre thing I could imagine. The same feeling of impotent rage I had felt over Addy washed back over me.

Only this time, I suddenly saw it.

All at once it became clear that this wasn't about the political machinations of a church committee any more than it was about our family pet or an angry staffer. This was a theme that had been plaguing me all my life!

Why did I find myself in a job where I wasn't allowed to be angry and didn't have enough authority to do my work? It was because I'd been accepting responsibility and giving away authority voluntarily for most of my life!

Sure, it was always frustrating. It always made me feel dissatisfied and angry. But until my rage and frustration had been driven to these new heights, I'd managed to keep it hidden from myself. Now my own nasty habit was as clear to me as day.

I'd been doing it with my family and my church, behind my own back, for years.

In the case of my family, I worked very hard to meet their needs. Yet when it came to making decisions about how the kids were to be raised or where the money would be spent or what sports the children would take part in or what pets we would have, I always abdicated to Jacquie's wishes. Why? Because I didn't ever think it was worth fighting over. Jacquie and I were heavily invested in the idea that we never fought. Ours was a marriage of two poster children.

The payoff was that it allowed me to harbor a seething resentment—which I kept secret, even from myself. It also allowed me to let Jacquie make the difficult decisions of child rearing while I could feel magnanimous for giving her the authority! This freed me for work. It also freed me to be the armchair quarterback when something went wrong.

In the case of the church, I worked very hard to meet its needs. Yet when it came time to making decisions about how the church kids would be taught, where the money would be spent, what extracurricular activities we would support, and what our pet projects would be, that was the session's responsibility. Why? That was the Presbyterian way. Besides, I was heavily invested in the idea that we were a church that seldom fought. We lived in harmony.

But the real payoff was that, in ceding authority to the session, I was freed from the burden of claiming my own voice. The truth was that, for many years, I had felt deeply that the Christian tradition, as it was popularly portrayed, was way off track. I believed it was promoting a profound misunderstanding about who Jesus was and what his mission was.

After my own experiences, I felt firmly that the denial of mystical realms had left the church in a spiritual vacuum.

There were few things I believed more passionately than this. Yet, although I felt that conviction in my bones, I dared not say it out loud. I was afraid I might offend the wrong people.

I often complained that the ministry demanded so much time for administration, visitation, teaching, and worship leadership that it kept me from doing what I thought was crucial. The truth was, these activities helped to shield me from my deepest fear: taking responsibility for speaking publicly and clearly about what I knew to be true. My lack of time shielded me from the consequences of speaking my mind.

Third Time's a Charm

This moment of clarity dawned on me the day before I had scheduled a third spiritual retreat for members of my congregation. It was to be a repeat of my first seminar, dealing with Healing as Spiritual Practice. We had gotten such a good response from that first group that new people had signed up. Some of them were what I would have considered the least likely prospects for such an unconventional journey.

Yet as the weekend progressed, even the most conservative participants began to sense the amazing and exhilarating power of the hidden spiritual dimension. Those who were sure they had all the answers discovered ranges of inquiry they had never before considered.

During breaks, Jacquie and I would take walks in the pristine mountain trails, discussing our future. In light of everything that had happened, I saw that future so much differently now. For the first time, I could see myself leaving the ministry.

As Jacquie and I talked, we dreamed of a new life. It was both exhilarating and thrilling. Suddenly the future was filled with promise, and I was ready to claim authority for my life. Right or wrong, I would be making the decisions from here on in.

It was time for me to claim my own voice and my own life. Strange as it seems, I had been hiding behind the authority of the church to avoid my true calling.

Baptism

It was the last day of the seminar. In the morning, Jacquie and I went out for another walk. The air was brisk, and sunlight glistened off the rippling waters of the small stream flowing through the retreat center. We made our way to the middle of the flowing water across steppingstones covered with moss.

Once there, we crouched down and spoke from the heart.

"You still sure about this?" I said to Jacquie, knowing that leaving the ministry meant that we'd be embarking on a life of extreme uncertainty.

"Paul, I've watched you struggling with this for far too long," Jacquie said. There was a long pause, and then she looked up at me. "How would you feel if we switched roles for a minute?"

"No problem. What did you have in mind?"

Jacquie reached down into the water and raised a handful above my head. "Paul Lawrence Rademacher, I baptize you into your new life."

She let the cold water trickle over my scalp and down my neck. I stifled the impulse to cry out from the shock of the icy fluid.

"In the name of the Father, and the Son, and the Holy Spirit—especially the Spirit."

It was a passing for both of us. So I returned the favor, baptizing her to mark the new direction of her life.

After I finished, Jacquie reverently cupped her hands into the water once again, then she threw it in my face. I slapped the surface and soaked her good. We came back to the seminar sopping wet.

After we returned to the church the next evening, I spoke to the session and informed them of my resignation. I needed time to write, I told them. It was important for me to devote more of my life to my passion.

Most were surprised. A few saw it coming.

After the stunned silence, there were questions about what I would do for a living, expressions of gratitude, and wishes for great success.

The day I walked out of the church, I felt a tremendous weight lifted off my shoulders. There was no doubt in my mind that it was the right decision.

Three months later, I was once again at the bottom of the food chain, finding backbreaking ways to move concrete, smashing my thumb with a hammer, crawling under houses through cobwebs, mud, and itching insulation. I was never happier.

A Minor Celebrity

Speaking with your own voice, however, isn't always appreciated by others. It can be especially perilous when you're speaking with a voice that doesn't conform to public values.

In the Bible Belt, when someone leaves the ministry, it's big news. It rocks the boat and upsets the image that congregations work so hard to keep in place. It's regarded as a betrayal of Jesus.

When news of my impending departure leaked out, I was interviewed by the local paper. Letters to the editor were written about the damage I had done to Jesus' work.

One pastor wrote in to say that "unlike Mr. Rademacher," *he* had been able to make the difficult choices to balance his family and work lives. He was obviously dismayed by my lack of dedication. "What would have happened if Jesus had left the ministry?" he offered rhetorically.

I had to laugh. As far as I could tell, Jesus had lasted somewhere between one and three years in the ministry before they killed him. I'd hung in there for fifteen years. I can live with that.

An Invitation

Four months after leaving the church, I got a call from The Monroe Institute in Faber, Virginia. They asked me if I would like to become a residential facilitator there.

I could hardly believe my ears. In the moment I'd first read Bob Monroe's book so many years before and found out that he had created an institute, two thoughts had popped into my mind: *Wouldn't it be amazing to go there some day?* and *Wouldn't it be amazing to work there?*

At the time, I was sure neither one of them would happen. But I'd gone to the Institute. And now, suddenly, inexplicably, my most far-fetched dream had come true.

It's amazing the way life rewards us for taking chances. If I had stayed in the pastorate, I would have never been able to devote the time necessary to become a facilitator. But soon after I left the church, out of the blue, the doors were opened.

And another door has also opened. This book, which I've been carrying inside for more than twelve years, has also come to pass. It's my way of speaking "after all these years, in my own voice, before it was too late to turn my face again."[117]

That's the task of incarnation. It's the quest to give voice to our deepest yearnings and to see the wonder of our own uniqueness. When we honor that inner yearning, the strangest things begin to happen. We begin to receive assistance in the most unexpected ways.

CHAPTER TWENTY-ONE

Tips for the Spiritual Hitchhiker

Sometimes I feel like a spiritual hitchhiker, thumbing a ride on an incredible highway. Through accidents that revealed a glimpse of glory, through struggles as a pastor, through meditating at ETC, and through the path of training at The Monroe Institute, I've been traveling toward the hidden dimensions of life—opening ever more to the radiance that lives within every aspect of creation. Though I often fail to take notice, still the spirit beckons me into an ever-deepening mystery. A world that once seemed impossibly difficult, even depressing, has taken on the resonance of joy.

An indescribable richness awaits each of us. Yet it is not something we can attain by a frantic search for security. It doesn't lie in distant and exotic lands. It's as close as your next thought. That thought requires a conscious decision to turn away from fear—away from viewing the world as a dangerous place that we must hammer into submission.

It means letting go of our preconceptions about what *should* be, so we can embrace the wonder of our next breath and realize, in that breath, the magnificence of our own creation—which extends beyond the physical world and touches dimensions beyond imagination.

Imagine for a moment what it would be like to *know* that you were more than your physical body. Daily interactions with nonphysical dimensions would open up unimagined possibilities. It would mean being in touch with an inexhaustible creativity as you begin to move in concert with your deepest passion and ultimate purpose.

The limits of this world would cease to be unyielding barriers of frustration and would instead become new opportunities for unexpected growth and insight. Life would lose its oppressive heaviness and begin to sparkle with the lightness of spirit.

TRUSTING OUR UNIQUENESS

The paths of spirit are boundless and varied. There are as many paths as there are seekers. The important thing is to find the way best suited to your own particular makeup and to honor it.

The journey begins by trusting and valuing our own uniqueness—especially when it comes to perceiving spirit.

We all have dominant modes of perception. Some are primarily visual. Others are primarily auditory. A few are highly sensitive to smell and taste.

Those who are sensitive to touch are the kinesthetics. They gather and process information through their bodies. My wife, Jacquie, is one of these. At first, I could not understand this way of experiencing, because visualization came so easily to me.

Because Jacquie found it hard to see internal mental pictures, I considered it my mission to help her realize that she was much better at it than she thought. I would ask her to do things like picture the living room in which she grew up. Because she was able to do these things over time, I was sure her "problem" was just that she undervalued her visual capacities.

It didn't occur to me until much later to honor her primary mode of perception—touch. Like a misguided evangelist, I was bent on trying to make her like me.

When Jacquie took her first program at The Monroe Institute, she at first was baffled. All around her the visual types were exploding like fireworks with reports of their thrilling journeys.

The only thing Jacquie saw was black. True, the black had subtle differences from time to time. Sometimes it was really black and other times it was just sort of black. But black wasn't what she had signed up for at all.

So, in utter frustration, she went into one of the meditation sessions shaking her fist at whoever was listening on the other side.

"Why can't I *see?*" she screamed.

The answer she received was, "Because, first, you must learn how to feel." Jacquie first had to honor who she was and how she was made. By doing that, she would know herself to be perfectly suited for receiving information in her own way.

When Jacquie came home and told me about the message, I suddenly understood Jesus' saying that "the first shall be last and the last first."[118] We've been conditioned to dismiss touch and to value sight. In the process, we may have overlooked one of the most essential perceptual modes for the kingdom of heaven.

It's no accident that Jacquie embarked on a career as a massage therapist, with incredible abilities to sense the human body through her hands.

INGREDIENTS FOR THE JOURNEY

While no one can know your path but you, there are, however, a few ingredients I can offer as aids to sustain your inner journey.

First, give yourself the gift of time. So often we try to do everything on the run. A little voice inside our heads is convinced that if we can squeeze one more activity in, finish one more project, make one more phone call, it will put us ahead of the game, and then we'll be able to find some peace and quiet.

When I was a builder, I was always tempted to stretch the day in this manner. In the morning, I would plan out the things that needed to be accomplished in order for it to be classified as a productive day. If I failed to get them done—virtually all the time—I would try to make up for it by lengthening the day. The more I did this, the worse things seemed to go.

The old Amish saying, "The hurrier I go, the behinder I get," is spiritually astute. The idea that I will ever get ahead by working harder or faster is just an illusion. When things go wrong, the universe is telling me that I'm missing a very important point. Seldom do I get the lesson, and seldom do I say thanks for it.

The truth is that moving into the states of awareness that Jesus called the kingdom of heaven takes time. The mind is resistant to slowing down, and so it will put up a strong fight if there's not enough to entertain it. It will continue looking for new dramas to nurture long after the exterior environment has calmed down.

The trick is to not give in to this desire for activity and to simply watch the number of maneuvers the mind will use to liven things up. Eventually, however, it will give up and allow the kingdom of heaven to peek through.

A Cumulative Effect

In this regard, I've found that enrolling in a workshop that is four to seven days long will usually provide enough time and space for the world to open up. This length is necessary for what I call the *cumulative effect*. That is when small efforts become mutually reinforcing.

Years ago, Nikola Tesla, a genius who was fascinated with physics and electricity, among other things, began to experiment with this idea of the cumulative effect. He theorized that a small impact could be magnified exponentially if it were timed with the natural reverberations of a larger body. To test his idea, he invented a small contraption that delivered a hammer blow at specified intervals.

One day, while no one was watching, he affixed this unit to the side of a steel column of a building under construction. He adjusted the interval of the hammer blow to coincide with the echo of the reverberation within the steel skeleton.

The first blows had little impact. But as each successive blow was added to the previous reverberations, the entire structure began to sway and jerk to the point where it would have collapsed if Tesla hadn't turned off his little box.[119]

The same effect can be achieved with a sustained period of spiritual practice. Normally when we engage in meditative practices, our efforts are sporadic at best. Even if we can manage to stay awake during the exercise, we're immediately called back by the demands of ordinary awareness.

The baseline of our consciousness is not altered significantly. If we're able to shift awareness at all, it's like the seed sown on the path of Jesus' parable. The birds come along and snatch it up right away. Each meditation, then, must stand on its own with no chance to be reinforced by other sessions.

Devoting extended time to moving progressively further into the mystical realm allows each exercise to build on the previous work. It's like laying a foundation upon which a whole new structure of awareness can be built. The reason many people are not able to enter altered states is because they don't allow enough time for this cumulative effect to take place.

GROUP SUPPORT

Second, find a group of people who can share your interest. Because our society is oriented in such a different direction, it's very challenging to maintain your focus on this work. One of the best ways to combat this problem is to create cells of like-minded people, so you can nurture one another in your spiritual quests. If enough of these cells are formed, eventually the dominant thrust of our collective psyche will shift. In fact, this is already happening at a rapid rate.

Having others along can also be much more fun. Years ago, we had a group of people who went on an annual skiing trip. It was something Jacquie and I looked forward to with great enthusiasm, because it was a time when we laughed almost continuously.

These were in my younger days, when I still had something to prove athletically. One time, I was a little dissatisfied with the slow pace and tame demeanor of our skiing group, so I decided to go off by myself to more challenging slopes. I planned on catching up with my friends later.

Unfortunately, I couldn't find them the rest of the day. It was the most miserable time skiing I've ever had.

What I found was that skiing, as much as I loved it, was nothing compared to the joy we experienced as a group. It's a lesson I've never forgotten.

A group will make you laugh. They will help you not to take yourself or your journey with such deadly earnestness. As many have said before, "Angels fly because they take themselves lightly." Close friends will not only encourage your spiritual journey, but they will also serve up a healthy portion of humility.

In a retreat setting, the combined efforts of the people gathered flow together to create a sacred space. Unified concentration produces a mutually reinforcing support for the work.

It's much like gathering helium-filled balloons. One by itself isn't enough to provide sufficient lift to take a person airborne. But if balloons are added one at a time, eventually there will be enough to pull even the heaviest individual aloft. In this way, a group can hold space for individual exploration.

CHANGE SELF, CHANGE WORLD

Many times we turn away from giving ourselves the gift of time to explore the inner world because we consider it to be self-indulgent. We have learned from an early age that truly good people are unselfish.

But viewing spiritual work in this manner overlooks the fact that we all contribute to the ethos in which we live. We're deeply connected at a soul level, far more than we know. When each of us embarks on the spiritual quest, the degree to which we alter our awareness not only affects us but also has an impact on the world in which we live. The only real hope for any kind of peace in our world is through changing our collective awareness.

We can talk about sharing and justice all we want. We can nod our heads during sermons about giving joyfully to those around us, reaching beyond racial barriers, and turning away from war. But until we come to know—by direct perception—our essential unity with one another and the world, these noble ideas will inspire us for a moment and then fade away.

Only when the unity of the kingdom of heaven becomes part of our lived experience will we change. Only as each of us changes from within will the collective awareness shift toward peace.

So it's no small thing to alter one's consciousness. We do it as a legacy to our children and their children. In the end, it can be the most significant work we can do.

WE'VE BEEN WAITING FOR YOU

I can't help thinking about my first visit to that magical, otherworldly city of light in Focus 21. When I came into that huge hall filled with luminous people, I was surprised when one of them greeted me with the words, "We've been waiting for you."

"You've been waiting for me? Why?"

"Because what you are doing is very important to us."

At the time, I had no idea what could be so important about my haphazard forays into the spiritual realm. I was undisciplined, disorganized, distracted, and depressed most of the time, always yearning for something that was out of my reach. Their comment struck me as almost comical.

But now I understand those words in a whole new way. Maybe it's true after all. Maybe what I'm doing *is* important, not only to me but also to an unseen world more beautiful than anything I could have ever dreamed.

Maybe it's true for all of us when we follow our unique path. Our actions suddenly become precious, even essential.

Whether you stumble into it by accident or inch toward it deliberately, I hope you find that sacred calling that is your unique gift. When you discover it, you may be surprised to find that there is a multitude waiting to celebrate with you.

Here's to your passion.

Here's to your purpose.

Here's to the genius that is yours alone.

ENDNOTES

1. Willis Barnstone, *The Other Bible: Ancient and Alternative Scripture* (San Francisco: Harper, 1984), 301. All other biblical references are from the *New Oxford Annotated Bible, New Revised Standard Version* (New York: Oxford University Press, 1994).

2. Carlos Castaneda, *The Teachings of Don Juan: A Yaqui Way of Knowledge*, Deluxe 30th Anniversary Edition with a New Author Commentary (Berkeley, CA: University of California Press, 1998), xiii.

3. John 14:12.

4. Joseph Campbell, *The Hero with a Thousand Faces*, 2nd ed. (Princeton, NJ: Princeton University Press, 1968), 51.

5. Carl Reiner (director), *The Man with Two Brains* (motion picture) (United States: Warner Bros., Inc.), 1983.

6. Philippians 4:7.

7. Matthew 13:44.

8. Matthew 13:45.

9. Joseph Campbell, *The Hero with a Thousand Faces*, 2nd ed. (Princeton, NJ: Princeton University Press, 1968), 49–58.

10. John 10:10.

11. Luke 12:22–31.

12. Matthew 5:44.

13. I first came across this quotation in a pamphlet produced by Priority Associates. The full pamphlet can be viewed online at www.ipriority.com. I discovered a different translation of this excerpt in another edition of *The Gulag Archipelago:* "Gradually it was disclosed to me that the line separating good and evil passes not through states, nor between classes, nor between political parties either—but right through every human heart—and through all human hearts." Aleksandr I. Solzhenitsyn, *The Gulag Archipelago 1918–1956* (New York: Harper & Row, 1985), 312.

14. Matthew 9:12–13.

15. Matthew 25:40.

16. Christianna Brand, "The Sins of the Fathers," *What Dread Hand: A Collection of Short Stories* (Great Britain: Ian Henry Publications, 1977), 122–131.

17. Matthew 16:4.

18. Luke 11:53–54.

19. Matthew 12:40.

20. Jonah 1:2.

21. Jonah 3:10.

22. Jonah 4:1, 2.

23. Exodus 34:6.

24. Jonah 4:10, 11.

25. David Brock, *Blinded by the Right* (New York: Three Rivers Press, 2002), 53.

26. Genesis 1:31.

27. Genesis 1:3.

28. Eckhart Tolle, *The Power of Now* (Novato, CA: New World Library, 1999), 148.

29. Henry David Thoreau, *Walden* (New York: Thomas Y. Crowell & Co., 1910), 8.

30. Luke 18:16.

31. Evelyn Underhill, *Mysticism*, 12th ed. (New York: New American Library, 1974), 3.

32. Cool Quotes http:/home.Columbus.rr.com/nasheet/quotes.htm (accessed 7/23/2004).

33. C. S. Lewis, *A Grief Observed* (San Francisco: HarperSanFrancisco, 2001), 5, 6.

34. John 20:25.

35. John 20:29.

36. Hans Wilhelm, *All for the Best* (Charlottesville, VA: Hampton Roads, 2003).

37. Deuteronomy 6:4.

38. Robert A. Johnson and Jerry M. Ruhl, *Balancing Heaven and Earth* (San Francisco: HarperSanFrancisco, 1998), 7.

39. John 8:14, 15.

40. Matthew 7:1, 2.

41. Exodus 20:4, 5a.

42. Matthew 10:26.

43. Matthew 5:14–16.

44. Aldous Huxley, *The Doors of Perception and Heaven and Hell* (New York: Harper & Row, 1954, 1955, 1956). First Perennial Library edition (New York: Perennial Library, 1990).

45. Evelyn Underhill, *Mysticism*, 12th ed. (New York: New American Library, 1974), 6.

46. Ezekiel 1:11–14.

47. Mark 4:30–32.

48. Revelation 21:4.

49. Matthew 26:41.

50. Luke 18:17.

51. Robert Tallon, *The Alligator's Song* (New York: Parents Magazine Press, 1981).

52. E. H. Harburg and Harold Arlen, "Over the Rainbow," from *The Wizard of Oz* (motion picture, MGM, 1939).

53. Luke 9:24, 25.

54. Carl Jung, *Memories, Dreams, Reflections* (New York: Random House, 1961; New York: Vintage Books, 1989), 91. Citation is to the Vintage Books edition.

55. John 11:16.

56. John 11:21.

57. John 11:22.

58. John 11:23.

59. The Bhagavad Gita (New York: Harper Torchbooks, 1973), 277.

60. Ibid., 286.

61. Isaiah 6:4, 5.

62. John 11:24.

63. John 11:25.

64. John 11:32.

65. John 11:37.

66. John 11:43.

67. John 11:44.

68. Studs Terkel, *Working* (New York: Ballantine Books, 1985), 5.

69. John 13:12–17, 20.

70. John 15:15.

71. John 13:21.

72. John 13:27.

73. John 12:5.

74. Exodus 33:19, 20.

75. Exodus 33:22, 23.

76. John 10:30.

77. John 5:19.

78. John 8:58.

79. John 14:8.

80. John 14:9, 10.

81. John 14:12.

82. John 17:20–24.

83. John 3:16, 17.

84. Evelyn Underhill, *Mysticism*, 12th ed. (New York: New American Library, 1974), 357.

85. II Corinthians 12:2–4.

86. Robert A. Monroe, *Far Journeys* (New York: Doubleday, 1985).

87. Genesis 1:1.

88. Rabbi David A. Cooper, *God Is a Verb* (New York: Riverhead Books, 1997).

89. John 8:51.

90. John 8:52, 53.

91. John 8:57.

92. John 8:58.

93. John 17:21–23.

94. Peter Russell, *The Global Brain: Our Next Evolutionary Leap,* video recording (London: Chris Hall Productions).

95. Terry Gross, "Interview with Rabbi Burton Visotzky," *Fresh Air*, NPR, April 10, 1998, Transcript by FDCH under license from WHYY, Inc.

96. Genesis 12:13.

97. Revelation 21:4.

98. Revelation 21:23.

99. Excerpts from Revelation 21:10, 11, 18, 19, 23.

100. I Corinthians 15:35–40, 42–44.

101. Matthew 22:25–28.

102. Deuteronomy 25:5, 6.

103. Matthew 22:29–32.

104. Robert A. Monroe, *Far Journeys* (New York: Doubleday, 1985).

105. Isaiah 11:6–9.

106. Revelation 21:3, 4.

107. Romans 8:18–23.

108. Joseph Campbell, *The Hero with a Thousand Faces*, 2nd ed. (Princeton, NJ: Princeton University Press, 1968), 216.

109. Mark 4:3–8.

110. Mark 4:13–20.

111. John 1:1–5.

112. John 1:14.

113. I Kings 19:11–13.

114. John 1:9.

115. Matthew 6:25, 26, 28–30, 34.

116. Marianne Williamson, *A Return to Love: Reflections on the Principles of a Course in Miracles* (New York: Harper Collins, 1996), 190, 191.

117. David Whyte, "All the True Vows," *The House of Belonging* (Langley, WA: Many Rivers Press, 1997), 25.

118. Matthew 19:30.

119. Margaret Cheney, *Tesla: Man Out of Time* (New York: Touchstone, 2001).

ABOUT THE AUTHOR

Paul Rademacher graduated from Princeton Theological Seminary with a master of divinity degree in 1985 and served as a Presbyterian pastor for fifteen years. Currently, he is executive director of The Monroe Institute in Faber, Virginia, world-renowned for the exploration of human consciousness. The building industry has been a major focus in Paul's life, where he has spent many years as a laborer, journeyman carpenter, general contractor, and designer. He is also an acclaimed public speaker, seminar leader, artist, closet musician, husband, and father of three.

Hampton Roads Publishing Company

. . . for the evolving human spirit

Hampton Roads Publishing Company
publishes books on a variety of subjects,
including spirituality, health, and other
related topics.

For a copy of our latest trade catalog,
call toll-free, 800-766-8009,
or send your name and address to:

Hampton Roads Publishing Company, Inc.
1125 Stoney Ridge Road
Charlottesville, VA 22902
E-mail: hrpc@hrpub.com
Internet: www.hrpub.com